PHILADELPHIA–
THE FEDERALIST CITY

Kennikat Press
National University Publications
Series in American Studies

General Editor
James P. Shenton
Professor of History, Columbia University

CE

RICHARD G. MILLER

PHILADELPHIA– THE FEDERALIST CITY

A Study of Urban Politics

1789 – 1801

National University Publications
KENNIKAT PRESS // 1976
Port Washington, N. Y. // London

Manufactured in the United States of America

Published by
Kennikat Press Corp.
Port Washington, N.Y./London

Library of Congress Cataloging in Publication Data

Miller, Richard G
Philadelphia–the Federalist city.

(Series in American studies) (Kennikat Press national university publications)
Bibliography: p.
Includes index.
1. Philadelphia–Politics and government.
2. Political parties–Pennsylvania–Philadelphia–History. I. Title.
JS1266.M54 320'.9748'1103 75-44384
ISBN 0-8046-9135-5

TO MY MOTHER

and

IN MEMORY OF MY FATHER

CONTENTS

PREFACE

The study of the American city during the early national period has been for the most part overlooked by historians. All too little is known about urban political developments, party formation, social structure, and demographic character. Historians have concentrated their efforts on the national and state level and have neglected to explain adequately why people formed political organizations and voted the way they did at the local level. Previous studies tracing the development of the first party system have focused almost exclusively on political issues and have overlooked the influence that the social structure had on political behavior. A case study of party formation in an urban center encompassing a social analysis of party character and changing voter loyalties can shed some new light on American politics during a seminal phase of its development. Such an examination of urban politics and voter behavior will permit a better understanding of American society during the first years under the Constitution.

Philadelphia, Pennsylvania, seems an ideal candidate for such a study. First, as the nation's capital it was at the center of the political turmoil that erupted during the decade, a turmoil that strongly influenced the way Philadelphians responded to political issues. Second, the city had two political parties which created lively competition for political office in the 1790s. Third, since Philadelphia had a larger population than any other American city, an understanding of its political development would go a long way toward explaining urban politics during the early national period. Fourth, Philadelphia, with a large German and Irish population, differed noticeably in demographic complexion from other American cities. Fifth, Philadelphia's rapid growth from 1790 to 1800 provides an opportunity to examine the political effects of the influx of large numbers of immigrants into the city's economy—a process which would occur in other cities in the nineteenth century. Although most of these conditions were common to other American cities they were more salient in Philadelphia.

Urban politics in the 1790s involved clashes between different interest groups within the upper class. These clashes reflected the high degree of political and social tensions found in an urban area. The group conflicts engendered by class and ethnic rivalries stimulated political activity. The great exposure of urban citizens to newspapers, broadsides, pamphlets, speeches, and meetings also tended to stimulate political awareness and a sense of political duty. The extent to which Philadelphians participated in politics had a direct relation to their immediate political expectations, which were greater than those held by people living in rural areas. The urban dweller, generally more highly educated than the rural citizen, also felt the effects of class, social, and ethnic cleavages more than his counterpart in the country. Philadelphians tended to refute the common assumption that the backbone of democracy rested in the rural area. Obviously, the development of the party system in Philadelphia, and with it the greater participation of the common citizens in the political process, had brought the beginnings of political democracy even before the 1790s, but it was the events of the final decade of the eighteenth century which markedly accelerated the trend.

The political process in Philadelphia involved the whole fabric of society with the interrelationships of the human actors at the very core. This study explores why the development of two readily identifiable parties caused greater participation among voters in the political process. More people came to the polls and more came to feel a loyalty to one party. The interest groups that formed the political coalitions of the 1790s were for the most part small and local, not broad and national. Studies of political parties on the national or even the state level often inhibit any specific identification of the men who led or supported political parties. Political parties must be considered not merely as institutions, but broad-based social forces through which the voter at the local level relates himself to the broader society. Parties represent a means through which men seek to implement their social and economic values. Elections, then, are much more than mere contests between institutions; instead, they represent conflicts between men adhering to different socioeconomic value systems. As a result, men seeking political office in Philadelphia found themselves forced to widen their appeal to include a broad spectrum of the city's heterogeneous population, and in the process an urban political machine emerged.

The completion of this study would not have been possible without the aid, encouragement, and advice of many people and institutions along the way. Grants from the Organized Research Fund at the University of Texas at Arlington enabled me to make numerous trips to Philadelphia to complete the research. Thanks are due to the Editor of the *Rocky Mountain Social Science Journal* for permission to use a portion of chapter one, which appeared in that periodical in an early version. I owe much to Lisle Rose, of the State Department, Jack Sosin, Benjamin Rader, and James Rawley at the University of Nebraska for providing incisive criticism during the early stages of the project. My colleagues at the University of Texas at Arlington read, listened to, criticized, and helped me refine many of my ideas. I owe a special thanks to John Hudson, head librarian at UTA, whose sharp skills as an editor improved the manuscript in many ways. The courteous and informed cooperation of the staffs of the Historical Society of Pennsylvania and the Library Company of Philadelphia greatly facilitated my research. Other libraries that provided aid and assistance include the Library of Congress, the American Philosophical Society, and the New York Historical Society. The staff of the computer center at University of Texas at Arlington were also generous with their time and advice. To Linda Mack and Jo White, who typed and helped edit several drafts of the manuscript, I owe a great deal. Finally, to my wife, Karen Pisacka Miller, whose understanding and encouragement allowed me to complete this project, mere words cannot adequately express my gratitude.

PHILADELPHIA–
THE FEDERALIST CITY

LIST OF ABBREVIATIONS

The following abbreviations have been employed. Other sources will be described in the footnotes.

APS	American Philosophical Society, Philadelphia, Pennsylvania
CUL	Columbia University Library, New York, New York
HL	Huntington Library, San Marino, California
HSP	Historical Society of Pennsylvania, Philadelphia, Pennsylvania
LC	Library of Congress, Washington, D.C.
LCP	Library Company of Philadelphia, Philadelphia, Pennsylvania
MHS	Massachusetts Historical Society, Boston, Massachusetts
NYHS	New York Historical Society, New York, New York
NYPL	New York Public Library, New York, New York
PCA	Philadelphia City Archives, Philadelphia, Pennsylvania
PMHB	*Pennsylvania Magazine of History and Biography*
PHMC	Pennsylvania Historical Museum Commission, Harrisburg, Pennsylvania

Chapter One

GENTRY AND ENTREPRENEURS

Over the last few years historians have shown increasing interest in the social structure of eighteenth-century America. They have tried to explain the stratification of society through an analysis of the economic system, the political structure, and the ideology or values that eighteenth-century Americans embraced. By examining these independent variables historians have been able to tie the social profile of a society to its political movements and cultural values.[1] Though they have centered their attention chiefly on the years preceding and immediately following the Revolution, their methodology is applicable to a study of American society in the 1790s. By using studies of colonial America as a foundation we can determine whether the social structure of the post-Revolutionary era became more egalitarian[2] or whether it became more differentiated, causing a tendency toward political elitism.[3] Another possibility, as Professor Gary Nash suggests, might be that social attitudes became more democratic while the social structure became less so.[4]

This study will undertake an analysis of social stratification in Philadelphia during the 1790s by using the distribution of wealth as a means of understanding the city's society. Such an examination will provide a more accurate view than is generally obtained of the number of variables involved in influencing voting behavior and party formation. This does not mean that occupation and wealth necessarily determine voting. Rather, it recognizes that man's total social milieu and a number of potentially relevant variables help influence his outlook on society. Through this integration of the distribution of wealth with the socioeconomic groups of Philadelphia the residency patterns among the occupational classifications will emerge, indicating what occupational groups owned property and where they lived. As a preliminary to this social analysis, the manuscript returns for Pennsylvania's septennial census for 1793 and 1800 and the Philadelphia tax rolls were used to determine occupational classification, distribution of wealth, and the residency patterns for the socioeconomic groups.[5]

By the 1790s Philadelphia had developed a distinct urban social structure. The city that William Penn founded on the banks of the Delaware River reached the peak of its influence in the decade following the adoption of the United States Constitution. With a larger population than any other city in North America (44,096 in 1790 and 61,559 in 1800, including its suburbs), it served as the state capital until 1799 and the national capital until 1800.[6] Philadelphia easily surpassed its nearest rivals, New York and Boston, and became the nation's leading banking and commercial center. Its growth during the eighteenth century was due primarily to its location and the quality of its leadership. Philadelphia was heavily involved in the re-export trade, and this represented one of the main sources of its prosperity. Moreover. the city had a vast hinterland, from which it drew raw material and farm products to trade for manufactured goods. This enabled Philadelphia to establish a large carrying trade, whose far-flung commerce opened many avenues of achievement for its people and made the social structure more complex and diverse.[7] By the end of the century Philadelphia had attracted thousands of immigrants representing many cultures, which gave the city a distinctly cosmopolitan air. One observer remarked that Philadelphia of the 1790s had turned into "one great hotel or place of shelter for strangers."[8]

The city itself stretched from the Delaware River on the east to the Schuylkill River on the west and nine blocks north to south. Within its confines Philadelphia had well-planned right-angle streets, most of which were paved in the city's core and edged with raised brick sidewalks. In the central section Philadelphia gave the appearance of a city whose citizens had ample opportunities to make a comfortable living. Philadelphia was big–noisier, richer, and busier than any other urban area in North America.[9] In addition to the many small shops that dotted the city, Philadelphia boasted of having the largest outdoor market in the country. This colonnaded shed stretched for two city blocks down the center of High (now Market) Street. Conestoga wagons lumbered through the city from early morning till well past dusk, which, along with the many coaches, chaises and drays, created an almost deafening noise.[10] Yet many Philadelphians rejoiced at this activity, for it meant prosperity and the means to live comfortable and enjoyable lives.

Basically, Philadelphia was a city of entrepreneurs. Here aspiring artisans produced a variety of goods, from wagons and fine silverware to tailored suits, incorporating the latest styles from Paris. Most of the artisans and craftsmen retailed their wares in their own shops, but some sold to contractors on a job-for-job basis. The bulk of these shops were one-man operations with some making use of apprentices or family members as workers. The artisans and craftsmen were the "tradesmen" and "mechanics," whose number and prosperity had made them a strong force in Philadelphia.[11] Below the mechanics were the laborers, apprentices, servants, and free blacks, who, while not enjoying the experience of entrepreneurship, found work in the midst of what seemed an ever-expanding urban economy.

The general prosperity of Philadelphia reflected the ease with which some Philadelphians increased their wealth. Philadelphia, with its economic freedom and abundance, provided many opportunities for ambitious merchants and artisans.[12] Nonetheless, in spite of this appearance of economic opportunity and prosperity, the distribution of wealth in Philadelphia followed a pattern similar to that of other commercial cities and towns in eighteenth-century America. By 1800, for example, 23.2 percent of the taxpayers owned 76.8 percent of the taxable property valued at over $50 (see table 1). Three occupations—merchants, lawyers, and gentlemen—owned the bulk of the city's real property valued at over $50. Moreover, these three occupations owned 70.0 percent of the property valued at between $7,000-10,000 and 77.8 percent of the property valued at more than $10,000. Even more revealing is that many who classified themselves "gentlemen" were in fact retired merchants and most of the lawyers were relatives of successful merchant families.[13] However, it should be noted that taxable wealth measures only a part of Philadelphia's total wealth. Thus the city's merchants with their vast commerce controlled and directed Philadelphia's economic life and enjoyed much of the profits. They owned the ships and the shipyards, and they collected the farm products and other raw materials for trade. Furthermore, these men of commerce and trade reinvested much of their capital back into the city's economy, enabling Philadelphia to have a continuous growth spiral throughout much of the eighteenth century. This inequitable distribution of wealth demonstrates that while opportunity existed for men to earn a living in Philadelphia there was little economic equality. The ownership of real property indicates that one socioeconomic group was vested with great prosperity and economic power.

This striking inequality of wealth distribution in Philadelphia becomes even more apparent when the population as a whole is examined. By means of the federal and state censuses taxpayers may be categorized by residency pattern and socioeconomic classification. Since both the federal and state censuses reflect only heads of households and taxable men and women, it is nearly impossible to accumulate any significant data about the very poor in Philadelphia. But some observations are possible. Out of a labor force of over 10,000 in 1800, there were only 6,818 taxables. This means that nearly one-third of the working population rarely lived above subsistence levels. Moreover, 58.4 percent of the taxable population owned no real property, indicating that over half of Philadelphia's working class lived on or just above subsistence levels.[14]

TABLE 1
DISTRIBUTION OF TAXABLE WEALTH IN PHILADELPHIA, 1800

Assessment in Dollars	*Number in Category*	*Percentage of Taxpayers in Category*
None	3,962	58.4
50	1,248	18.4
51-100	200	2.9
101-250	200	2.9
251-500	171	2.5
501-750	161	2.4
751-1,000	136	2.0
1,000-2,000	301	4.4
2,001-5,000	319	4.7
5,001-7,000	51	.8
7,001-10,000	20	.3
10,000+	18	.3
Totals	6,787	100.0

Source: *Manuscript Returns for Pennsylvania Septennial Census, 1800, PHMC; Philadelphia City Tax Assessment Books, 1800, PAC.*

Philadelphia's population was distributed unevenly throughout the city's twelve wards (see figure 1). In Philadelphia's seven core wards (North, Chestnut, Walnut, High, Middle, South, and Lower Delaware) the demographic complexion presents a picture of a wide distribution of occupations, reflecting the early settlement pattern of the city (table 2). As the oldest section of the city, the population clustered in the immediate vicinity of the docks and wharves stretching for about eight blocks west from the Delaware and four blocks north and south. In this core area lived many of the oldest and most firmly established families, such as the Biddles and the Rawles, along with a number of the city's merchants and other tradesmen as well as some skilled craftsmen. Of Philadelphia's 6,818 taxables and heads of households in 1800, forty-eight percent resided in these core wards. This distribution of population ranged from a high of 12.5 percent in the North ward to a low of 2.0 percent in Walnut ward. The population in each of the core wards generally was smaller than in the peripheral wards; North, with a population of 4,126 in 1800, represented the only exception, indicating that the city's growth spread to its peripheral wards. This trend toward the suburbs can be attributed in part to the small land area of the

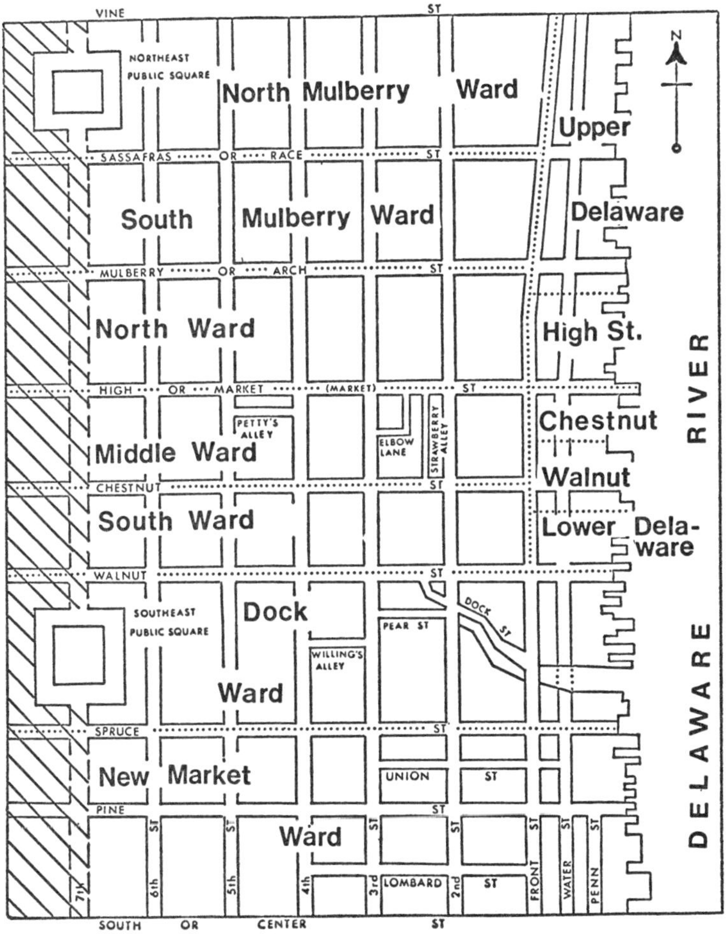

FIGURE 1
PHILADELPHIA'S 12 WARDS

inner city wards, which allowed little room for expansion. Moreover, many people wanted to retreat from the heavy population density of the core wards.[15]

TABLE 2
CORE AND PERIPHERAL RESIDENCE OF OCCUPATIONAL CLASSIFICATIONS, 1800

Occupational Classification	*Core*		*Peripheral*		*Total Taxable Population*	
	N	%	N	%	N	%
Public Office Holders	33	39.8	50	60.2	83	1.2
Professionals	154	31.6	341	68.4	495	7.1
Tradesmen	217	54.5	181	45.5	398	5.9
Clerks	127	40.3	190	59.7	317	4.7
Building Trades	161	23.9	514	76.1	675	9.9
Clothing Trades	302	36.4	516	63.6	818	12.1
Food Trades	150	32.1	318	67.9	468	6.9
Marine Trades	10	19.6	42	30.4	52	.7
Metal Trades	103	40.8	153	59.2	256	3.7
Wood Trades	47	31.9	104	68.1	151	2.2
Misc. Trades	295	50.5	290	49.5	495	7.2
Services	212	46.1	248	53.9	460	6.6
Mariners	42	23.6	136	76.4	178	2.6
Unskilled Laborers	128	24.6	401	75.4	529	7.9
Gentlemen	94	39.4	144	60.6	238	3.5
Widows and Unknown Occupation	131	39.0	205	61.0	336	5.0
Merchants	293	40.4	433	59.6	726	10.7

Source: Manuscript Returns for Pennsylvania Septennial Census, 1800, PHMC.

Though smaller in population than the peripheral wards, the core wards contained a higher percentage of the city's wealthy. In fact, more than 60 percent of the city's population who owned property valued at over $1,000 resided in the core wards. On the other hand, of those men and women who owned no real property, only 25.2 percent lived in the core wards. This indicates that the middle and poorer socioeconomic groups tended to reside more frequently in the peripheral wards than in the core wards.

Some idea of eighteenth-century urban life can be obtained by examining one of the core wards in some detail. North ward, bounded by Mulberry Street in the north and by High Street in the south, stretched to the Schuylkill River in the west, although settlement reached only to about

Ninth Street, and bounded by Second Street in the east. The center of the city's traffic pattern ran through North ward, as High Street was the main artery for the large quantities of farm produce and raw materials that poured into the city, much of it for sale in the High Street outdoor market.

North ward's population in 1800 stood at 4,126 including slaves. The inhabitants of the ward represented every degree of condition from the very rich to the unemployed free blacks. Some of Philadelphia's leading citizens had their residences in North ward. They included Charles Biddle, a leader in state government during the Revolutionary era, Lawrence Seckle, a Federalist political leader, and John Steinmetz, a wealthy Republican leader during the 1790s. The population density in the ward reflected the poor method of land division that had all but destroyed the best laid plans of William Penn when he originally laid out his "Green Town."[16] The alleys that laced their way through North ward were lined with the poorly constructed homes of the city's poor. Urban pollution was already a problem. Streets and alleys were littered with garbage, and human and animal waste was washed by rain into the creeks and rivers that flowed through and surrounded Philadelphia. These conditions obviously led to severe public health problems and an almost annual outbreak of yellow fever, beginning with the great epidemic of 1793.[17]

The taxable population of North ward in 1800 stood at 855, about 20 percent of the total population. The composition of the ward's socioeconomic groups varied, but more professionals, tradesmen, and artisans resided there than did the unskilled, unemployed, and poor. A high percentage of federal and state officeholders along with 17.9 percent of Philadelphia's lawyers, the highest percentage of any of the core wards, and 25 percent of the city's ministers lived in North ward, while merchants and retailers living in North ward comprised 16.9 and 18.4 percent of those two groups in the city as a whole. Moreover, a large percentage of the city's artisans such as coachmakers (34.0), stonecutters (26.3), saddlers (26.2), ironmongers (22.9), and blacksmiths (16.4) lived in the ward. Of the city's unskilled laborers only 9.1 percent lived in North ward. Thus merchants, doctors, and lawyers shared the ward's narrow dimensions with carpenters, cordwainers, weavers, grocers, blacksmiths, coachmakers, and porters. This wide divergence of socioeconomic groups gave North ward, along with many of the other wards in Philadelphia, a residency pattern the city would later lose when it moved into the industrial age.

The distribution of wealth within North ward followed the general pattern for the city, with 31.8 percent of the taxpayers owning 68.2 percent of the taxable property valued at more than $50. The tax records reveal (see table 3) that of the 855 taxable citizens, only five people had taxable property valued at over $10,000. Conversely, 336 people, or 39.3

percent, owned no real property and 246, or 28.8 percent, had property valued at less than $50. Furthermore, nearly one-third of those who owned property in excess of $7,000 lived in North ward. When wealth was compared with occupation, the merchants of North ward had the highest mean assessed property valuation, $1,407, although those who classified themselves "gentlemen" had a mean of $3,822. Moreover, artisans such as those engaged in the food and clothing trades had a mean assessed wealth valued at $738 and $602, respectively, while professionals had a mean wealth of $540.18. These figures demonstrate that ownership of property belonged to men who possessed marketable skills and trades for the expanding commercial economy of Philadelphia. However, the distribution of wealth also signifies that 72.3 percent of North ward's population owned property valued at $100 or less (see table 3).

TABLE 3
DISTRIBUTION OF TAXABLE WEALTH IN NORTH WARD, 1800

Assessment in Dollars	*Number in Category*	*Percentage of Taxpayers in Category*	*Percentage of City Total Wealth*
None	336	39.3	8.5
1-50	246	28.8	19.7
51-100	36	4.2	17.5
101-250	38	4.4	18.5
251-500	27	3.2	15.7
501-750	32	3.7	19.6
751-1,000	19	2.2	14.0
1,001-2,000	48	5.6	15.8
2,001-5,000	61	7.1	18.9
5,001-7,000	6	.7	11.5
7,001-10,000	1	.1	4.8
10,000+	5	.6	27.8
Totals	855	100.0	

Source: *Manuscript Returns for Pennsylvania Septennial Census, 1800, PHMC; Philadelphia City Tax Assessment Books, 1800, PAC.*

Philadelphia's peripheral wards (North Mulberry, South Mulberry, Upper Delaware, Dock, and New Market) exhibited a somewhat different settlement pattern from that of the core wards. This held true not only for the occupational diversity, but the religious and ethnic origin as well. These wards underwent accelerated growth from 1790 to 1800. In part, this could be attributed to the large influx of immigrants who poured into the city from Ireland, England, France and Germany. The exact increase in the population of Philadelphia's periphery is difficult to determine since the 1790 census did not break the population down by wards as the 1800 census did, but the increase was approximately fifty percent.[18] Before the Revolution most of Philadelphia's German population settled in North and South Mulberry wards, an ethnic clustering that continued during the 1790s. In addition to the German concentration, Mulberry and Upper Delaware wards had large Quaker populations. This area north of High Street, although exhibiting ethnic clustering, should not be associated with the ethnic ghettos of the late nineteenth and twentieth century American city. In Philadelphia's southern edges the growth pattern appeared much the same, except that Dock and New Market wards became the residence of many of the Irish immigrants. In fact, the southern wards, with the neighboring district of Southwark, had the highest concentration of Irish in the greater Philadelphia area.[19] This does not mean that the inhabitants of these areas were all immigrants and their descendants, since many of Philadelphia's wealthiest and oldest families also made their home in these wards.

An examination of the occupational classifications shows that the peripheral wards were as marked by diversity as the central core. Artisans in large numbers, as well as those men employed in the service trades and unskilled laborers, made their homes in the peripheral wards. Moreover, the area south of Walnut Street was primarily the residence of men in such marine trades as mastmaking, rigging, and sailmaking. Dock and New Market wards contained 55.2 percent of the city's sailors and 55.8 percent of the sea captains. Skilled Philadelphians tended to prefer peripheral areas to the core of the city, as did members of the clergy. The more prosperous occupational groups also resided in the outer wards. For example, 59.6 percent of the city's merchants lived in the five peripheral wards along with 68.4 percent of the professional classes. New Market ward had living within its boundaries the highest percentage (19.6) of merchants in Philadelphia.[20]

A study of one of the peripheral wards will underline the differences and similarities between the two areas. New Market ward has been selected because it had the largest population in the city–in 1800 it was 4,865, including slaves. Furthermore, it had a high concentration of foreign-born or children of foreign-born and it represented one of the fastest growing areas in the city. Clustered within the confines of Spruce Street on the north and Cedar Street on the south and running from the Delaware River to the Schuylkill River in the west lived a diverse population. In fact, New Market ward represented a microcosm of Philadelphia as a whole. In 1800, New Market ward had 1,276 taxables comprising a whole series of crafts and trades. New Market ward was in the center of Philadelphia's commercial and marine life. Wharves and docks lined the Delaware where the city's merchants had their countinghouses on or near the docks. These storefront operations usually employed one clerk and laborers to load or unload the cargos consigned to a particular merchant. Retail shops, along with the homes and shops of artisans, also dotted the streets that led to the docks. Maritime trades also played an essential role in New Market ward's economy. The center of the city's shipbuilding, located here, provided jobs for a number of artisans and laborers. In fact, a high percentage of the marine artisans such as sailmakers (28.6), mastmakers (75.0), and blockmakers (28.6) lived in the ward. Similarly, 55.0 and 35.2 percent of the city's sea captains and sailors resided in New Market ward. This merchant and maritime economy also spilled over into the Southwark district of Philadelphia county.[21] New Market ward was also the largest ward in terms of land area and many Philadelphia farms were located in its western extremity, especially west of Seventh Street. This large area also prevented some of the overcrowded conditions that prevailed in the core wards, although the clustering of houses near the docks out to Fourth Street also brought with it poor sanitary conditions and related health problems.

By occupation the population of New Market ward ranged from some of the city's wealthiest merchants to the poorest unemployed immigrants. As in North ward, New Market ward contained a high percentage of public officeholders, along with a number of professionals, although a comparison of the percentage of the city's lawyers living in North and New Market wards shows that the former had 17.9 percent while the latter had 9.0 percent. New Market's percentage of tradesmen was smaller than that of the core wards. The building crafts mark a pattern that prevailed throughout the peripheral wards. New Market ward included 25.1 percent of the city's carpenters, 28.6 percent of the plasterers, 26.2 percent of the joiners, and 17.7 percent of the painters. A similar pattern occurs among the other skilled artisans. In the service trades New Market ward contained higher percentages of the city's hairdressers (20.0), carters (27.0), coachdrivers (29.6), gardeners (50.0), innkeepers (13.3), and waiters (80.0). It is not surprising, then, to find the ward had the greatest percentage of the city's laborers (27.0 percent), a large part of whom were Irish immigrants.[22] Thus, while New Market was the largest ward in Philadelphia it contained in proportion to the core wards a smaller percentage of the city's professionals and tradesmen. This fact emphasizes that eighteenth-century Philadelphia settlement patterns were in marked contrast to the living patterns of the industrial city, where the core area became the slums for unskilled laborers while the professional and middle class fled to the peripheral areas.

The distribution of wealth in New Market ward was more unequal than in Philadelphia as a whole. In New Market ward 61.9 percent of the taxpayers owned no real property. This indicates that most of the ward's population were either skilled artisans or unskilled laborers trying to earn a living in an expanding commercial economy. In fact, only 24.1 percent of the ward's taxables owned property valued at over $50 (see table 4). By

TABLE 4
DISTRIBUTION OF TAXABLE WEALTH IN NEW MARKET WARD, 1800

Assessment in Dollars	*Number in Category*	*Percentage of Taxpayers in Category*	*Percentage of City Total*
None	793	61.9	20.0
1-50	180	14.0	14.4
51-100	50	3.9	24.3
101-250	58	4.5	28.3
251-500	51	4.0	29.7
501-750	38	3.0	23.3
751-1,000	29	2.3	21.3
1,001-2,000	48	3.7	15.8
2,001-5,000	27	2.1	8.4
5,001-7,000	3	.2	5.8
7,001-10,000	3	.2	14.3
10,000+	2	.2	11.1
Totals	1,282	100.0	

Source: *Manuscript Returns for Pennsylvania Septennial Census, 1800, PHMC; Philadelphia City Tax Assessment Books, 1800, PAC.*

translating these percentages to occupational classifications one can determine what groups owned the bulk of the ward's real property. One of the wealthiest occupational groups in Philadelphia–the merchants–had a mean assessed property valuation in New Market of $1,129. A comparison of this mean against all other occupational classifications shows that the ward's merchants ranked below only the "gentlemen" ($1,323), many of whom were themselves former merchants. The skilled artisans show very little variation in their mean assessments, with the exception of those engaged in marine trades, where the mean was $773, and in woodworking, where the mean was $892. The unskilled owned little or no real property and what they did own was of low assessed value. In terms of real property the merchants or those groups related to them owned the bulk of the city's property, and the skilled artisans followed a distant second.

An interesting pattern emerges, however, that qualifies some of these conclusions. While the professional class as a whole had a much lower mean assessed wealth in Philadelphia ($860) and in New Market ward

($398), the lawyers' mean wealth for the city ($1,982) and New Market ($1,303) was higher, placing them above the merchants. The explanation for this trend seems clear. Successful lawyers handled the accounts of the merchants and thus benefited from their prosperity. Furthermore, many of the lawyers were the sons of wealthy merchant families who continued, though classifying themselves lawyers, to engage in commercial trade.

Those skilled artisans who prospered accumulated real property in sufficient amounts to call themselves successful men. But the distribution of property reveals that most artisans owned very little if any property and unskilled workers owned almost none at all. It appears obvious that while many men could earn a living, especially those with skills, they had little surplus wealth with which to acquire real property. As the city's population grew in the 1790s competition for jobs increased, and those without established position had an increasingly difficult time in gaining a foothold in the city's economic life.

Status, or social values, though an independent variable with its own dynamics for change, was closely related in Philadelphia to wealth and occupational classification. Social status was defined and accepted by the city's population on the basis of occupation and how much wealth a man had obtained.[23] Philadelphia's role as a commercial center had enabled its merchants to attain a high status because of the productive role they played in the social system. Though the city had a few wealthy artisans and retailers, their status never matched that of the successful merchants and lawyers. Philadelphia's wealthy merchant families had established, well before the Revolution, a distinct and privileged elite. This class, jealous of their position, sought by social and political exclusiveness to strengthen the barriers which separated them from those of lesser wealth and occupational status. This did not mean that men who acquired wealth could not gain entrance to the charmed circles; but their task by the 1790s was extremely difficult. Wealthy merchants established social institutions such as the Library Company of Philadelphia, the Dancing Assembly, and the Colony in Schuylkill, (a fishing club) to delineate the differences between those who had attained wealth and status and those who had not. By drawing clear distinctions the wealthy sought to maintain control of the city in the hands of a few men. By the 1790s these social organizations admitted few new members; one gained acceptance either by birth or else through marriage or a business alliance with an original family.[24] Skilled artisans or the middle class had neither the money nor time to compete with the gentry. Instead artisans spent the bulk of their time trying to earn a living and acquire the wealth that they hoped would one day allow them to become part of the upper class. Philadelphia's social classes, established during the colonial period, followed clear lines and changed little during the 1790s.

In addition to the exclusive social institutions of the gentry, urban life provided both the means and the leisure time for many less prosperous inhabitants to associate according to their occupations and tastes. By 1790 there were over 200 taverns licensed by Philadelphia's city government, one to suit the taste of almost anyone. The taverns ranged from the "grog-shop" near the docks to the City Tavern, patterned after the famous London models and intended for the city's gentlemen. One observer remarked that the City Tavern represented "the largest and most elegant house occupied in that way in America." Most men associated with others of their occupational class. Thus carpenters, tailors, blacksmiths, cabinetmakers, and clerks each had their own favorite tavern where they would meet on a regular basis.[25] These weekly or nightly meetings offered men the opportunity to exchange business and political news and to hear the latest ideas from Europe. This form of social intercourse enabled each man to form a sense of identity with the events of the day and strengthened the feeling of community that many Philadelphians had about their city.

Political structure represents another independent variable used to measure social stratification. By computing the distribution of wealth and relating it to the political composition of the Federalist and Republican parties in Philadelphia, a clearer understanding of the city's social structure can be attained (table 5). In addition, this information will shed some light on the development of the first American party system at the local level.[26]

TABLE 5
DISTRIBUTION OF WEALTH BY PARTY CANDIDATES, 1800

	Under $100	*Under $500*	*Under $1,000*	*Under $5,000*	*Under $10,000*	*Plus $10,000*
Federalist	10.8%	.7%	.7%	25.2%	22.3%	40.3%
Republican	22.7%	3.6%	9.1%	28.2%	13.6%	22.7%

Source: *United States Direct Tax of 1798, Tax List for Philadelphia, and Manuscript Returns for Pennsylvania Septennial Census, 1800, PHMC.*

Federalists drew more of their leaders from the wealthier classes of society than did Republicans. Of the sample 139 Federalist candidates during the 1790s, 40.3 percent owned property valued at $10,000 or more, while only 22.7 percent of the Republican candidates owned as much. Only 11.5 percent of the Federalists owned property valued at less than $500, while 26.3 percent of the Republican candidates owned this little property. In fact, over half the Republican candidates owned property valued at less than $5,000.[27] Richer than many of their Republican counterparts, Federalist leaders were chiefly merchants and lawyers, 36.8 and 22.8 percent respectively. The percentage of Republican leadership from these occupations was 18.2 and 9.1 percent. Aside from merchants and lawyers, Federalists drew their candidates for the most part from retailers (3.7%), carpenters (2.9%), marine tradesmen (2.9%), grocers (3.7%), printers (2.9%), and brewers (2.2%). Republicans, on the other hand, turned to the skilled crafts and trades much more frequently for their candidates. They ran more retailers (8.2%), carpenters (5.5%), tailors (3.6%), sugar refiners (2.7%), printers (4.5%), and woodcrafts, (3.6%) than their Federalist counterparts. From this evidence it appears that Republicans wanted to encourage support from as many groups as possible to indicate that they represented the aspirations of Philadelphians trying to gain a foothold in the socioeconomic life of the city.

Representing older, more established wealth, Federalists drew their leadership from both Quaker and non-Quaker families. While 34.0 percent were Quakers, 43.3 percent of those Federalist candidates who were non-Quaker were Anglican; and only 11.3 and 10.3 percent, respectively, were Lutheran and Presbyterian. As table 6 shows, Republicans also drew over

TABLE 6
RELIGIOUS AFFILIATION OF PARTY CANDIDATES

	Federalist (%)	*Republican (%)*
Anglican	43.3	30.9
Quaker	34.0	29.1
Presbyterian	10.3	23.6
Baptist	0.0	5.5
Lutheran	11.3	9.1
Roman Catholic	1.0	1.8

half of their candidates from the Anglican and Quaker community, but many more of their leaders were Presbyterian, Lutheran, Baptist, and Catholic. The large percentage of Anglicans and Quakers among Federalist leaders seems to indicate that they represented the heirs of the colonial gentry who had become dominant in Philadelphia through economic, social, and political ties and alliances. They included such Anglican families as the Willings, Binghams, Powels, and Coxes. The Quaker families included the Pembertons, Fishers, Norrises, Whartons, and Merediths. Endogamy played an important role among these families and contributed to the unity of the Federalist party during the 1790s. For example, among the non-Quaker families Thomas Willing, who became president of the Bank of the United States, was connected to Samuel Powel, a wealthy merchant who served as mayor of Philadelphia, and William Bingham.[28]

This gentry completely dominated each of Philadelphia's major financial institutions. The Bank of North America was the oldest and largest bank in the country in 1790. Of its thirty-four directors during 1782-1801, thirty-one, in addition to its two presidents, Thomas Willing and John Nixon, came from Philadelphia's Federalist circles. Federalists such as Thomas Willing, Samuel Powel, Samuel Meredith, Robert Morris, William Lewis, Thomas Fitzsimons, and George Latimer served as directors for much of the period. The board of directors of the First Bank of the United States further demonstrates the clannishness of this Federalist junto. Thomas Willing served as president while his son-in-law, William Bingham, served as a director; John Nixon and his son were also on the board. These men were joined by Thomas Fitzsimons and John Nesbitt, who had held similar posts with the Bank of North America.[29]

Republican leaders lacked the social prestige of the Federalists. They represented ambitious types who had achieved some degree of wealth and sought entrance into the upper circles of Philadelphia life. Among them were such men as the lawyers Alexander J. Dallas and Thomas McKean, the Jewish innkeeper Israel Israel, the merchants Stephen Girard and John Swanwick, and doctors Michael Leib and James Hutchinson.[30]

The differences in wealth between the two parties becomes even clearer when the leaders from both parties are compared by their occupational classification. Federalist lawyers had a mean wealth of $9,355, while Republican lawyers had a mean of only $2,950. Differences in wealth extended to merchants of both parties, although it was not as pronounced; the mean for Federalists was $17,387; for Republicans, $12,387. This pattern continues even when the wealth of artisans is compared. For example, Federalists engaged in the building trades had a mean wealth of $7,478, while Republicans in the same trade had a mean of $3,165. The disparity of wealth between Federalists and Republicans is also predictable when the leaders are compared by religion and by occupation. Federalists who were Anglicans had a mean wealth of $15,811, while Republican Anglicans had a mean wealth of $12,917. Moreover, Quaker Federalists had a mean assessed wealth of $17,463, while Republicans of the same denomination had $9,030. Only in the case of those candidates who were Presbyterians did the Republicans have a slightly higher mean assessed wealth—$7,991 to $7,757 for the Federalists. This represents the only exception; in all other religious affiliations Federalist candidates prove to have had the greater wealth.

The differences in wealth between Federalist and Republican candidates are also reflected when wealth is compared by offices sought (see table 7). When the wealth of candidates is compared by party it shows a mean of $12,176 for the Federalists as against $6,651 for the Republicans.

Moreover, this comparison demonstrates that in every instance Federalist candidates' mean assessed wealth far surpassed that of their Republican opponents. The variance in some cases is striking; note, for example, the differences in assessed wealth between Federalist candidates for United States Congress and their Republican opposition ($55,363 as opposed to $19,130). In those offices where the Republicans sought to include some of the city's prosperous artisans, usually the Common and Select Council of city government, the differences are obvious. In fact, Federalists made little effort to include many artisans in their selection of candidates, instead holding fast to the notion that they were the natural leaders as demonstrated by their economic success. This pattern is further underlined

TABLE 7
MEAN WEALTH OF CANDIDATES BY OFFICE

	Federalist	*Republican*
Common Council	$ 9,626	$ 4,891
Select Council	8,359	8,184
Alderman	16,824	8,133
State Assembly	18,823	8,606
State Senate	39,613	18,529
U.S. Congress	55,363	19,129
Other Offices	13,989	9,232

Source: United States Direct Tax of 1798, Tax List for Philadelphia, and Manuscript Returns for Pennsylvania Septennial Census, 1800, PHMC.

when the wealth of Federalist and Republican candidates is compared by ward. Federalists who resided in North ward had a mean assessed wealth of $15,695, while Republicans had $9,215. In New Market ward the trend repeated itself, the Federalists having a mean wealth of $6,186 and Republicans $2,363. In every ward, with the exception of High Street and Middle, Federalists' wealth surpassed that of their Republican opponents.

The distribution of wealth in Philadelphia during the 1790s suggests that while the city's economy provided opportunities for its citizens, the popular myth that any man could acquire wealth and status and rise to the top of the socioeconomic ladder seems far from the truth. Instead, the prerequisites for upward mobility in Philadelphia appear to have been dependent in large part upon the inheritance of wealth and standing. Substantively, it demonstrates that occupation and wealth were correlated and that a select number of the city's merchants and lawyers controlled much of the socioeconomic and political life of Philadelphia. Although both political parties nominated wealthy men as candidates, the skilled artisans of the middle class found greater opportunities in the Republican party than in the Federalist party. Conversely, a larger proportion of Federalist leadership came from the wealthy, well-entrenched families who had dominated the economic and social life of Philadelphia since the colonial era.[31] Philadelphia, then, had developed a well-defined differentiated society following the pattern of other eighteenth-century American cities and towns. Moreover, Philadelphia's social structure and political leadership provides an early forecast of the highly rigid state of urban society in the 1830s and 1840s.[32]

Chapter Two

THE ORIGINS OF THE FEDERALIST AND REPUBLICAN PARTIES, 1776-1790

To understand politics in Philadelphia during the 1790s requires more than an analysis of short term forces. The explanation of how and why the Federalist differed from the Republican party and the reasons for their formation necessitates an understanding of the impact of the Revolution on political institutions and the political alignments in Philadelphia after the Revolution. "No decade in the history of politics, religion, technology, painting, poetry and whatnot ever contains its own explanation."[1] Therefore, to discover the means by which the Federalist and Republican parties were constructed in Philadelphia, it is necessary first to look for their roots in the years immediately following the Revolution.

The American Revolution tore Philadelphia's colonial gentry apart. The conflict did not divide Philadelphians along class or occupational lines but rather reflected each citizen's personal attitudes toward the revolutionary government established in Pennsylvania. The turbulent and complex events of 1775-1776 resulted in an extremely democratic constitution for Pennsylvania. This constitution granted the franchise to almost every white male over twenty-one who paid taxes in the state; it abolished Philadelphia's city charter, with the reins of government assumed by the state assembly; and it established a single-house legislature subject to annual elections.[2] In one sweep the colonial gentry lost political power, and their efforts to regain this power comprise the origins of the partisan battles in the years following the Revolution.

As a result of the Revolution the exclusiveness of the colonial gentry broke apart, and many newcomers made their way into Philadelphia's upper circles. Men such as Robert Morris, a self-made man who had been a business partner of Thomas Willing before the war, assumed a leading role in the gentry's struggle with the radical whigs who controlled the state government. Other such men included merchants who had amassed fortunes during the war: Thomas Fitzsimons, who had immigrated from Northern Ireland before the Revolution and served as a captain in the militia during the war; Francis Gurney, who served as a lieutenant colonel in the Continental Army; George Latimer, who also served in the Continental Army and later became collector of customs in Philadelphia; Levi Hollingsworth a flour merchant who built a successful business trading with the West Indies and England and served in the Continental Army; John Innskeep, who served in the militia. These men, and others like them, added a patriotic flavor to the gentry, which included many neutrals and tories. Some of the gentry who were branded tories and removed from Philadelphia for part of the war included Samuel Powel, the mayor of the city; Benjamin Chew, a former alderman; Edward Shippen, a former councilman and judge of the Court of Vice-Admiralty; and Henry Drinker, a wealthy Quaker merchant. On the whole the position of much of the colonial gentry towards the Revolution was an acceptance of independence but little beyond that.[3] The men of new wealth who won admittance into Philadelphia's gentry during and after the Revolution had done so by their political and military service in the war and by business alliances with the descendants of the colonial families.

Between 1776 and 1789 this new coalition of Philadelphia's gentry engaged in a bitter political struggle against the supporters of Pennsylvania's democratic constitution of 1776. The events of those years were exceedingly complex with some men shifting sides with the prevailing political winds, but during the course of the contest the gentry of Philadelphia forged a political organization whose goals were twofold: first, to regain and solidify their political power lost in 1776; and, second, to win a new and far less radical state constitution. To develop a political organization, the gentry had to adopt the democratic ideals unleashed by the Revolution in order to win the broad-based support necessary to defeat the radical "Constitutionalists." To accommodate democratic practices the gentry were required to increase their personal contact with voters and acquire the flexibility to modify positions, concessions which resulted in some alteration of the elitist traditions of the colonial era.

This conservative political organization, or junto, called itself the Republican party, or the Anti-Constitutionalists. They feared the democratic constitution of Pennsylvania, feeling that its single-house legislature, unchecked by any other authority, was subject to corruption by the passions of the people. The junto had little faith in the ability of the people to govern themselves unless guided by the natural leaders of society—the wealthy and well-born. Philadelphia's junto seemed willing to adopt democratic practices by actively soliciting voter support, but felt strongly that the men the voters chose should be selected from the upper class. Moreover, Republicans saw that the Constitutionalists opposed government aid to business. Issues such as banking reform, tariffs, trade, and protection of private property were extremely important to the merchants, lawyers, and artisans of Philadelphia.[4]

The political struggle which ensued found the junto, after the elections of 1786, in complete control of the city's legislative seats. In fact, from 1786 until the call for the state constitutional convention in 1789 the junto-led Republican party controlled the state legislature. These victories resulted from the willingness of the city's gentry to use democratic campaign practices to win political power. In the election of 1786 and afterwards the junto actively solicited the votes of artisans and ethnic groups in Philadelphia. Their campaign rhetoric implied that the Constitutionalists denied artisans and tradesmen an equal opportunity to succeed by burdening them with heavy taxes and by attempting to remove the charter of the Bank of North America, which provided loans to artisans and tradesmen. Though appeals were framed to these groups, few artisans and tradesmen bothered to vote; indeed, in any given election, the average turnout was only slightly over 20 percent of the eligible voters.[5] But, by their implications the junto convinced a number of voters that the economic prosperity of the city was at stake and the goals of a free and open society threatened.

After the federal constitution was submitted to Pennsylvania in 1788, the junto played the leading role in winning its ratification. The businessmen who formed the backbone of the junto thought the new federal constitution reflected an ideal community based on the aims of private economic gain, and they tied their political organization to supporting the new central government.[6] Robert Morris, William Bingham, Thomas Fitzsimons, and James Wilson had established a close rapport with George Washington and Alexander Hamilton during the war. This provided them with exclusive ties to the leaders of the new federal government. As a result of these friendships and support, the junto obtained control of the federal patronage for Philadelphia throughout the period 1789 to 1801.[7]

At the same time, the Constitutionalists lacked the unity and stability needed to prevail against Philadelphia's entrenched gentry. The party achieved some success at the polls in Philadelphia during the war years but failed to establish a solid, organized party apparatus that could compete with the political machine developed by the junto. Philadelphia's Constitutionalists were led by Dr. James Hutchinson, a man Charles Biddle described as "fat enough to act the character of Falstaff without the stuffing." To Hutchinson, who derived great pleasure from the business of politics, fell the task of organizing the party in the city. He was assisted by three other Philadelphians: Jonathan Sergeant, a lawyer and member of the Continental Congress; Blair McClenachan, an Irish-born merchant who had achieved some success during the Revolution in establishing a counting-house; and George Bryan, justice of the state supreme court.[8]

Although the party remained strong in other sections of the state, after the junto's victories in the 1786 elections it rapidly deteriorated in Philadelphia.[9] The Constitutionalists' failure resulted from their inability to realize that they could no longer rely on war hysteria and the resultant anti-British sentiment as effective political issues. Constitutionalists further hastened their decline by the opposition many voiced in 1787 to the federal constitution, which had strong popular support in Philadelphia, where many voters sought a national government more responsive to the needs of an expanding commercial city.

The junto, in winning control of Philadelphia in 1786, had taken advantage of the favorable conditions prevailing in the city to establish a highly organized political machine. The environment of Philadelphia, with its high population density, the availability of many weekly and daily newspapers to dispense political news, and the high level of education, provided the gentry with the means to construct a political organization. In addition, because the city served as the state and federal capitals, Philadelphians felt a keen sense of being at the center of events, where their votes had a great effect in the outcome of any election. This sense of efficacy allowed the political leaders to rally an urban population and bring them out to vote. This remarkable feeling of community among Philadelphians helped spur the building of a political organization and enabled the junto to arrange mass meetings, in addition to using broadsides and newspapers, to win support for a new state constitution. Consequently, the acceptance the junto had won in the election of 1786 and subsequent elections carried over into the decade of the 1790s, when new issues challenged their political organization.

Those Philadelphians who had struggled throughout the 1780s to achieve some form of economic success had supported the junto in its efforts to build a political organization and win a new state constitution. These same men, who by the 1790s had secured an economic foothold, sought rewards from Philadelphia's entrenched gentry in the form of admittance into their exclusive social organizations and a share in the political spoils. Some of these *nouveaux arrivés* included Alexander J. Dallas, Thomas McKean, Israel Israel, John Swanwick, Stephen Girard, and Dr. Benjamin Rush. These ambitious types had taken an active role in winning ratification of the federal constitution in Philadelphia and had worked to defeat the Constitutionalists by supporting a call for a state constitutional convention in 1789.

After the Revolution the fluidity of wealth and class in Philadelphia created an atmosphere whereby men had expectations that they could rise in the community. Those who achieved economic success, such as Thomas Fitzsimons and William Bingham, had won, through business and marriage alliances, admittance into the upper circle of Philadelphia society. On the other hand, men, such as Dallas and Swanwick, who wanted to become full participants in the city's social and political life found the junto unwilling to open its doors to those who lacked business connections and/or family ties with the older colonial families. Other men, such as McKean and Rush, thought their services during the Revolution and the support they had given the federal and state constitution entitled them to a place in the city's decision-making councils.[10]

As the junto won its goals with the calling of a state constitutional convention in 1789, these men seeking political and social position, along with some other frustrated politicians, began to split with the established gentry. This rift became apparent soon after the calling of the state constitutional convention, when the junto neglected to include any of the new aspirants among its candidates for state and local offices. Frustrated and bitter, many of these ambitious men started to look outside the junto for their rewards.

One contemporary observer of Philadelphia's society noted,

> . . . there are several classes of company–the *Cream,* the *New Milk,* the *Skim Milk,* and the *Canailee*! . . . In private parties and in public meetings, the distinctions here are accurately preserved. The Cream generally curdles into a small group on the most eligible situation in the room. The New Milk seems floating between the wish to coalesce with the Cream and to escape from the Skim Milk, and the Skim Milk . . . laughs at the anxiety of the New Milk.[11]

During the 1790s the men excluded by the junto coalesced under the leadership of John Swanwick, Thomas McKean, Michael Leib, and Alexander J. Dallas with such former Constitutionalists as Dr. James Hutchinson, George Bryan, Blair McClenachan, Dr. William Shippen, and George Logan to form a political alliance. At the outset their distrust of the junto's control of Philadelphia held these men together. Unity came slowly and hesitantly and only after the former state parties had lost their reason for existence with the calling of a state constitional convention. As it emerged, this faction encompassed men who had supported the state constitution of 1776 and those who had opposed it. It included both radical whigs and moderate whigs, those who supported the federal consitution and those who had reservations about it. The struggle that ensued between this faction and the junto became not one of class warfare but a struggle for political power among some of the most affluent men of Philadelphia.

This rift within the gentry had its antecedents in the 1789 city elections to form a new municipal government under the Act of Incorporation passed by the state legislature that same year. This city charter provided for governmental control of Philadelphia to pass from the state executive council and the assembly to a city council composed of aldermen and a common council and headed by a mayor. The city government would be chosen at an election held in April, 1789. The board of aldermen would be elected by the freeholders of the city for a seven-year term, while the common councilmen would be elected by the freemen for a three-year term. The aldermen would elect the mayor from among their own number. The law-making power would rest with the aldermen and common council assembled together. The aldermen would also function as justices of the peace. The new municipal charter appeared well received by the junto; although framed on "popular principles," it provided them the opportunity to win control of the city government through democratic means.[12]

Immediately after the passage of the Act of Incorporation, the junto launched its campaign to win control of the city council. They sponsored a town meeting to select a committee that would form tickets for alderman and the common council. This committee would then make its recommendations to another public meeting which would officially endorse the tickets.[13] This method of nominating candidates had developed during the colonial era, when the wealthy families selected candidates from among their own number. These meetings had a twofold purpose: to win widespread popular approval for the tickets, and to give the voters the illusion that they had a voice in the selection of candidates.

The junto's candidates for aldermen and common council came only from the ranks of the "old" wealth and completely ignored those men of "new" wealth. This lack of recognition came, no doubt, as a serious blow to many who had actively supported the junto in its struggles with the Constitutionalists. The men the junto selected included such merchants as Joseph Swift, John Nixon, Joseph Ball, and Samuel Miles, along with former tories Samuel Powel and Benjamin Chew. The junto also named a city election committee, which would have 3,000 tickets printed and distributed throughout Philadelphia. The ticket would also appear in the various city newspapers. Although the gentry faced no solid opposition, they wanted to elect all the men on their tickets through an organized campaign effort. The junto framed its campaign appeal in traditional elitist terms, claiming that the voters should choose only men of wealth, men whose affluence prevented them from "trespassing on the community." In the election all fifteen candidates backed by the junto won handily over candidates proposed by unorganized groups.[14]

The campaign for the common council appeared more bitter and closely contested than the aldermanic races. The junto told the electorate that its candidates would look out for the general interest of the community, which meant it would strive to maintain, as the only goal of government, a setting wherein each citizen would have the opportunity to seek private wealth through his own industry. The opposition, composed chiefly of Constitutionalists, tried to convince the voters that the junto's candidates, who were all freeholders, would not look out for the workingman's interests. One writer appealed to the freemen to select candidates who "are in your station in life–men who will not *betray* your interest." Another, who called himself the "Old Mechanic," asserted that the poor rate, the streets, the "watch and lamp tax," and many other important issues that concerned the freemen would be passed by the new city council. Only by sending their own men, he claimed, would the freemen be heard and "taxes judiciously laid."[15]

Despite these efforts Philadelphians elected twenty-two of the junto's thirty-three candidates. All of the eleven men not on the junto ticket came from the ranks of the established gentry. Moreover, only about 24 percent of the eligible voters bothered to cast their ballots.[16] This voter apathy is attributable to two factors: one, the lack of political issues that would stir the interest of the voters; and, two, the absence of alternative candidates who would provide voters with a clear choice. It seemed to many Philadelphians that the candidates all came from the gentry and that once elected they would pursue policies that few people found unacceptable. The election returns demonstrated that Philadelphians willingly placed their trust in a group of wealthy merchants and lawyers who had supported the federal constitution and who called for the adoption of a new and less democratic state constitution. The opposition lacked the issues and, more importantly, the organization to challenge successfully the junto at the polls. The junto had taken advantage of the good feelings generated by the adoption of the federal constitution in Philadelphia and had used it to win control of city government. In addition, during the course of the campaign, the junto had reinforced its claim that once in power it would preserve a free and open economy where each man would have the opportunity to gain economic prosperity.

Nevertheless, the election success of the junto caused some bitterness within the ranks of the Federalist gentry. The men of "new" wealth saw that the older elements of the upper class had not included them either as candidates nor sought their advice during the campaign. This neglect caused some apprehensions as to what their place would be and what political offices they could hope to hold. This resentment in no way meant that the dissatisfied Federalists formed a distinct faction within the junto, but rather they had begun to question what the future held for each of them. For the moment, however, they put the disappointments behind them and concentrated on winning a new state consitution.

A few days after the passage of Philadelphia's city charter, those members of the state assembly who opposed the current state constitution met at City Tavern to determine how to bring about a call for a new state government. They decided to ask the people to express their sentiments about calling a convention "for altering and amending our state constitution." The address reflected the reasons why the junto believed the state needed a new constitution: the federal constitution must predominate, and the single-house legislature needed a greater check upon its powers.[17]

Opposition to the resolution came from Constitutionalists, who claimed that a few men wanted to destroy the constitution and "throw the state into confusion for the sake of gratifying the ambitions and mercenary views of our aristocratic faction [in Philadelphia]."[18] Many of Philadelphia's political leaders, on the other hand, saw an opportunity to defeat and destroy their "Constitutionalist" opponents. As one junto supporter put it, the convention would have a "direct Operation in dissolving that Party Combination which has so long kept this state in Broils and Discontent."[19] The junto formed a committee to obtain signatures on petitions to demonstrate that Philadelphians supported the call for a constitutional convention. This committee had handbills distributed throughout the city and sent copies to other parts of the state, requesting support for the petitions. They claimed to represent a "number of respectable Citizens" of Philadelphia who wanted a constitutional convention.[20]

The *Federal Gazette* launched a campaign to win support for the constitutional convention by claiming that the state constitution appeared to work against bringing the federal capital to Philadelphia. The state and federal governments, the paper contended, could not remain in harmony since the former was unicameral and the latter bicameral. The *Gazette* noted that the people who opposed change in the state constitution were in a small minority, based on the number who had opposed the resolutions in the assembly. The paper contended that the forty-one who voted in favor represented 41,000 people, while the seventeen opposed spoke for only 17,000 residents.[21]

In Philadelphia only the *Independent Gazetteer* opposed the call for a convention. It termed the state constitution the "anchor of the people's liberties" and called for its retention until the passage of the Bill of Rights. The paper charged that a "certain aristocratic party joined with those" who had not supported the Revolution sought to destroy the state constitution.[22] Constitutionalists appealed to class bias when they told Philadelphians to reject the junto which represented only the upper class. By such an approach they wanted to scare voters into believing the loss of the state constitution would endanger their liberties and bring a government dedicated to the enhancement of the gentry. These tactics had some effect, for the number of petitions received by the assembly in favor of the convention was not at all what the junto had expected.[23]

When the assembly reconvened in September, 1789, Anti-Constitutionalists, after several days of debate, pushed through a report calling for a constitutional convention. All but one member of the Philadelphia city and county delegation voted in favor of the report. William Lewis opposed it on the grounds that the results of the constitutional convention should be submitted to the people for their approval. He considered the resolutions of the assembly as an "unwarrantable assumption of power."[24]

In the city elections held during the fall of 1789, the voters would select members for the assembly and delegates to the constitutional convention to be held in November. In its campaign the junto told the voters that only "inflexible federalists" should be elected to serve in the assembly. It nominated only men who had supported the federal constitution and those who had taken leading roles in advocating a change in the state's constitution. At a meeting held at the State House, the junto framed its ticket for the assembly and convention. All the assembly candidates came from the ranks of the entrenched gentry. The selection of two of the candidates, William Bingham and Henry Drinker, aroused opposition because some thought at least two of the assembly candidates should be from those not closely associated with the established gentry.[25]

On election day this split widened into an open breach. Those who opposed the nomination of Bingham and Drinker appeared at the State House, the polling place for Philadelphia, passing out tickets that did not include the names of Bingham and Drinker. Finally, after much haggling, both sides agreed upon Francis Gurney, an Anglican merchant, and William Rawle, a Quaker lawyer, and hand-written tickets bearing their names soon appeared at the polls.[26] This compromise was possible only because Gurney and Rawle had declared that they had no further political ambitions. These declarations allowed the opposing camps to reach an agreement rather than see some candidates from the Constitutional faction win an assembly seat. In the assembly races this compromise assured the election of junto candidates. The returns showed that Seckle and Hiltzheimer had run four hundred votes ahead of Gurney and three hundred ahead of Rawle, indicating, that many voters either did not vote for all the candidates or split their votes among miscellaneous candidates where returns are unavailable.[27]

With the meeting of the constitutional convention in Philadelphia on November 24, 1789, the *Federal Gazette* heralded the extinction of "party spirit in Pennsylvania." It saw the composition of the constitutional convention as providing the opportunity to compromise the basic differences between the Republican and Constitutional parties. With such political realists as Thomas Mifflin, Thomas McKean, and James Wilson leading the convention, some form of agreement appeared certain. Most of the state's politicians seemed to desire a constitution with a two-house legislature and a strong executive officer. As congressman Thomas Fitzsimons realized, it would not do to press the Constitutionalists too hard, since after the constitution was written power in both the city and state would be at stake. He also foresaw a "considerable revolution" in state politics, where the "Quakers and old Tories" would join the Constitutionalists rather than the Republicans and with the deserters from the latter, "will rule the roost."[28] Accordingly, it was important that both sides come to an agreement wherein each felt it had an opportunity to win control in the city and the state.

A constitution soon emerged that seemed to satisfy the vast majority of the delegates. It called for a bicameral legislature. Members of the senate would be elected from districts and serve three years, while delegates to the house would be elected from the counties and the city of Philadelphia and serve one-year terms. The executive was placed in the hands of a popularly elected governor, who held veto power over legislation, plus numerous patronage positions, in addition to being commander-in-chief of the state militia. The governor's term ran for three years, with the stipulation that no man could serve more than nine out of twelve years. It granted suffrage to any white adult freeman who had lived in the state for two years preceding an election and had paid state or county taxes assessed at least six months before voting. This suffrage law was one of the most liberal in the new nation. The constitution, which went into effect on September 2, 1790, represented a compromise that satisfied many of the demands of both parties. Each thought it had a great opportunity to win control of the state.[29] In that effort the largest city in the nation would play an important role.

Even before the constitutional convention completed its work, politicians in Philadelphia began to search for the proper man to run for governor. This office, with its vast patronage and executive authority, represented an important post, as it could firmly establish one group in power for a long time. "Nine years is a long term," Senator William Maclay explained to Benjamin Rush, "and I think it two to one that the person who wins the first election, will hold it for that period." Maclay indicated that Philadelphia politicians must unite around one man or their influence in the state would be diminished. "How much respect ought to be paid to them [Philadelphia] in the chair of Chief Magistrate is obvious."[30]

During the spring of 1790 Philadelphia's leaders centered their attention on four possible gubernatorial candidates: Thomas Mifflin, the president of the state and popular revolutionary general; Robert Morris, United States senator, wealthy merchant and a leader of the junto; Samuel Bryan, justice of the state supreme court and a leader of the Constitutionalists in Philadelphia; and Frederick Muhlenberg of Philadelphia county, Speaker of the United States House of Representatives. Party loyalty had little to do with the choice for governor, for, with the adoption of the state constitution, new issues and new alliances began to take the place of old state parties. Most politicians in Philadelphia wanted to unite around one man, but with the decline of the Republican party that proved impossible. As a result, the junto divided into two camps, with one faction centering around the city's congressional delegation opposing Mifflin's candidacy and another faction composed of men of "new" wealth along with some of the older, more entrenched gentry supporting him.

The remnants of the Constitutional party in Philadelphia, though favoring Bryan, seemed willing to throw their support to Mifflin. "Desponding owing to an ignorance in our strength," explained Samuel Bryan, Jr., "has led to the idea that Mifflin would be the best bet we could carry." To many politicians throughout the state Mifflin was not closely identified with either of the old state parties, and once in office he might be persuaded to reward certain groups. Moreover, many thought that because of his great popularity, a result of his wartime service, he had the best prospects of winning; and with no party loyalties to bind them, politicians began to proclaim his virtues. Dr. James Hutchinson took a leading role in supporting Mifflin, as did many other Constitutionalists.[31]

Nevertheless, Philadelphia's congressional delegation, along with others in the junto, opposed the candidacy of Mifflin from the outset. They feared that their policies would not be followed by the state government and that they would have no voice in patronage distribution. At their weekly dinner in New York City, with James Wilson in attendance, Thomas Fitzsimons told the group: "Gentlemen, it is expected of us that we should fix the governor of Pennsylvania." This antipathy towards Mifflin stemmed from his conduct as president of the state, when he had thrown little or no patronage in their direction. They obviously wanted a man they could more easily control. At this weekly dinner Morris and Muhlenberg agreed that their friends should determine the contest between them. Morris closed by declaring to Muhlenberg; "May you or I be Governor." Shortly after the meeting Fitzsimons wrote to Rush and urged his friends in Philadelphia to take an active part in defeating Mifflin. Having little faith in the people's ability to judge the candidates objectively, he feared the election of Mifflin.[32]

The Fitzsimons faction did not choose a candidate until September, when Morris announced his decision not to run. At the same time Fitzsimons discouraged Muhlenberg from seeking the faction's endorsement for governor. Fitzsimons had told Muhlenberg of the power and dignity of the house speaker's post and assured him his continuance in it if he declined to run for governor. Muhlenberg soon afterwards indicated that he would not run against the wishes of his "republican friends."[33] Early in September this clique threw its support to General Arthur St. Clair. St. Clair had served in the British army before settling in Pennsylvania, where he had held a series of offices in the western counties. During the Revolution he held a commission from and served in the Continental Congress. In 1787 he was named governor of the Northwest Territory.[34] Yet, he was not as well known to the voters as Mifflin.

After the adjournment of the constitutional convention, the Fitzsimons faction issued a broadside congratulating Pennsylvanians on their new constitution and proclaiming the candidacy of Arthur St. Clair. Those signing the appeal were all Philadelphia politicians and members of the state Republican party.[35] After issuing the broadside Fitzsimons wrote to St. Clair indicating the support he had and told him that "some of your friends will not spare pains to accomplish what they believe would prove highly advantageous to our country." Tench Coxe declared that St. Clair would make a fine chief magistrate and that he would bring the state in line with the more patriotic objectives of the federal government. He noted that the men who supported St. Clair by signing the broadside would have great weight in the election.[36]

In their public appeals St. Clair's supporters emphasized that as a friend of General Washington he could get more accomplished for Pennsylvania than could Mifflin, who, they hinted, might be at odds with the president. However, even with the addition of more Philadelphia political leaders, the St. Clair cause stirred little excitement. Thomas Fitzsimons soon complained, "our opposition to Mifflin is feeble in the extreme, a thousand circumstances combine to render it so. As . . . may be presumed from appearances at present it will be given up." The candidacy of St. Clair had served to unite Mifflin's supporters, who, Fitzsimons implied, were all members of the old Constitutional party. The "Republicans have ever been Indolent," he concluded, "except on extreme necessity." St. Clair also believed that the Constitutional party had supported Mifflin.[37]

In Philadelphia former Constitutionalists did support Mifflin. But, for that matter, not all of the junto had endorsed St. Clair. This point seemed logical when most of St. Clair's Philadelphia supporters were drawn from the ranks of the congressional delegation or held some federal position. Men such as Robert Morris and Fitzsimons had felt that Mifflin lacked the favor of General Washington, which eliminated his effectiveness in acquiring federal patronage.

While St. Clair had difficulty arousing support, Mifflin had no trouble at all. At a meeting held at Epple's Tavern in Philadelphia, supporters of Mifflin issued an appeal that attempted to play down partisan differences. At the same time they sought to assure Philadelphians that Mifflin had a record of protecting private property, as well as concern for all classes of people. In subsequent newspaper attacks they painted the backers of St. Clair guilty of class bias. "These self-sufficient gentlemen have had the effrontery to step forward and endeavor . . . to tarnish . . . the character" of a man who has the respect of most people in the state.[38]

The race for governor did not overshadow the important contest for the state senate and the five assembly seats from Philadelphia. One writer for the junto defined the talents necessary for the city's representatives and revealed the junto's strong attachment to elitist rule: first, representatives should have an intimate knowledge of the city's commercial interests which would allow them to use the vast machine of wealth and resources; second, a full knowledge of finance was needed as well as support of the public credit; and, third, they should be of independent means, " in order to add dignity and weight to the city's representation." The junto held two public meetings for the purpose of framing tickets for the senate and assembly. The politicians who managed these affairs came from the gentry; they seemed to have selected the nominees beforehand and then submitted the names to the meetings in order to give the appearance of popular choice.[39]

The day after the meetings a split within the ranks of the Federalist junto became evident. Discontented Federalists objected to the exclusive practices followed by the junto in framing its tickets. To demonstrate their resentment, they held their own meeting and nominated for the assembly three of the junto's candidates plus two candidates of their own choosing.[40] In forming their tickets these disaffected Federalists served notice on the junto that they no longer would support the practices and the candidates of the older establishment.

Election day brought more than the normal number of Philadelphians to the polls to cast their ballots for the establishment of the new state government. In the governor's race about 26 percent of the voters turned out, up from the mean of around 20 percent. The results of the election provided little in the way of surprises. Thomas Mifflin routed St. Clair in Philadelphia, getting 94.8 percent, while in the state at large he received 90.8 percent of the vote.[41] Mifflin owed his victory to his great popularity, for he had little organization and no rousing campaign was launched in his behalf. Mifflin found support from a wide sector of the community. He received the almost solid support of Constitutionalists in the city and state, and had strong backing from many former Republicans in Philadelphia. The campaign of his opponent, on the other hand, started with a small clique, organized in Philadelphia, which after one week lost all interest when they found little support for their candidate.

Samuel Bryan said of Mifflin's victory that he had emancipated "himself from the servile thralldom of a junto" that allowed no "deviation from their monopolizing dictates." But Robert Morris touched the hard realities of Mifflin's huge majority when he observed that those men gave out St. Clair's name "promising to support him, but never gave themselves any further trouble . . . therefore Mifflin's industry and promises carried him almost unanimously."[42] Morris, of course, had not included himself in the clique that wanted to defeat Mifflin and had promised to back the candidacy of St. Clair.

In the contests for the senate and assembly seats from Philadelphia the candidates supported by the junto organization won easy victories. In the senate races the lowest junto candidate garnered 63.3 percent of the vote. In the assembly races three of the five junto candidates won handily. The other two won by margins of 54.0 and 52.8 percent respectively. The number of Philadelphians who voted in these contests dipped to 25 percent, a slight decline from those who voted for governor.[43] The junto candidates won because they had the support of a well-organized clique. The opposition lacked the unity and issues to mount a serious campaign to oust the entrenched gentry, who had won the loyalty of Philadelphians who believed that elected office should be bestowed on men who had demonstrated their abilities by acquiring wealth and status. But the results indicated that opposition to the Federalist junto had a chance to succeed if more Philadelphians could be enticed to the ballot box. As yet, this huge, untapped mass of Philadelphia voters, chiefly middle- and lower-class artisans and unskilled laborers, saw no real differences between the candidates. This vast number of Philadelphians would have to be organized and convinced that their own self-interest demanded that they take an active role in political affairs.

After Mifflin's election a struggle ensued among Philadelphia's politicians to influence the governor in the appointment of the newly created post of Secretary of the Commonwealth. This position would carry with it great influence in patronage, since the man who held the office would be the chief advisor to the governor. Constitutionalists of Philadelphia supported Samuel Bryan, claiming that his appointment would draw the line between the "Aristocratic and democratic interests," consolidate Constitutionalists, and keep the governor "from the wiles of the other party who will practice every finesse and alienate him from his present views." The junto tended to support Charles Biddle as the lesser of the two evils, realizing that it would have little voice in the final selection.[44] When Mifflin appointed Alexander J. Dallas, a young attorney from Philadelphia, it shocked the city's gentry. Dallas's appointment soon provided a rallying point for those discontented politicians and men from the "newer" wealth who demanded free and equal access to the city's social and political institutions.

Although Philadelphia's politicians fought over the election of a new city government and the establishment of the new state constitution, they appeared united on one issue—their desire to have the federal capital moved to Philadelphia.[45] After the ratification of the federal constitution, Philadelphians made every effort to have the capital moved from New York City. Even before Congress met in the spring of 1789, Tench Coxe wrote to James Madison indicating his great concern that the first meeting place of the new government should be in the Quaker city. He explained that the nation would benefit from the city's close ties with Europe and its cosmopolitan atmosphere. Benjamin Rush also made an effort by supporting John Adams for vice-president, thinking that Adams would back such a move. Rush indicated to Adams that he, Morris and James Wilson had helped win the vice-presidential seat for him, and he hoped that Adams' influence would "be exerted immediately in favor of a motion to bring congress to Philadelphia." He wanted to see the capital moved at once to Philadelphia to prevent "the seat of government [moving] to a more southern . . . and less republican state" in the future. Rush pointed out that Philadelphia was the "headquarters of federalism" and had few anti-federalists, and "when discovered they are so contemptible in point of character" that even the "disaffected in Congress would not associate with them."[46]

During the first year-and-a-half of the new government's existence, prominent Philadelphians actively corresponded and lobbied with the delegation in New York. According to Peter Muhlenberg, congressman from Pennsylvania, most delegates wanted to move out of New York. Pennsylvania could acquire the capital, he thought, if the matter was brought up by some other state. Muhlenberg seemed a little surprised to find "what strange prejudices some of the Members have implied against" Philadelphia. They seem to fear, he explained, "the commercial influence," but that could be overcome in time "if the city could be fixed upon as the temporary seat of Congress, until a permanent one is established." He suggested how this aversion might be overcome. Congressmen passing through the city should be flattered with attention. He, himself, would take the first opportunity to "accompany Mr. Fisher Ames, and others of the Eastern [New England] delegation to Philad[elph]ia, to take the benefit of the fresh air in the *open enclosure* at the State House" and speak to them of "the friendly Assistance of Mr. [Tench] Coxe, to get them acquineted [sic] in the city."[47] Robert Morris declared that he intended to get the "General Government Seated as near to the City . . . as possible." He indicated that Pennsylvania held the balance between the southern states and the "Eastern interests" and that if the Pennsylvania delegates delayed they "would lose the power of fixing the Government within our boundaries."[48]

Philadelphia newspapers carried out an active campaign to bring the capital back to Philadelphia. They printed petitions from various groups and societies to Congress requesting that Congress move to Philadelphia. The *Federal Gazette* warned that confidence in Congress would fall as a consequence of "staying in an improper place." The paper later explained that Philadelphia was filled "Chiefly with Americans who exhibit the ancient simple republican manners of our country."[49]

The recently elected city officials also lobbied for the removal of Congress to Philadelphia. The city council wrote to Thomas Fitzsimons advising him that the new court house, erected on the same square as the State House, could provide Congress with the space it required. When Fitzsimons pointed out that in addition the city would need to provide a house for the president and make other buildings available to the federal government, the city council complied by voting the funds necessary to remodel the court house and by using a lottery to raise the funds for the building of a new city hall which could be used by the federal government. The city council also provided funds to have the home of Robert Morris remodeled for the use of the president.[50]

The importance of bringing the capital to Philadelphia cannot be overemphasized; both Philadelphians serving in Congress, Thomas Fitzsimons and George Clymer, had declared that they could not vote for the assumption of state debts incurred during the Revolution unless Congress moved to their city. Both men strongly favored assumption and their votes were needed for its passage, but both felt the necessity to strike a bargain in order to save their political lives.[51] No politician representing Philadelphia could expect reelection if he had not extended every effort to bring the capital back to what Philadelphians considered its rightful home. By July, 1790, a compromise had been reached and the question settled by granting a temporary residence to Philadelphia for ten years, with the permanent location to be on the Potomac River. This agreement was reached after the bill calling for the assumption of state debts had been tied to the residency plan, with the supporters of both agreeing to vote for both bills.[52]

Philadelphia received news of the capital's transference with great joy and excitement. Many believed that once the capital was in Philadelphia it would not move again. Politicians from all factions tried to claim credit for the move. Some asserted that Robert Morris played the leading role, but most of the city's political leaders, especially those connected with the city government, credited Thomas Fitzsimons with supporting the compromise that brought the capital to the Quaker city.[53] With that kind of support Fitzsimons had the edge over any challenger in the coming contest to retain his congressional seat.

The two years that followed Pennsylvania's ratification of the federal Constitution had seen the junto win a new state constitution and city charter. The junto's victory in 1786 had generated the support it needed to defeat its old rivals and gain political ascendancy in Philadelphia. By 1790 the threads of a new political interest began to emerge around the frustrations and ambitions of the newer gentry who wanted to take their place in the power structure of Philadelphia. Moreover, the increased prosperity of the 1790s and the growth of the city's population added to the fluidity of the political atmosphere; one obvious result of a large population was a surplus of potential leaders. By the 1790s a man whose wealth placed him among the most wealthy fifth of the taxpayers found himself one of 1,377 of equal substance. This increasing number of prosperous taxpayers put greater pressures on the Federalist elite to include them in the distribution of the spoils. When Federalists refused many in the upper-class looked elsewhere for political rewards.

Chapter Three

FERMENT AND OPPOSITION, 1789-1792

Alexander Hamilton's First Report on the Public Credit provided the first test of stability for the federal interest in Philadelphia. The debate over the deposition of the domestic war debt and federal assumption of state debts caused Philadelphians to assess their position in the light of their own self-interests and the effect of these interests on the future of the new federal government. The importance that many Philadelphians attached to settling the national debt and thus securing a stable financial condition cannot be overemphasized in a city whose economy depended chiefly on trade. The question of how best to handle national and state debts caused some alienated Federalists to split off and form their own political faction.[1] This question, coupled with the exclusive political practices of the city's Federalist junto, drove a wedge between the gentry and forced those who opposed the junto to bring their own case to the voters.

Speculation in federal securities centered in Philadelphia. Those involved included some Federalist leaders, such as William Bingham and Robert Morris. These and other speculators as early as 1789 had petitioned Congress to act in funding the domestic debt.[2] In fact, the vast majority of Philadelphia's political leaders strongly favored funding as essential to the city's economy and their own self-interests. William Bingham wrote to his friend Alexander Hamilton urging the adoption of a funding program and the creation of a national bank. Other Philadelphians saw in the proposals an ideal opportunity to increase their own wealth as well as strengthen the city's ties to the new federal government. Philadelphia public creditors generally supported Hamilton's plan that continental bonds be redeemed from their present owners at face value plus four percent accumulated interest payable in specie or western lands.[3]

To aid in a speedy passage of a funding law, many Philadelphia Federalists pressured Philadelphians to lobby for the legislation. They believed that only by its passage could the union be secured and the national debt stabilized.[4] William Bradford urged that the sooner a funding law was adopted the sooner the public mind would rest, and the sooner "these papers came to a settled value, the better for the country." Clement Biddle, one of the largest bondholders in Philadelphia, also cautioned that Congress should act immediately to pass a funding bill else a "less favorable plan" be approved that would not satisfy those Philadelphians holding and speculating in the securities. Other Philadelphians argued that the funding measures were practicable "and just towards the public creditors." Although Hamilton's plan did not give the holder cash, one writer said, "pray! have not thousands lost by the ravages of war, by tender laws, by the many depredations of anarchy." Thomas Fitzsimons claimed that the plan made equal provisions for all and that discrimination was not a practicable solution.[5]

While most public creditors in Philadelphia favored some form of a funding law, they opposed assumption of state debts incurred during the Revolution. William Bradford warned that assumption had "created alarm and desponding among the public creditors" in Philadelphia. Clement Biddle claimed that many of the original bondholders considered assumption "as a millstone about the necks of the whole system which must finally sink it." When Hamilton later connected assumption with the removal of the capital to Philadelphia, many Philadelphians who opposed assumption seemed willing, though reluctant, to accept the plan.[6] Most of Philadelphia's public creditors opposed assumption because they felt their holdings might be endangered, but after the measure was tied to moving the capital to their city they seemed willing to place any short term economic gain behind the long term gains that having the capital in Philadelphia would bring.

Meanwhile, Philadelphia's public creditors still lobbied for a strong funding bill. In July, 1790, public creditors organized a town meeting in support of such a bill. The meeting approved a committee to draft a petition to Congress which would indicate the city's support for the bill.[7] The self-interests of the public creditors cut across party lines, with Federalists and anti-Federalists supporting a funding bill modeled after Hamilton's plan. The support given to the funding plan demonstrated that Philadelphia's public creditors saw it as a means of enhancing their own wealth. This was a case of men placing their own interest behind the national good.

At the same time opposition appeared to any funding of the war debt. Some Philadelphians, chiefly former Constitutionalists, believed that funding would only strengthen the federal government, and they opposed any plan that would create a strong central government. Constitutionalists feared that a funding bill would mean "governing by debt," which could lead to constitutional subversion. They were concerned that such a plan would destroy republican government by undermining the independence of the legislative branch. To Constitutionalists the funding plan would entrench a few "leading nabobs, tory whigs . . . and their self important company brokers" in political power in Philadelphia and the federal government.[8] In fact, this attack initiated many of the themes used in the following years by Republicans, who always painted Federalists as an exclusive organization serving only the needs of the upper class and therefore a threat to republican government.

By the summer of 1790, the loud debate over funding and assumption had begun to arouse strong passions among the gentry. Men who had found themselves on the same side during the struggle over both the federal and state constitutions suddenly found themselves opposing each other. Funding and assumption had won the support of most politicians who had favored the federal Constitution. But opposition to these measures had begun to form from some disaffected Federalists who saw in it the opportunity to advance their own political ambitions and by others who genuinely felt that funding and assumption represented a threat to the Constitution. This opposition centered around the growing dissatisfaction with the exclusiveness of the junto and took the form of supporting the discrimination plan introduced in Congress by James Madison. This plan proposed to discriminate between the original bondholders–persons who had rendered services or supplies during the Revolution–and the later purchasers of the securities, who usually paid only a fraction of their face value. Madison called for an equitable division of the profit, which otherwise would have gone only to the purchaser at the time the debt was funded. As this opposition coalesced, it came under the leadership of Dr. James Hutchinson and Alexander J. Dallas. To win support for the discrimination plan, this faction sent a petition through Philadelphia "with a view that it should be signed by the late army praying discrimination to be made" in favor of the original bondholders.[9]

The petition forced Federalists to defend the funding plan. One newspaper asserted that the original bondholders had not supported the petition. Thomas Fitzsimons wrote to his friend Benjamin Rush indicating his satisfaction with the funding bill in its original form. He claimed that on principle it was the best, and he knew that in "public life it is too often necessary to sacrifice to public opinion . . . but there are occasions when every man in public life ought to act on his own."[10] Rush remained unconvinced. He and other Federalists saw funding as an economic program that made stockholders of Congressmen and whose economic interest committed them to the executive branch. Rush feared that the executive branch through its control of the treasury department could apply economic pressure on those Congressmen who held public securities. The presence of such Congressmen, Rush believed, would destroy that body's independence and endanger balanced government. Rush saw the beginning of an American aristocracy and with it constitutional degeneration. To him the whole structure of republican government was at stake. He concluded that funding could cause a majority of Philadelphians to oppose the measure or at least support Madison's resolution in favor of discrimination.[11]

Rush and James Hutchinson extended their opposition beyond petitioning when they started an active campaign to arouse public opinion against members of Congress who supported Hamilton's funding plan. In fact, Rush broke with his old friend Fitzsimons over funding. Rush told Madison that in the next election he thought that no congressmen from Philadelphia who voted against Madison's proposal could expect to be reelected. "The Quakers and Germans," he said, "who *now* govern directly or indirectly . . . our city . . . possess very few certificates." He charged that Fitzsimons had differed in his character as a man of understanding with "our best citizens by becoming a *midwife* of a system" which he claimed to oppose when elected to Congress.[12]

At this same time Philadelphians learned of a proposed federal excise tax on distilled liquors designed to help fund the national debt. The opposition it aroused represented the strongest protest to any measure since the Revolution. This bill hit hardest the artisans and German population, who saw that the tax would make liquor more expensive and thus have a decided effect on their life style. Here many Philadelphians could see how national economic measures had a direct bearing on their lives. One outraged member of the assembly, Richard Wells, cried that if the language he uttered against the excise was the language of sedition he wished it in his powers "on behalf of the liberties of the people to extend his voice as a trumpet till the tyranny fell before him as did the walls of Jericho."[13] As the debate continued in Congress, meetings were held and petitions circulated through Philadelphia opposing the excise tax as an "infringement of the liberties of the People." A meeting, chaired by George Logan, passed resolutions which described the excise as a "dangerous violation of our natural and inalienable rights" and insisted that Congress had no right to interfere with the use of distilled liquors.[14] This interference by the government in the private affairs of Philadelphians seemed a threat to their right to strive for wealth without being restricted by laws or institutions. Philadelphians were firm in their beliefs that the only role of government was to maintain a setting wherein each citizen could search for wealth in a free and open economy. They therefore viewed the excise tax as a threat to their "liberties."

As a result of this pressure the assembly of Pennsylvania voted to instruct the state's delegation in Congress to oppose the excise bill. In the vote all the members from both the city and county, with the exception of William Bingham and Blair McClenachan, supported the motion. Bingham held that the state had no right to interfere with the actions of the federal government.[15] He and other Federalists placed support of administration policies ahead of what their constituents wanted. But this in part could be explained because most Federalist leaders had already achieved economic success, and the tax on distilled liquors would do little if any harm to their economic interests.

Bingham's position found support in Philadelphia among Federalists, who took a dim view of any state action that challenged the authority of the federal government. This opposition appeared in the state senate, where the junto had more influence than in the assembly. The senate narrowly defeated the assembly resolution nine to eight, with Philadelphia's senators voting with the majority. The long range political effects of this struggle escaped the Federalists. They did not see that for the first time a segment of the community which had been politically apathetic had come out strongly against Federalist financial measures and in the process were being organized politically by the opponents of the junto. Moreover, this opposition to excise taxes represented a mere prelude to the uproar caused in 1794, when Federalists enacted additional duties.[16] This was an explosive issue that allowed Republicans to make inroads on Federalist sentiment in Philadelphia.

Meanwhile, the introduction of the national bank bill in Congress found widespread support from among the gentry of Philadelphia regardless of their political affiliation. Even many of those who had opposed funding and assumption came out in support of the national bank. In addition, the Bank of North America, which was controlled by the junto, threw its weight behind the proposed national bank. Other Philadelphians saw that while the national bank might temporarily take money out of the city's economy it would still represent an economic advantage to the commerce of Philadelphia.[17]

This support represented only a logical development of the city's great interest in maintaining its leadership as the financial and commercial center of the nation. Furthermore, Philadelphians believed that the government was fulfilling its proper role in proposing a national bank, since the bank would help create a setting in which each individual would have the opportunity to attain his own wealth in a free and open market. With this wide backing supporters of the national bank used all their influence to win public approval. After the bank bill had passed Congress, Thomas Willing, president of the Bank of North America, was named president of the Bank of the United States, as a reward for the valuable assistance given by the city's Federalists.[18]

Nevertheless, the bank brought mixed blessing to Philadelphia's economy. By late summer the city had come under a wave of speculation in Bank of the United States stock. Benjamin Rush wrote that the city "is one great theater of fraud and rapine. You hear nothing but *script* . . . at every corner. Merchants, grocers, shopkeepers, sea captains, and even apprentice boys have embarked in the business."[19] This speculation binge had lasted for more than a month when the bottom fell out of the market. The result was a major financial panic in Philadelphia, where, Jefferson said, "ships are lying idle at the wharfs, buildings are stopped, capital withdrawn from commerce, manufacturing, arts, and agriculture."[20] This crisis was short-lived, but another even more devastating crisis followed it ten months later. Rush declared that merchants, artisans, "tradesmen, draymen, widows, orphans, oystermen, marketwomen, churches, and even common prostitutes were caught in the credit squeeze."[21]

The effects of these two financial crises had an important impact on party development in Philadelphia. Men whose economic self-interest suffered blamed the policies of the Federalist party for their miseries. Funding, assumption, and the panic provided politicians disenchanted with the exclusiveness of the junto with issues that could win them support from the electorate. Fisher Ames noted a growing opposition to Federalists in Philadelphia that had "generated a regular, well-disciplined opposition party, whose leaders cry 'liberty,' but mean . . . 'power.' " Tench Coxe also expressed the concern of Philadelphia's Federalists that funding and assumption provided the opposition with the means to arouse public sentiment against them.[22]

In the midst of the financial panic of 1791 the junto had to turn its attention to winning a congressional election. Pennsylvania had not held its election for representatives to the Second Congress in the fall of 1790 because the state assembly had failed to pass an election law. In the election for the First Congress, held in January, 1789, candidates ran on an at-large basis. Philadelphians in the assembly favored such a plan, but assemblymen from rural counties preferred election by districts. The junto supported at-large elections because they could maintain control of the large population centered in the southeastern portion of the state and thus assure that the friends of government continued their control of Pennsylvania's congressional delegation.

In January, 1791, members from the west introduced in the assembly an election bill calling for election by districts, and after a month of debate the committee appointed by William Bingham, speaker of the assembly, reported a bill along this line. Supporters of the district plan asserted that in the past a few persons from Philadelphia had controlled the appointment of every office "of note" and that it did not seem surprising that "they are alarmed at the faintest attempts to thwart their views." One member explained: "Let the Drones of Philadelphia . . . sip the honey they have made in welcome, but do not suffer them to put gall in your cup." That kind of appeal worked effectively against the junto in winning support from members from other counties. The district election bill passed, thirty-three to twenty-eight, with all members from the city and county, save one, opposed. In the senate the district bill passed on March 10 with all Philadelphia's senators opposing the measure. The new law divided the state into eight districts, with Philadelphia and Delaware counties as one district.[23] This law thus deprived the junto of much of its power to affect elections outside the Philadelphia area.

The Dallas and Hutchinson faction opened their campaign by attacking the arch supporter of Hamilton's financial policies, Thomas Fitzsimons, who was running for reelection. But neither Dallas nor Hutchinson could find anyone in Philadelphia willing to challenge Fitzsimons and the junto organization.[24] As the campaign progressed neither issues nor candidates appeared to excite the interests of the voters. The junto, as it had done in the past, held its meeting to nominate candidates for Congress and the state legislature. Party leaders made no real effort to mount an active campaign, since the opposition appeared unable to run a ticket against them. In fact, the Hutchinson faction had found almost no support to run a slate for the city's five assembly seats. What Hutchinson and Dallas had thought during the summer of 1791 would make lively campaign issues—Hamilton's financial plans—appeared to work in favor of the Federalists. A majority of Philadelphians seemed willing to continue their support of men who had returned the capital to Philadelphia and brought the headquarters of the new national bank to the city. The economy appeared stabilized and the voters pleased with the settlement of the funding law. It was no surprise when Fitzsimons and the junto's candidates for the assembly were all elected.[25]

Soon after the 1791 elections a bill calling for state-wide elections for the Third Congress was introduced in the assembly in the spring of 1792. The Philadelphia delegation rammed the bill through before the federal Congress had voted on the number of congressmen the state would have. The election bill that passed called for every voter to return a handwritten ticket with the names of as many persons as the state was entitled to in Congress. The bill had the solid support of all the members from both the city and county.[26]

With the passage of this general election law Philadelphia would again exert its power and influence in determining the complexion of the state's delegation to the national Congress. Accordingly, the law forced the men in Philadelphia who opposed the junto to organize on a statewide level and develop campaign tactics that would aid them in their efforts to oust the ruling clique from political control of Philadelphia.

After the second financial panic the measures adopted by the federal government had begun to draw more critics than some Philadelphians, after the election of 1791, had thought possible.[27] Opponents of federal policies began to unite and hold meetings in homes such as George Logan's to discuss the political situation and means they could adopt to win support at the polls. James Hutchinson, Alexander Dallas, Benjamin Bache, editor of the *General Advertiser* and grandson of Benjamin Franklin, and at times Thomas Jefferson, met to decide how to form and build a political organization. This faction realized that they had to develop issues and organize voters who in the past had been apathetic or unwilling to vote.[28] Philadelphians who took the trouble to vote had traditionally accepted that the city's successful businessmen should be the political leaders of the community. Any group challenging the city's elite would have to convince Philadelphians that the junto was not entitled to office by virtue of birth or wealth. Some Philadelphians began to accept the idea that political parties or factions were not only unavoidable but necessary in a society where opposing interests existed.

Junto leaders realized that they would face a severe challenge in the upcoming congressional elections. To prepare for it they met privately and adopted a plan which called for public meetings to be held in each county beginning with Philadelphia in late July to form a ticket. At the completion of these meetings, delegates appointed by the gatherings would meet in Lancaster at the end of August to set the Federalist ticket. The junto, led by Thomas Fitzsimons, wanted to place on the ticket only the most popular men who adhered to federal sentiments. Consequently, before the Philadelphia meeting in July the junto had decided whom they wanted to nominate, thus setting the tone for the other meetings throughout the state. In revealing their plans to Adams, Tench Coxe indicated that the ticket would be acceptable to a majority of the state "as to insure its decided Success." He did not believe it would be "more favorable to national views than those on the former two occasions," but there would be more energy.[29]

Philadelphians who opposed the Federalist junto also held a series of private meetings. Both Hutchinson and Dallas thought the most effective means of winning voter support would be a ticket composed of moderate Federalists and opponents of the policies of the federal government.[30] By this method they could attract voters from a broad segment of the community and at the same time fend off charges that they were anti-Federalists bent on destruction of the federal government.

The depth of political division among Philadelphia's gentry became obvious during a town meeting called by the junto to select its delegates to the Lancaster convention. This meeting and others that followed during the summer of 1792 revealed that opponents of the junto intended to challenge their political domination of Philadelphia. The first meeting, held on July 25, was attended by both supporters and opponents of the junto. When junto leaders tried to name their slate a long series of bitter debates ensued between the two opposing sides, causing the meeting to break up with nothing decided. The failure of this meeting to name a slate of delegates led to a series of other town meetings called for that same purpose. At these meetings supporters of each camp broke into bitter and sometimes violent debates over the methods of selection and the men to be selected, resulting in each side's naming its own tickets of delegates. This series of town meetings demonstrated to Philadelphians that the Federalist junto was no longer united and that another political organization was forming to challenge it. Opponents of the junto justified their opposition and the subsequent development of a political party on two grounds: one, the methods of the junto in selecting candidates were undemocratic; and, two, the men chosen by the junto intended to use their offices for the enrichment of a few wealthy men.[31]

The opposition's only hope of success was to organize and appeal to those Philadelphians who in the past had taken little interest in politics. The emerging Republican party had to convince large numbers of middle- and lower-class artisans, unskilled laborers, Germans, Irish, Protestants, and Catholics that they had a vital part to play in the political process by appealing to their self-interest. This could be accomplished only by demonstrating that this new party wanted every citizen to have an equal opportunity regardless of his economic status. This concept represented a direct challenge to the notion held by some Philadelphians that only the wealthy should govern society. Thus the opponents of the junto sought to use the ideals and goals of the Revolution to form a heterogeneous urban political party that solicited support from many diverse socioeconomic groups. In so doing they represented their party as the direct antithesis to the exclusive homogeneity of the gentry.

Federalists feared the acrimony of the meetings might result in the establishment of another political party in Philadelphia. "Parties run high here in their selection of representatives and electors. The contest is now brought to such a point, that two opposition tickets, without any name being the same in both, will be vehemently supported." According to one observer, Thomas Fitzsimons appeared to be in some political trouble unless the "old republican party should be found more numerous" than the old Constitutional party, "for altho' the designations are now lost, the members of them continue unchanged in their temper to each other." Thomas Adams, an attorney and son of Vice-President John Adams, also compared the junto with the old Republican party. When "any important Question is agitated here—the distinctions of party are quite as familiar as they were formerly—every man knows his side of a Question."[32]

Following the meetings the Hutchinson-Dallas faction received additional support from a very astute political organizer, John Beckley, clerk of the House of Representatives. Beckly saw in the "tumultuous proceeding" that the Republicans, as he referred to the Hutchinson faction, had a good chance against the junto. With Beckley's active aid the Hutchinson-Dallas faction felt they could mount a serious challenge to the junto's continued domination of Philadelphia.[33] By his connection with congressional sources Beckley added another dimension to the local Philadelphia political scene. This instance demonstrates the importance to Philadelphia politicians of being able to draw on the talents of political leaders serving in the capital city.

Hutchinson seemed buoyant over the prospects of his ticket. He had no doubt that it would carry the city and Philadelphia county. Yet the Hutchinson-Dallas faction was having difficulty finding someone from Philadelphia to place on the ticket. Hutchinson wanted Charles Thomson, a former president of the Continental Congress and a very popular figure in Philadelphia, to run but Thomson seemed reluctant. "We are much embarrassed and tho' our opponents are defeated and the Majority of the people are favorable, yet we cannot fix on a Man." Moreover, he seemed uncertain as to which Philadelphians would appear on the junto ticket, predicting either Fitzsimons, Bingham or the Muhlenbergs. Apparently the Republican leadership was forming its ticket without the advice of the people whose support it so actively sought during the meetings of July. This represented nothing unusual, since both sides designed their efforts to solicit popular support, not reflect popular opinion. In a circular letter the Hutchinson-Dallas faction claimed that it wanted to "obtain the sense of the people in the different parts of the state, respecting the characters proper to nominate as Representatives in Congress" and electors.[34] The letter was nothing but a ruse intended to gain a political advantage for their faction which actively claimed to represent the wishes of all Philadelphians.

As the campaign entered its final stages Hutchinson and his faction seemed confident of victory. He reported that the "aristocrats" of Philadelphia had been totally defeated and the whig spirit regenerated in the people. "The Aristocrats," Hutchinson added, "have not as yet agreed on their ticket;" but he thought they would run Bingham and Fitzsimons. He noted that Republicans had completed their ticket, and it would win approval in the eastern part of the state: where "the Whig spirit is up, and we feel alive, we shall at least equal and I believe exceed our opponents in the city and county of Philadelphia."[35]

Dallas also shared Hutchinson's optimism. "Nothing but the want of concert and unanimity can prevent our rising in honorable triumph in the present contest." The apprehensions, he added, of the Federalists appeared high and if "we fail it would be our own fault," not their ability. Beckley, for his part, was confident that despite the junto's attempts to seduce the Dutch and German voters by circulating a ticket with "six Dutch names and seven approved Treasury men," it would come too late to offset their claim of having the ticket chosen by the people.[36]

Madison came to the aid of the fledgling Republican interest by writing for the *National Gazette.* In it he struck the keynote of Republican rhetoric which sought to characterize that faction as a broad-based party which would vigorously protect the welfare of all classes. It appeared that the emerging Republican party wanted to encourage support from a wide number of interest groups. Republicans had to persuade Philadelphians that their own self-interest suffered as a result of Federalist policies. Only by soliciting the votes of the middle-class and ethnocultural minorities could they hope for success. The Hutchinson-Dallas followers used just this appeal during the closing weeks of the campaign in a broadside addressed to the "Freemen of Pennsylvania." This appeal claimed that the gentry had only their own interests in mind and would not represent all Philadelphians.[37]

Late in September, Republicans published a list of names submitted to their correspondence committee from the general public on the choice of election tickets. This list appeared in the papers well after they had framed the ticket. The committee, however, told the readers that from the names submitted they would form a ticket based upon the men who had received the most support from the people.[38] By this means Hutchinson and Dallas hoped to neutralize the criticism they had already received and at the same time prove that they represented the true interests and sentiments of the people.

Meanwhile, the junto went ahead with its original plans to hold a convention in Lancaster to form a ticket, despite an almost complete lack of interest from the other counties, except those near Philadelphia. Philadelphia's representatives, William Lewis and Robert Waln, almost completely dominated the meeting. The junto seemed overjoyed at the result in Lancaster. Tench Coxe told John Adams that the ticket contained more "firm friends to a complete execution of the power of the general government than any we have yet had," although it contained some representatives of an opposition sentiment; but "never are so few malignant Characters among them." He added that the ticket would have enthusiastic backing among the Federalists of Philadelphia.[39]

In an obvious attempt to discredit the Lancaster meeting, Hutchinson asserted that the Federalists lacked authority from the people to hold such a convention. This convention could serve as a weapon in the campaign, he pointed out, by adding to Republican claims that the junto represented only the interests of a small minority of Philadelphia aristocrats. Federalists countered in a broadside issued about a week before the election. In it they sought to associate the Hutchinson-Dallas faction with anti-Federalists who wanted to promote opposition to the "mildest and most rational of governments." To prove their charge, Federalists pointed out that John Smilie, who appeared on the "anti-Federalist ticket," had opposed the adoption of the federal Constitution.[40]

The duel for control of the congressional delegation did not completely overshadow the race for the city's five assembly seats. A week before the election, the junto held two meetings to form their slate for the assembly. Lacking the organization of the junto but wanting to challenge them, the Hutchinson-Dallas faction ran a ticket that included four men the junto had nominated: George Latimer, Jacob Hiltzheimer, Benjamin Morgan, and Henry Kammerer. But for the fifth place on the ticket they named John Swanwick. It was for this seat that the Hutchinson-Dallas faction conducted a rousing campaign.[41]

Republicans circulated a broadside urging Philadelphians to cast their votes for the "ticket to support the Rights of Man." The broadside warned against the "consummate display of the presumption and boldness of the Aristocratic junto" in nominating William Lewis for the assembly. Purportedly he had opposed the Revolution and during the state constitutional convention advocated depriving the people the right to elect members of the state senate. He had also opposed freedom of the press and the principle of representation. "What act of public spirit, or patriotism has William Lewis ever performed? On what occasion has he shewn himself attached to the welfare of the people, or friendly to the cause of liberty?" With that type of appeal the Hutchinson-Dallas faction sought to discredit the junto by claiming that only John Swanwick could adequately represent all the interests of Philadelphia. Swanwick, while not opposing the Revolution, was not an average citizen as the faction who supported him implied; in fact, Swanwick was a man of considerable wealth and influence in the city.[42]

The junto, on the other hand, made little attempt to mount a campaign against Swanwick beyond the two campaign meetings where they agreed on their ticket. When the broadside attacking Lewis appeared two days before the election, the junto had little time in which to refute the charges, and, in any case, made no effort. Federalists must have assumed that the voters would continue to give their ballots to the men they recommended for these local offices.

In examining the election slate of both tickets the voter saw that each slate had seven of the thirteen candidates in common. The struggle came down to six candidates.[43] Both sides spared no effort in their attempts to elect their entire slate, with charges hurled at one another of representing aristocratic interests and opposing the rights of the people. In Philadelphia the junto faced a challenge which, if successful, would threaten its political control. If the Republicans, on the other hand, could have a majority for any of one of their six candidates it would brighten their prospects that in the future they could win political control of Philadelphia from the junto.

When the polls closed in Philadelphia on election day, October 9, the junto had carried a majority for all its candidates. Furthermore, voter turnout had increased to about 30 percent of those eligible, a jump of almost 6 percent over the previous elections in 1790. This fact indicates that competition for office caused greater voter participation and shows that Republicans were partially successful in widening their base of support among those in the past who had not voted. The seven men who appeared on both tickets captured the most votes, with only ninety-nine votes separating the top vote-getter, Frederick Muhlenberg, from the bottom, Peter Muhlenberg. In the balloting for the six contested seats, the Federalists received a majority for all their candidates. In the county the results were reversed, with the Republicans winning a majority for their six candidates. In the state at large each side elected three of its candidates; for the Federalists, James Armstrong, Thomas Fitzsimons, and Thomas Scott; for the Republicans, John Smilie, Andrew Gregg, and William Montgomery.[44] Only one Philadelphian, Thomas Fitzsimons, was elected on either slate.

In the race for Philadelphia's assembly seats, Republicans won what must be considered a stunning upset with John Swanwick's defeat by sixty-five votes of the junto candidate, William Lewis. This represented the only bright spot for Republicans in the city elections.[45] The victory offered the hope that if Republicans campaigned on the issue of representing the interests of all Philadelphians, in contrast to the narrow interests of the junto, they had a chance of winning. What Republicans had to accomplish was to organize a heterogeneous urban party that could draw out those voters who still remained apathetic. Republicans, in losing, demonstrated that they could mount a serious challenge to the junto, but they lacked the one means to win elections—an effective campaign issue that would arouse sufficient interest from voters to turn the other party out of office. But another important factor in Swanwick's victory was the lack of an exerted campaign effort on the part of the junto. In the congressional race the junto had demonstrated that when it made an all-out effort using all the campaign techniques available—newspapers, broadsides, and public meetings—it could win elections in Philadelphia. In winning, Federalists proved that the electorate would continue to support the party that allied itself with the policies of the federal government.

Commenting on the elections, Thomas Adams declared that the results appeared "to be Federal," but he added that "there was a very formidable interest" in Republicans, who were "indefatigable in their endeavors to carry their Ticket, but are obliged to knock under at last." He thought Philadelphia had disgraced itself by the "countenance given to Rank Anti's" and that the state would never have a "splendid Representation" while so many "distinct interests" were present. Other Federalists did not appear as pessimistic as Adams. That Federalists had carried their ticket in the city against strong opposition seemed to please most of them. Some indicated that perhaps in the future they would go with the district plan, and not oppose it as they had in the past.[46]

In surveying the election results Hutchinson asserted that in Philadelphia, the "Whigs" had many problems, but on the whole "were close on the heels of our opponents." Other Republicans seemed more pessimistic over the Federalists' success in Philadelphia. The only ray of hope was the victory of Swanwick. Hutchinson declared that Lewis had been run for the avowed purpose of choosing a Federalist in the coming election for a United States senator. The Federalists, he proclaimed, "strained every nerve to carry him but were defeated by 65 votes; it is impossible to conceive the chagrin of the Aristocrats on this occasion." John Beckley saw the hand of Alexander Hamilton in the contest, which indicated to him that the Federalists wanted to "preserve *them* a proper Senator." Moreover, he saw the results as a great blow to Federalist hopes, more so than if their entire ticket had failed.[47]

In contrast to the heated contest for Congress, the election for presidential electors appeared dull and uninspiring. Washington's reelection was taken for granted; the only concern among Federalists appeared whether Republicans would field a slate of electors and if they would oppose the reelection of John Adams. There had been reports that some in Philadelphia would support George Clinton or Aaron Burr of New York in place of John Adams. But the reports brought little enthusiasm among either Republicans or, more importantly, the voters. Hutchinson felt that they had little chance of electing a "Whig" ticket, but he did want to offer some aid to Republicans in other states in their efforts to replace Adams as vice-president. Republicans did not nominate an electoral ticket until October to oppose the one offered by the Federalists.[48]

From the outset Federalists appeared confident of gaining Pennsylvania's entire electoral vote for Adams. Samuel Otis reported to the vice-president that he thought Federalists of the city would work for him. Hamilton also thought that nearly all Philadelphia Federalists would support Adams. Tench Coxe told Adams that the "antifederal people are not as much animated . . . as their leaders," and that the

Federalists had received a large portion of the vote from the city and county. He felt confident that seventy-five or eighty percent of the electors of Pennsylvania would be "for you and against Mr. Clinton or any other person that may be attempting to run." In fact, the lowest count for a Federalist elector was 338 more than that for the nearest Republican.[49] The lack of competition for political office caused a marked decline in the number of voters who participated in the selection of electors. In the contest for representatives and the assembly about thirty-four percent of Philadelphia's electorate voted, while for electors it was only about eleven percent.[50]

The years 1789 to 1792 marked a period of transition from political warfare fought over issues relating to the adoption of a new state constitution, to political conflict between new groups formed as a result of issues arising from the policies pursued by the new federal government. This description does not mean that state and local issues played no important role in elections, but that politicians began to associate themselves on either side of federal policies. In the Philadelphia elections of 1791 and 1792 the issues revolved around which political group would control Philadelphia—the Federalists, as the junto called itself, or the Republicans who followed the leadership of James Hutchinson and Alexander Dallas. These labels were not rigid but were rather loosely applied during the campaigns. Those who opposed the junto did not do so out of a conviction that the policies pursued by the federal government were wrong, but because such issues provided a means to challenge the entrenched leadership of Philadelphia. Issues in 1791-92 played a small role in the elections, in part because Philadelphians felt in general that the Hamiltonian program suited the needs of a commercial city devoted to the goals of private wealth. Moreover, those politicians dissatisfied with their exclusion from political office or dissatisfied with what they considered their lack of reward did not know how to take advantage of issues and organize a campaign around them.

The men who formed the opposition during these years came from the upper class and were men of wealth who wanted to gain political and social position. With the exception of James Hutchinson, they had supported the federal Constitution, and they had belonged to the former state Republican party. But they opposed the junto in order to break its exclusive political and social hold on Philadelphia. In the elections of 1791-92 this newly formed political interest showed that it had established a crude organization that could attract large numbers of voters. In the years that followed, the developing Republican interest would attempt to formalize this organization by taking advantage of the urban conditions that had allowed the junto earlier to build its party into a political machine.

Chapter Four

THE POLITICS OF NEUTRALITY AND EXCISE TAXES, 1793-1794

Philadelphia politics underwent a dramatic upheaval during 1793-1794. The tensions among the upper class increased as events in Europe and at home caused men to take positions on issues that hastened the development of the two-party system. The impact of the neutrality crisis and the passage of additional excise duties had a direct effect on the livelihood of many Philadelphians. Politicians saw that these issues excited strong passions in the electorate and caused renewed political interest among previously apathetic Philadelphians.

The French Revolution from its outset in 1789 won the approval of a majority of Philadelphians. Most citizens felt a strong attachment toward France for the aid she had provided during the American Revolution.[1] During the first three years of the furor Philadelphians expressed general admiration for the actions taken by the French people and viewed the French cause as their own. Philadelphia newspapers often devoted more space to the French Revolution than to the affairs of the city.[2] Some Philadelphians even went so far as to hold parades and dinners in honor of the French Republic.[3]

A number of Philadelphians, however, viewed the events in France with disdain, fearing them as a threat to the social structure of the United States if carried too far. Others, especially many merchants, who formed the nucleus of Philadelphia's Federalist leadership, saw that the European war might cause severe damage to their extensive trade with Great Britain. They favored a policy of strict neutrality and strongly opposed any preferential treatment to France under the 1778 treaty of alliance. As William Bingham noted, the "interest of Commerce, as connected with politics, are so striking, that it is difficult to separate one from the other." He observed that the vast majority of people favored neutrality, for they saw the need of a commercial nation to remain at peace. These apprehensions were heightened when the French Revolutionary government executed Louis XVI and proclaimed a republic.[4]

Events in Europe, then, planted the seeds that caused American foreign policy to become a point around which political factions could rally support for local causes. The debate over American involvement in the European war involved Philadelphians in a passionate argument that ebbed and flowed with the tide of the war. This emotional binge grew directly out of Philadelphia's interest in trade with England and France and out of concern for the effect non-neutrality might have on the nation's honor and future.

When President George Washington issued the Neutrality Proclamation, a number of Philadelphia merchants addressed a petition to him expressing their approval "of the wisdom and goodness which dictated your late Proclamation." The petitioners included many of the leading merchants who traded with England. As merchants they carried on a large trade which would be affected should the United States become involved in the war. The city government, controlled by the Federalists, added its support by a resolution that prevented armed privateers from using the port. The city council directed this slap at the French, whose privateers had been operating in Delaware Bay against English shipping.[5]

Federalist sentiments did not seem to represent the majority opinion of Philadelphia's citizens. When the French Republic appointed Edmond Genet as minister to the United States, Philadelphians made elaborate preparations to receive him in the capital city. One writer explained that Philadelphians had the opportunity to give Genet a great welcome and to show their high regard for republicanism. He deplored the refusal of the general government to allow the firing of cannons when the French minister arrived, asserting that the freemen of the city should not be bound by rules of conduct prescribed by the government, since "the arbitrary mandates of a PITT are not *as yet,* adapted to the tempers of Americans." Alexander Hamilton, expressing the views of many Federalists, said of the planned reception that he hoped that the "good sense and prudence of Philadelphians would guard them against any public demonstration for Genet."[6]

Federalists' views to the contrary, when a French ship bearing the flags of two captured British vessels arrived in Philadelphia on May 5, 1793, it received a fifteen-gun salute. Large numbers of people lined the wharves to greet the ship representing the French Republic. According to Jefferson, the "yeomanry of the City (not the fashionable people nor the paper men) showed prodigious joy when flocking to the wharves."[7]

Genet arrived on May 16, 1793, and received a tumultuous greeting from a huge crowd that escorted him to the center of Philadelphia. The same evening a meeting held at the State House appointed a committee to prepare an address to the French minister. The committee, firmly controlled by the city's Republican faction, was headed by Alexander J. Dallas and James Hutchinson. The address prepared by the committee and adopted at the meeting asserted that the people of Philadelphia saw in the French struggle the interest of freedom and equality, which, added to the affection the people felt towards France, rendered "the cause of France important to every republic, and dear to the human race."[8] The Republicans' address demonstrated that they associated themselves with the notion that every man had the right to participate in public life regardless of his station in society. By such leveling appeals Republicans hoped to attract support from Philadelphia's diverse ethnic and religious minorities, as well as from middle- and lower-class artisans and laborers. Republicans had to encourage more Philadelphians to take an active role in politics, and by so doing they would construct a broad-based urban coalition composed of those who had not voted in the past.

Viewing the greeting given Genet by Philadelphians, Alexander Hamilton claimed that the city's newspapers had incorrectly reported the size of Genet's reception. He asserted that only a small number went out to greet Genet and that only forty to a hundred attended the meeting at the State House. That meeting, he argued, represented the real test for the opposition, for "tis there we are to look for the real partisans of the measure," and with that he affirmed that not a tenth of Philadelphia's population participated in it. Hamilton saw that those who prepared the address to Genet were the same men "who have uniformly supported the enemies and the disturbers of the Government." He would not have been surprised to see a "curious *combination* growing up to control its measures, with regard to foreign policy, at the expense of the peace of the Country."[9]

Until the affair of the *Petite Democrate,* Philadelphia's Federalists saw the popular enthusiasm generated by Genet's arrival as a serious threat to their political power. When news arrived that under Genet's orders the French had armed the captured British ship *Little Sarah,* renamed her the *Petite Democrate,* and ordered her to sail in violation of the Neutrality Proclamation, a storm broke over the city. Both Alexander J. Dallas and Jefferson had tried to prevent the sailing until clearance could be secured from Washington, but Genet paid little heed to them, feeling that he had the backing of the people and that the Neutrality Proclamation did not have the support of the nation. Immediately after the ship sailed, many of the city's merchants, supporters of the Federalist junto, called a meeting, where they claimed that the arming of privateers violated the treaty of

1778 with France. They decided to inform Governor Mifflin that they would raise six thousand dollars for the defense of the port against such privateers. The Federalist junto saw in Genet's conduct an opportunity to discredit the pro-French Republicans and thus weaken their political opponents. They also hoped that this incident would allow the government to abrogate the French treaty.[10] In spite of Federalist attacks local Republicans endorsed Genet's action, indicating that they had no immediate intentions of abandoning their pro-French position. In fact, their action demonstrated that Republicans could not afford to lose the support of the large French community in Philadelphia.[11]

In the midst of the Genet controversy Republicans proved their pro-French sympathies by the support they rendered Gideon Henfield during his trial for privateering. Henfield had been arrested while his privateer, the *Citoyen Genet,* was in the port of Philadelphia. This trial excited the interest of politicians and statesmen alike. William Rawle presented the government's case, arguing that an American citizen could not engage in hostile action against a friendly power. Local Republicans Peter DuPonceau and Jonathan Sergeant handled the defense. They contended that the treaties cited by the government did not specifically rule out the type of action undertaken by Henfield. The jury found Henfield not guilty.[12] The verdict split Philadelphia politicians along partisan lines with both sides trying to use the case to win public support. But Republicans seemed to have lost the battle for public approval. Most Philadelphians found Genet's conduct and the Henfield verdict unacceptable.[13] The passions aroused by Republicans had not succeeded in winning widespread popular endorsement. Indeed, by the end of 1793 Republicans found their efforts to build a broad-based urban party no closer to completion than before Genet's arrival. The foreign affairs crisis of 1793 had created a climate that intensified already existing divisions among the city's upper class and laid the groundwork for political warfare during 1794.

In fact, Jefferson had seen before the Genet crisis that the line between the two factions was drawn by the policies of the federal government. According to the Virginian the junto had the support of the fashionable circles of Philadelphia, the merchants trading on British capital, and the men who speculated in currency and bonds. He added that "all the old tories are found in one of these deceptions." The other side, he explained, received the backing of merchants trading on their own capital: Irish merchants, and "tradesmen, mechanics, farmers and every possible description of our citizens."[14]

Republicans soon after the Henfield trial began to abandon Genet. Jefferson wrote that the people of Philadelphia were beginning to make their disapprobation of any opposition to their government by a foreigner and were declaring their support of the President. "Philadelphia, so enthusiastic for him before his proceedings were known, is going over from him entirely." He later declared that Hutchinson had told him that Genet had totally overturned the republican interest in Philadelphia. Even though the conduct of Edmond Genet had caused many in the Quaker city to lose their enthusiasm toward France, the people generally remained at least sympathetic to France in its war with England.[15]

At the same time the first of the Democratic Societies was formed in Philadelphia. This political club carried on an active campaign in support of the French cause in the debate raging throughout the city. This Democratic Society and others formed throughout the country came neither as a result of Genet's arrival nor as an attempt to mirror the Jacobin Club in Paris. The Society founded in Philadelphia was organized by James Hutchinson and Alexander Dallas to advance the Republican position. It served as a focal point for men active in opposing the junto, and as a means of advancing propaganda in the city's newspapers. The membership of the club included most of the city's active Republicans. Within six months of its formation the club listed 320 members. In fact, the Philadelphia club had the largest membership in the country. About one-fourth of the members were artisans, about fifty-one had some relation to the city's manufacturing and mercantile interest, and the remainder had a variety of occupations ranging from doctor to innkeeper. On the whole the members' occupations show a marked similarity with the socioeconomic status of Republican candidates for public office during the 1790s.[16] This heavy concentration of artisans, manufacturers, and maritime interests reflected the concern many Philadelphians had for trade with France and her colonies and their opposition to excise taxes.

Another political club was organized at about the same time as the Democratic Society. The German Republican Society was formed to organize German voters in Philadelphia and the county. The club's leaders also came from the ranks of those actively opposed to the junto and its support of the Washington administration's policies. The leaders, who included Henry Kammerer, Michael Leib, and Peter Muhlenberg, wanted the German population to be active in politics and desired to cultivate support from among this segment of the population for future campaigns.[17] Later in 1794 this society would join with the Democratic club in support of the ideals and goals of the French Revolution, and would become an important instrument in winning the German vote in the northern wards of the city.

Federalists saw these clubs as tools of the French and an arm of French policy. Fearing their propaganda, Federalists sensed the political dangers that the clubs along with the growing political opposition could cause their party in future elections. But supporters of the clubs claimed that Federalists represented the enemies of republicanism and equal rights. The *National Gazette* warned that a parcel of "little hawkers who had somehow wriggled themselves into wealth from carrying perhaps pedlar's [*sic*] pack" and had through the events of time acquired "the lofty air and strut of gentlemen" could not bear the "thoughts of *political equality.*" Popular clubs were a "deathstroke to them and baffled all their hopes of ever arriving to be lords, dukes, or kings." Republican rhetoric implied that Federalist policies constituted a threat to balanced government which could lead to constitutional decay. They seemed fearful that the executive branch would encroach on the legislature in an attempt to seize all power for itself.[18]

In addition to the bitter political struggles during the summer of 1793, a devastating outbreak of yellow fever struck the city. In a three-month period beginning in August, the dreaded fever caused the deaths of over four thousand persons, including Republican leader Dr. James Hutchinson and the junto stalwart Samuel Powel. By September the spread of the fever had caused a great many Philadelphians to move to the surrounding areas such as Germantown and Frankford.[19] It was in this turmoil that Philadelphia had to conduct an election for governor. The incumbent governor, Thomas Mifflin, had declared that he wanted to seek another term, and he was to be opposed by Frederick Muhlenberg. The campaign itself aroused little excitement, since neither man received the endorsement of either of the two competing groups. Both parties saw little need for risking a campaign against Mifflin when he had not shown any partisan views.

In Philadelphia the election brought little campaigning because of the plague, which had caused the chief organs of political news—the newspapers—to shut down or reduce their size during September and October. Preoccupied with staying alive, Philadelphians paid little attention to an election campaign that had aroused no major differences of opinion. When the voters came to cast their ballots at the State House, they had to file by the coffins and the smoking tar barrels collected there to care for the dead. The usual excitement of election day was absent, as were the speeches, the ale, the crowds, and the competition. Very few voters ventured out, and Mifflin won handily. In fact, the number of Philadelphians who went to the polls declined 70.4 percent from the previous election for governor in 1790. The state-wide returns showed Mifflin received 64.6 percent of the ballots.[20]

The only real contest occurred in December in a special election for the state senate called because of the death of Samuel Powel. In this election both parties conducted a campaign for the seat. Federalists nominated William Bingham and Republicans ran Israel Israel, owner of a tavern in the city, an officer of the Democratic Society, and a strong advocate of the French cause. The junto carried on a campaign through the newspapers claiming that Bingham had the desired talents and integrity to fill the position, while his opponent lacked these attributes and had no experience in public life. Bingham easily carried the day with 62.0 percent of the vote, which represented only about 14 percent of the eligible voters. For Republicans to win in Philadelphia they had to induce a much larger percentage of the voters to come to the polls. The county, as in the congressional election of the previous year, voted against the Federalist candidate, although by a small majority.[21] This junto victory suggests voters distrusted Genet's conduct and Republican association with the French cause. Voters of Philadelphia, it appeared, saw little reason to turn out of office the ruling group that had controlled the city for so many years.

During the spring of 1794 another political crisis rocked Philadelphia—the passage by Congress of excise duties on loaf sugar, snuff, carriages, sales of spiritous liquors, and auction sales. It was the tax on loaf sugar and snuff that was particularly galling to Philadelphia manufacturers and artisans. By 1794 Philadelphia had become a manufacturing center where twenty-seven snuff and tobacco factories employed over four hundred workers. In addition, the city had refined about 350,000 pounds of sugar in 1794. The growth of these industries also stimulated expansion of the city's shipbuilding industry into one of the largest in the country.[22] Manufacturers of these products organized a vocal protest movement that found support from a large segment of the manufacturing interest, which numbered in excess of two thousand persons. Two rallies were organized by Thomas Leiper, a wealthy snuff manufacturer, and Jacob Morgan, a wealthy sugar refiner, which went on record as opposing the government's action.[23]

Leiper and Morgan, both active in the Republican organization, convinced other party leaders that opposition to the excise tax could win votes in Philadelphia. This issue struck directly the economic self-interest of a large percentage of the community. Here was a national issue that artisans, manufacturers, laborers, and tavernkeepers could see had a direct relationship to their lives. By exploiting Federalist support of it Republicans hoped to broaden their base of support to include men who, in the past, had either backed the Federalists or had not voted at all. Shortly after the manufacturers' protest meetings the city's Democratic Society went on record as opposing the excise taxes.[24] It soon became clear that Republicans intended to use the excise tax as a political issue to challenge Thomas Fitzsimons.

In addition, local Republicans threw their full weight behind Madison's resolutions aimed at restricting American trade with Great Britain. Madison had introduced these resolutions into the House of Representatives on January 3, 1794 in an attempt to give Republicans a national platform by offering an alternative to the policy pursued by the administration. The support these resolutions aroused throughout the Middle Atlantic states and New England led Federalist leaders to propose a special mission to England to negotiate the differences between the two countries.[25]

As early as the summer of 1793 Philadelphia merchants organized a committee to obtain redress for losses they experienced at the hands of the British and French navies. Thomas Adams reported that Great Britain had aroused "great apprenhension" among merchants and ship-owners by its depredation policy against American shipping.[26] But even during this crisis the city's merchant community split along established partisan lines. Federalist merchants, such as Thomas Fitzsimons, who had suffered losses to Great Britain, did not relax their pro-British sympathies; nor did Republican merchants who had lost ships to the French give up their loyalty to France. Republicans tried to arouse popular passions by supporting strong measures to protect American shipping and attacked those who had turned the Congress from debating the general good of America into "the House of Commons deliberating . . . for the benefit of Great Britain."[27] This growing sentiment for protection of American shipping aroused partisan debates, providing opportunities for ambitious politicians to use foreign policy as a political issue.

At a large public meeting held on March 8, Federalists, led by Thomas Fitzsimons, attempted to win popular support for a petition against Madison's resolutions. But their tactics boomeranged when John Swanwick won the support of the meeting against Fitzsimons by a margin of about three to one. After their defeat Fitzsimons and the others of the junto in attendance signed the petition. These Federalists obviously did not wish to be caught on the wrong side of a public issue that might have an important impact on the city's voters. Fitzsimons, thinking of his own reelection, declared that he and the other Federalists would take the petition through the city for signatures. Aroused by the debate, many in attendance demanded that more vigorous measures be adopted against the British. A few days later the Democratic Society of Pennsylvania and the German Republican Society added their voices to the growing clamor for Congress to take action against England.[28]

On March 18, another anti-British meeting was held in the State House yard. A resolution adopted by the gathering showed that the Republicans sought voter support by using the conduct of England as an issue on which to base their attacks on the policies of the general government. The meeting appeared under the control of Republicans and those merchants such as Stephen Girard who supported the Republican pro-French position. Girard was closely involved in trade with France and the French West

Indies. The resolutions reflected Republican views that Philadelphians still supported the French Revolution and opposed the government's policy of neutrality toward England when Great Britain would not respect that neutrality.[29] The Republican leadership presumed that those in Philadelphia who supported the government's policy toward England would find themselves out of favor with the voters and tied to a policy that no longer had any support. Moreover, meetings such as these demonstrated the relative ease with which an urban population could be organized for political action by a few skillful politicians.

Federalists in Congress, seeing the support aroused in Philadelphia and elsewhere, on March 26 helped pass an embargo for sixty days on American ships bound for foreign ports. The embargo seemed to have met with general approval from the citizens of the city. In fact, many of the city's sailors held a parade and later a meeting on May 23, 1794, at which they voted not to go to sea until they felt assured that "the country's flag would be respected." Reflecting this sentiment, Benjamin Barton wrote: "we are arising *with one mind* for our *defense* and for the preservation of the blessings of liberty and plenty." William Irvine claimed that "the real Republicans . . . have the lead when things look black because many who favored the schemes of the Monarchists or aristocrats . . . find their error and have turned." Even the leaders of the junto, he asserted, had proposed measures against Great Britain in order to revive their character.[30]

Friends of government, forced by the public's outcry against Great Britain to support an embargo, defeated Republican efforts in Congress to stop all trade with England until she paid for the damages inflicted on American shipping. Vice-President John Adams had written earlier that the embargo had cooled the public's temper in Philadelphia and that its economic effect would soon show that the people were wrong in supporting it. "Speculation mingles itself in every political operation," he asserted, "and many merchants had used the embargo to raise their prices." Adams then warned that the "foolish tradesmen and Labourous [*sic*] who were formerly to follow the heels of their scheming leaders are now put out of employment, and will lose 30 dollars a head by this Embargo."[31]

During that spring of 1794, Republicans made every effort to keep alive sympathy for France. On the streets of the city men with chopped hair and dressed in pantaloons, laced shoes and liberty caps greeted each other as "citizen." Everything that had any relation to royalty came under attack. A portrait of the queen of France that hung in a tavern had a streak of red painted around the neck, and a bas-relief of George II located at Christ Church was removed for fear some young Republicans would be forced to stay away from worship because of the "mark of infamy." On May 1, 1794, the Democratic and German Republican Societies held a large civic feast to celebrate the victories of the French Republic over the loyalists and aristocrats. The meeting, held at the country home of Israel Israel and attended by over eight hundred people, included all the leading opponents of the Federalist junto. Both Societies pledged themselves to work for the principles of the French Revolution and against the excise taxes. Other Republican organizations, such as the Society of St. Tammey, held similar gatherings during July to stir up interest against Federalist policies.[32]

To offset Republican advantages friends of the government urged Washington to send an envoy to England in an effort to stave off future trade restrictions and possibly war. Bitterly opposed to a special envoy, Republicans claimed that the administration wanted to tie the country to the monarchy of Great Britain. They also opposed the appointment of Chief Justice John Jay to the post. Washington wanted Jay to obtain a treaty which would secure compensation for shipping losses, evacuation of the northwest forts, and the right of American ships to trade with the British West Indies. When Jay departed on his mission on May 12, 1794, a mob aroused by some Republicans in Philadelphia hung him in effigy. Later, amidst cries from the "people," the effigy was guillotined and then blown up with gun powder.[33] But on the whole, Jay's departure was viewed with optimism by a majority of Philadelphians. Despite emotions aroused during the spring, most citizens did not favor a war with England, and this gesture by the administration seemed to dampen the public outcry against Great Britain.

Although Philadelphia's Federalist merchants generally supported the Jay mission, some had come to favor the Republican attitude on Great Britain. They believed that the British policies against American shipping and the "great abridgement of the freedoms of their [English] subjects in writing and speaking of men and measures," would work "powerfully against them in the minds" of the people, who could "judge what is arbitrary, tyrannical and unjust and what is not." Those who felt a strong attachment to Great Britain and who supported the junto had grave reservations concerning the conduct of England and the effects it had on public opinion in Philadelphia. To wealthy Quaker merchant Henry Drinker, it seemed that these policies provided Republicans with a ready-made opportunity to attack the government.[34]

During the critical summer of 1794, a revolt broke out in four western counties of Pennsylvania against the federal excise tax on distilled liquor. Rumblings of discontent were heard as early as 1791, but the crisis did not come until three years later. This revolt against federal authority presented Philadelphia Republicans, who had also bitterly opposed federal excise taxes, with a real dilemma; they could not support a revolt, else they might lose the favor of many in the city; nor could they forsake their Republican friends in the west who backed or supported the revolt. In an effort to appease both sides, at a meeting of the Democratic Society Republicans asserted that, although they opposed excise taxes as oppressive and hostile to the liberties of the country and "a nursery of vice and sycophancy," the Society highly disapproved "of every opposition to them not warranted by the frame of the government, which had received the sanction of the people." Republicans insisted that the excise should be repealed by constitutional means and that they would make legal opposition to all measures that endangered the freedom of the people.[35]

The friends of government in Philadelphia, at first hearing of the news from the west, thought they had an issue that could offset the advantages Republicans had been building during the spring and early summer. But Republicans, as reflected through the meeting of the Democratic Society and the support they gave the call by Washington for 5,200 militia from the state, offset Federalists' efforts in that regard. Philadelphians had responded with great enthusiasm in the call for troops, indicating their approval of Mifflin's statement that the government was "worth preserving." Even Hamilton grudgingly admitted that in Philadelphia "an excellent and productive zeal, embracing all parties has been kindled."[36] With the general support given the call for troops, Republicans had denied the junto an effective campaign issue in the coming congressional election.

Earlier in the year the legislature had passed a law which called for the state to elect its congressmen by districts rather than at large. This law provided that Philadelphia would elect one congressman. The bill had passed in spite of the opposition of the city's reperesentatives. In a dissenting motion Swanwick, Hiltzheimer, Kammerer, and Benjamin Morgan claimed the Constitution implied that the people of the whole state should elect members to Congress at large and not by political subdivisions.[37] The support given a general election law by Federalists Hiltzheimer and Morgan and Republicans Swanwick and Kammerer indicated both parties seemed to feel they could carry Philadelphia and use its voting weight in the state to help their party win control of the state delegation in Congress.

As the October election neared, Federalists decided to support the reelection bid of their stalwart, Thomas Fitzsimons. In his six years in Congress Fitzsimons had a clear record of supporting Federalist policies such as funding, assumption, the national bank, and the excise taxes. His opponent, John Swanwick, had, since his election to the state assembly in 1792, associated himself with other pro-French Republicans in supporting the embargo and opposing the excise taxes. Moreover, he was one of the leaders of the city's Democratic Society. The candidates very clearly represented the two opposing segments of the city's upper class. Fitzsimons represented the older, entrenched junto, which had dominated Philadelphia since before the Revolution; and Swanwick, the newer, rising wealthy, who demanded the right to take their place among the leaders of the community.

From the outset of the campaign, Swanwick directed his efforts to winning the votes of the artisans, tradesmen, unskilled laborers and ethnic minorities. His friends visited taverns of the working class, telling anyone who would listen that Swanwick had opposed the excise taxes and the debtor laws of the state. They also reminded listeners that Swanwick supported the French cause and had encouraged strong measures against England in reprisal for its raids against American commerce.[38]

Republicans wanted to keep alive the emotion-charged climate of the spring and summer. During the course of the campaign they charged that Fitzsimons, as a member of Congress, had knowledge of the precise time the embargo would take effect and had seen to it that his ships which were still in port left before the embargo became operative. Swanwick's supporters claimed that Fitzsimons by his conduct had greatly injured the other merchants of the city. Levi Hollingsworth, a wealthy merchant serving on the Federalist campaign committee, wrote a letter to the newspapers claiming as his motive "the cause of truth." Hollingsworth denied that Fitzsimons would have sent his ships out of the port before the embargo took effect and that, if he had, the law required them to return to port if they had sailed the same day the embargo had passed. He also rejected the claim that Fitzsimons had any intentions of injuring the other merchants and benefiting himself. But the Republican accusation received widespread circulation through Philadelphia, and Hollingsworth's rebuttal seemed to have little effect in dampening the uproar it caused among the electorate.[39]

In an added effort to excite widespread public interest for their candidate, Republicans held several town meetings in wards, such as North and South Mulberry, where a majority of the city's middle- and lower-class artisans, laborers, and ethnic minorities resided. By such tactics Republicans hoped to encourage apathetic Philadelphians to come to the polls. At each meeting Swanwick received the party's endorsement, but Republicans, not yet unified into a solid party organization, could not agree on a complete slate of their own to run for the state senate and assembly. In fact, they continued the practice of nominating some incumbent Federalists to their ticket, naming Jacob Hiltzheimer, Benjamin Morgan, and George Latimer. For the other three places in the assembly, the meetings divided between James Ash, Moses Levy, Lawrence Seckle, and Ferguson M'Elwaine. In the senate races Republicans supported three members of the junto, William Bingham, Robert Hare, and Nathaniel Newlin.[40] These meetings indicated that the Republican organization was still in its adolescent stage, since they directed their campaign only at winning the city's congressional seat and not electing an entire Republican slate. But Republicans had demonstrated that in the short span of three years, using the tools available to politicians in Philadelphia, such as managing mass meetings, newspapers, and political societies, a partisan organization could be constructed.

During the campaign Federalists attacked John Swanwick for his campaign tactics. One writer noted that in previous years the "friends of candidates were satisfied to use their influence in private amongst their own particular friends" while the candidate observed the reserve and decorum expected of a candidate for public office. But now, he asserted, Swanwick's conduct in actively seeking the office had changed that, and "we have before us the prospect of seeing all the arts of undue influence and corruption supplant the purity" which Philadelphians had come to expect in their elections. The junto also charged that Swanwick had supported the anti-excise cause only as a political expedient and that his real interest was in making money.[41] These accusations had little impact since most Philadelphians found the pursuit of private wealth an admirable goal. They saw no conflict between a man's desire to increase his own wealth while at the same time representing the interests of the people.

Federalists, with Washington taking the lead, vigorously denounced the Democratic Societies. Washington had placed much of the blame for the Whiskey Revolt in Pennsylvania on these societies. He contended that the societies "were instituted by the *artful* and designing" men who wanted "to sow the seeds of jealousy and distrust among the people," against the government by destroying all confidence in the administration of it.[42] Washington's attack provided the junto with an opportunity to discredit Swanwick by linking his membership in the Democratic Society to support of the Whiskey Revolt.

Moreover, the junto did not overlook the importance of the vote of the militia, which consisted of men who had been called upon to put down the revolt in the western counties. Many thought this vote might carry one candidate or the other in a close election. Federalists had the advantage in winning this vote, for the majority of the officers commanding Philadelphia regiments supported the Federalists. These officers used Washington's denouncement of the Democratic Societies to influence the men to vote for Fitzsimons. The commanders of the regiments also received tickets from the Federalists' campaign committee to distribute to the men on election day. Reports came back to Philadelphia that the commanding officers would use their influence to obtain the soldier's vote for Fitzsimons and the entire ticket and that they expected the ticket would "be carried unanimously."[43]

Federalists, sensing that Republicans might gain public support throug their numerous campaign meetings, scheduled one of their own for City Hall By calling the meeting for a central location, the junto hoped to attract a large crowd and give its ticket the illusion of popular endorsement. The meeting, held on October 11, nominated Thomas Fitzsimons for Congress. It also selected William Bingham to run for the state senate and George Latimer, Jacob Hiltzheimer, Benjamin Morgan, Lawrence Seckle, Robert Waln, and Francis Gurney for the assembly. But this did not prevent a large number of Swanwick's supporters from appearing at the junto meeting and making an attempt to win public endorsement for their candidate.[44]

On election day the campaign between Fitzsimons and Swanwick excited the whole city. Both candidates conducted rousing campaigns. Swanwick had used all the means available to bring his case to the voters. Fitzsimons, on the other hand, had calculated that his support of the administration and the backing of the junto organization would carry the day for him.[45] But the result of the election proved a shock to the junto. Their candidate lost the election to the upstart Republican by a narrow margin.

TABLE 8
VOTES CAST IN CONGRESSIONAL ELECTION OF 1794

Ward	*Federalist (%)*	*Republican (%)*
New Market	49.8	50.2
Dock	62.2	37.8
South	53.3	46.7
Walnut	66.7	33.3
Middle	48.7	51.3
Chestnut	62.7	37.3
Lower Delaware	42.7	57.3
Upper Delaware	43.2	56.8
North	44.4	55.6
High	50.7	49.3
South Mulberry	26.9	73.1
North Mulberry	25.0	75.0
Totals	48.8	51.2

Swanwick won the election on the strength of four factors: one, the sentiment against excise taxes common among the manufacturers, artisans, and unskilled laborers; two, Republican success in bringing about 34 percent of Philadelphia's eligible voters to the polls (this represents approximately a 4 percent increase over participation in the 1792 congressional election and it enabled Republicans to more than offset traditional Federalist support in the city's core wards); three, the accusations about Fitzsimons' misconduct at the time of the passage of the embargo; four, the emotional climate created by the debates surrounding American foreign policy. Edmund Randolph reported that the cry used by the Republicans,

"Swanwick and no Excise," seemed to have won him the support of the "less-informed classes of men." He also pointed out that the popular Thomas McKean had campaigned for Swanwick and that McKean had told a group on election day that the gentlemen of the city voted for Fitzsimons, implying that the Republicans had used class distinction as an issue in the election. In addition, the returns from the army gave Fitzsimons a majority of 170 votes, seeming to indicate the influence exerted by the city's militia officers in his behalf.[46] Republicans made acceptable to a majority of Philadelphians the idea of an opposition party. They seemed to have convinced the voters that they had the interests of balanced republican government at heart.

The data in table 8 indicate that Swanwick won seven of the city's twelve wards. His greatest percentage strength came in North and South Mulberry, Upper and Lower Delaware, and North wards. Fitzsimons found his greatest percentage strength in Walnut, Chestnut, and Dock wards, wards which ranked third, second, and first, respectively, in the percentage of merchants in the total of the potentially eligible voters who resided there. Moreover, Chestnut and Walnut wards had the lowest percentage of voters who owned no real property and the highest percentage of eligible voters who owned property valued at $1-100. However, Dock ward, which ranked third in Fitzsimons' percentage strength, had the third heaviest concentration of eligible voters who owned no real property and eleventh in eligible voters who owned property valued at $1-100. On the other hand, North Mulberry and Lower Delaware wards, which were first and third in Swanwick's percentage strength, ranked third and first in eligible voters who owned no real property, although North ward, which ranked fourth in Swanwick's percentage strength, ranked ninth in voters who owned no real property. The data provide still additional suggestive facts: the most heavily artisan wards, Lower Delaware and South Mulberry wards, were the third and second heaviest Swanwick wards, and the second heaviest Fitzsimons ward ranked eleventh in the number of artisans who lived there. Wards that contained high percentages of unskilled workers, such as Middle, New Market, and Dock, ranked sixth and seventh in Swanwick's percentage strength and third in Fitzsimons' percentage strength respectively.

The distribution of both the vote and the socioeconomic characteristics make it difficult to isolate many prevailing patterns. Some concise device is needed to point out relationships between the vote and the demographic data. For this purpose the Pearson coefficient of correlation has been used.[47] The relationships between the vote and the socioeconomic variables are presented in table 9. The data indicate that in only one instance did a significant correlation, i.e., over +.75 exist between the variables and party voting; this correlation suggests that merchants tended to vote for Fitzsimons rather than Swanwick. The other variables seem to indicate little relationship between socioeconomic variables and party voting. In fact, the magnitude of the correlations is not adequate to account for a major proportion of the variablility of the vote. However, it may be noted that in particular cases Swanwick fared quite well in voting units

TABLE 9
COEFFICIENTS OF CORRELATION BETWEEN CONGRESSIONAL VOTING AND VARIABLES, 1794

Variables	*Federalist*	*Republican*
Property Assessment		
None	-.49	+.50
1-100	+.55	-.55
101-1000	-.26	+.26
1001-5000	+.25	-.25
5001-10,000	+.54	-.54
10,000+	+.40	-.40
Occupations		
Public Officers	+.17	-.17
Professionals	+.35	-.35
Tradesmen	+.22	-.22
Merchants	+.77	-.77
Clerks	-.23	+.23
Building Trades	-.46	+.46
Cloth Trades	-.18	+.18
Food Trades	-.56	+.56
Marine Trades	-.33	+.33
Metal Trades	+.17	-.16
Wood Trades	-.23	+.23
Misc. Trades	+.01	-.01
Services	-.14	+.14
Mariners	-.05	+.05
Unskilled	-.17	+.17
Gentlemen	-.12	+.12

that had heavy concentrations of voters who owned no real property and had high percentages of artisans. There also might be some relationship between the ethnic composition of the wards and voting behavior. For instance, Swanwick received his greatest percentage strength from North and South Mulberry wards, where the bulk of Philadelphia's German population resided.

Swanwick's victory shocked Philadelphia's Federalists. One observer wrote that she could not understand how "he got in," as everybody spoke against and reproached him for belonging to the Democratic Society. The men in the army seemed to have reacted with total rage at Swanwick's success, many claiming that the Democratic Societies had aided the insurgents in the western counties and threatening "to kick him if he says a word in favor of Democracy." The *Gazette of the United States* asserted that the Republican victory came only because that faction had attacked the laws and system of government, claiming that by so doing they were strengthening the country.[48]

Republicans were overjoyed. Madison wrote that Swanwick's election as "a Republican by the commercial and political metropolis of the U.S. in preference to Fitzsimons" was of national consequence and was "so felt by the party in which the latter belongs."[49] In this Madison was quite right. Fitzsimons' defeat dealt a blow to the Federalists that weakened the basic foundation of their strength. Republicans had won their first major election and had proven that their efforts to organize a broad-based urban political party composed of manufacturers, artisans, unskilled laborers, and ethnocultural minorities had been partially successful.

In the election for the state senate and assembly the junto candidates won easily over those supported by Republicans. The three men nominated by the Republicans ran more than four hundred votes behind the lowest junto candidate, Robert Waln. In fact, Henry Kammerer, who had served in the previous assembly but had declared himself a Republican, went down in defeat.[50] Moreover, the outcome of these races proved that Philadelphians would vote for candidates on the strength of the issues. In the congressional race Republicans had used the excise tax and American neutrality to bring people to the polls. But in the senate and assembly contests Republicans had made little effort to campaign for their ticket and offered no reason to the voters why they should elect Republicans rather than Federalists. In previous years, Republicans had demonstrated they could win elections to the assembly, as when Swanwick had defeated William Lewis, but in 1794 they made no real effort to challenge the junto ticket.

While Federalists appeared satisfied with their sweep of the senate and assembly seats, they remained bitter and disappointed over Fitzsimons' loss. They aimed their resentment at the formation of political parties, asserting that the "antifederal faction is a disease like leprosy, which deforms, enfeebles and pollutes the victim [body politic] it is going to destroy. Republicans disliked the title anti-Federalist, one Federalist claimed, and instead preferred to be called Republicans "as the distinction of their party, as if the friends of government whom they slander and oppose were not republicans. If they wanted party names, let them wear the title they chose in 1787."[51] With this type of rhetoric Federalists hoped to brand Republicans as opponents of the United States government, not just its policies. By this method Federalists wanted to innoculate the voters with the view that all opposition was unhealthy for the country and should be stopped, and implied that the Americanism of the Republicans was in doubt.

The election of John Swanwick appeared as a climax to the events of 1793-94. The reaction among the electorate to the French Revolution and the war that followed and the passage of additional excise duties caused a division in public opinion that presented those seeking access to political power with emotional issues to arouse voter interest and support. The men who opposed the Federalists from the very ouset of the war in Europe sympathized with the French cause, while at the same time supporting Washington's policy of neutrality. But although Republicans supported neutrality they opposed the administration's inaction toward Great Britain, which allowed English war ships to seize American commerce. In addition, the excise taxes on snuff, loaf sugar, carriages, and liquor caused artisans and manufacturers to actively oppose Federalist policies. These issues brought many Philadelphians, including some previously uncommitted influential men, to support the Republican position. The emerging Republican party won the loyalty of a large portion of the electorate by using national issues to win local elections. The idea that voters on the local level could relate their self-interests to the broader society had an important impact on the formation of the two-party system in Philadelphia. At the same time Federalists found that their support of excise duties and their opposition to restrictions against shipping to Great Britain and compensation for American commerce losses provoked the ire of many Philadelphians. These political divisions, created in 1793-94, provided the basis upon which the differences between the two parties, as modified and consolidated in the future debates over the Jay Treaty, helped to determine the leading features of the first American party system in Philadelphia.

Chapter Five

"THIS DAMN TREATY"

In Philadelphia the Jay Treaty controversy became the means around which the first American party system was firmly organized on the local level. Both proponents and opponents of the treaty developed well-orchestrated efforts to win voter support for an issue that they believed vital for the future of the country. Inherent in the battle over the treaty was the struggle for political power among the upper class in Philadelphia. Some viewed the treaty as a betrayal of neutrality; others, as the only means of preserving neutrality. Each group saw in the other the evil effects of foreign influence. This foreign policy issue enabled local politicians to complete the process of constructing a two-party system in Philadelphia, one built at the grass roots level but tied to a national political movement. Philadelphians were particularly sensitive to the war in Europe since it had such a great impact on the city's economic life, affecting not only merchants but artisans and unskilled laborers as well. With their self-interest involved, it is easy to see why many Philadelphians took an active interest in the particular appeals from the Federalist and Republican parties.

During the harsh winter of 1794-95, after news reached Philadelphia that John Jay had signed a treaty with England, Federalists seemed satisfied that much of the partisan strife that had developed during the city's congressional election of 1794 would subside. Most Philadelphians wanted peace, but only if Great Britain would stop its raids on American commerce. But even before the treaty's terms were made public, local Republicans began to denounce the treaty, hoping to keep alive those anti-British passions that had helped them to achieve limited success at the polls in 1794. Fisher Ames noted that the intention of the Republicans in Philadelphia was to sound a "tocsin against the Treaty," pointing as evidence to a "little cloud . . . in Bache's paper that indicates a storm." He felt that Republicans would attempt to win support against the treaty, first by promoting the expectations of the public that Britain had granted everything and that the United States had given nothing in return, and second, after publication, by stating that the treaty had surrendered everything. Another Federalist, William Bradford, thought that the treaty would heal the wounds of the country and be good for the commerce of the city.[1]

The full clamor against the treaty developed when the terms became available to the public. Washington kept the contents of the treaty a secret until late spring. Filled with misgivings, he finally decided to submit it to the Senate for ratification. During the interim period political discussions of the treaty remained at a standstill. But William Bradford, along with others in Philadelphia's Federalist junto, felt confident that the treaty would receive the sanction of the Senate in spite "of the endeavor which our French friends have taken to prevent it." Philadelphia's Federalists strongly advocated ratification of the treaty, before knowing its contents, for they assumed it would prevent a war and preserve the strong economic ties that many of them enjoyed with Great Britain.[2]

After the Senate ratified the treaty by a close vote, Republicans attacked it in an effort to arouse public passions against the treaty supporters. The *Aurora* called the treaty "the *execution* of the United States." Benjamin Bache warned that it would be hostile "to our commerce, to the interest of republicanism, and to the great interest of the country." Alexander J. Dallas also feared the effects of the treaty on American relations with France. He felt that France had a right to resent the treaty and worried that it would create serious problems for the United States in its relations with the other countries in Europe. On July 1 Republicans added to the intensity of the conflict when Bache obtained a copy of the treaty and published it. The treaty, Republicans thought, confirmed the charges they had made during the past two years that the administration had favored Britain over France and that the rights of commerce would be exchanged for peace with England.[3] In the treaty's terms local Republicans had an issue that would win instant support from many segments of the community who felt that America's interests had been betrayed. To Republicans it represented an issue that could arouse the emotions of the voters and hence dampen the effects of the Whiskey Revolt and the excesses of the French Revolutionary government.

Philadelphia's Republicans, led by Alexander J. Dallas and John Swanwick, initiated three public meetings to protest the treaty. On July 4, 1795, they organized a parade that carried a transparency of Jay through the city's streets, proclaiming that Jay had sold out the country.

This group later burned Jay in effigy after they had a run-in with the militia, which had been sent out to break up the demonstration. Those attending the July 23 meeting appointed a committee to prepare an address to the president requesting that he not sign the treaty. Most of Philadelphia's Republican leaders sat on this committee.[4] John Beckley wrote that the five hundred people who attended the gathering all agreed with one voice to condemn the treaty. Beckley also noted that after the address had been approved, on July 25, Republicans planned to present it to each citizen in every ward for their signatures, "by which means we will discover the names and number of the British adherents, old Tories, and Aristocrats who modestly assumed the title of Federalists, and style themselves *the best* friends of our beloved President." By that method he and the other leaders hoped to demonstrate the mood of the "great commercial city of Philadelphia."[5]

A huge crowd gathered on July 25, 1795 to hear the committee read the address attacking the treaty. The address presented Republican views that the treaty did not provide for a fair and effectual settlement of the differences that existed between England and the United States. The treaty, Republicans asserted, required the federal government to accede to restraints upon American commerce and navigation; it embraced no principle of reciprocity and was in conflict with the rights of an independent nation. After the meeting had approved the address Blair McClenachan mounted the platform and addressed the crowd. Waving a copy of the treaty over his head, he cried: "What a damned treaty! I make a motion that every good citizen in this assembly kick this damn treaty to hell." Following his advice a mob stuck a copy of the treaty on a pole, marched to the home of the French minister, and from there to the home of the British minister, where they burned the treaty. A similar scene was enacted before the home of William Bingham, except that the mob broke some of his windows.[6]

A few days later the committee delivered the petition to Washington with the signatures of four hundred and thirteen people. Republicans emphasized that in spite of the treaty peace had not come nor could "business be carried on without interruption." After the mass meeting Republicans had copies of the treaty printed and distributed throughout the city. Dallas also wrote several articles for the newspapers stating the Republican case against it. The Republican leaders no doubt thought that if they could arouse the public against the treaty perhaps Washington would not sign it.[7]

While Republicans assailed the treaty Federalists did not remain inactive. They launched a propaganda drive using the appeals of peace and national security as a means of neutralizing the treaty's opponents. One paper claimed that the ratification of the treaty "must be a source of pleasing sensations . . . to all sincere lovers of their country." Another Federalist declared that the town was on fire. "We shall all be burned up alive by the mouth of the fool who cannot stop his clamor against the Treaty." It must be remembered, he observed, that a great nation like England would not accept America's terms as the basis for negotiations. William Bingham explained his vote for the treaty, declaring that it was in the best interest of the United States and that the country would benefit from it.[8]

In addition, friends of government began an organized effort to win support for the treaty. They wanted to convince Philadelphians that the treaty represented the best means of avoiding war and thus preserving the independence of the country. In August the city's merchants who supported the junto and who had trading ties with England organized a meeting and prepared a petition to the president which they circulated through Philadelphia. They supported the actions of the Senate and asserted that the merchants had a "more special interest in the Treaty than any other class." They felt that the advantages of the treaty far outweighed any disadvantages it had. The petition, when presented to Washington, bore the names of 412 Philadelphians. The number of signatures indicates that Philadelphia was evenly divided between pro- and anti-treaty sentiment.[9] By means of this petition the junto hoped to counter the popular excitement raised against the treaty and show Washington that Philadelphia was not a hotbed of Republicanism.

Benjamin Bache characterized the meeting: "select merchants and British agents . . . have had a meeting, privately assembled, and privately held on the subject of the Treaty" to counteract the "*rabble* in the State House Garden." But he added that the Federalists would find themselves alone in approbation of the treaty.[10] Obviously, Republicans were still trying to identify the junto as aristocrats who represented only a few, while identifying themselves as the party giving voice to the needs of all the "people."

The friends of the government in Philadelphia showed real concern over the anti-treaty sentiments Republicans had aroused and the possible political effects such opposition might have on future elections. The junto attempted to play down the significance of the meetings held against the treaty. One Federalist noted that only a minority of the population attended the meetings. "The merchants," he noted, "whose interests are most deeply affected appeared absent." He held in contempt those who attended, asserting that they appeared "so vociferous and so ridiculous" that he thought them incapable of comprehending any document that was as long as the treaty. "The conductors of the business generally appeared destitute of talent for informing the public mind."[11]

Oliver Wolcott observed that no more than fifteen hundred people took part and most of those from curiousity. "The actors were an ignorant mob, of that class which is disaffected and violent." Timothy Pickering agreed with Wolcott, describing those who attended as one-third spectators and Frenchmen. "Of the remaining two-thirds, judging from their appearance . . . at least one-fourth . . . had never read the Treaty." He denounced them as totally unqualified and impudent in their claim to express the sense of Philadelphia. Pickering had early declared that such a meeting could not possibly influence "the opinion of any man of sense and experience, who gives the reins, not to his passion, but to his reason."[12] This type of abuse implied that most voters were incapable of understanding the treaty's terms and indicates the disdain many Federalists held for common citizens. It seemed that Federalists expected the electorate to remain passive and take the advice of the upper class as they had traditionally done. But Philadelphia's Republican leaders, in their efforts to win political power, were encouraging each voter to take a more active political role and by so doing were destroying the basis of Federalist support.

Despite Republican efforts Washington signed the treaty on August 14, 1795. Before doing so he criticized efforts to discredit it. He asserted the desirability, after the "parozysm of the fever is a little abated," to determine the real temper of the people; for at "present the cry against the Treaty is like that against the mad-dog," with everyone wanting to run it down. Washington thought that the "foes of order" were deceiving the people and viewed Republican tactics in Philadelphia with great alarm.[13]

The bitter debate in Philadelphia during the summer of 1795 represented a mere prelude to the fall elections. Although the 1795 elections were for the legislature, both sides considered them a test of their treaty position. The junto realized that the winner would probably control the city in the years to come. Clement Biddle remarked that Philadelphia would have "a very warm contest this fall responding to the Treaty." "The opposition is very great," he noted, adding that "many respectable characters who [had] distinguished themselves during the Revolution" and who had long since retired had come forward in opposition to the treaty. William Bingham noted that the "public mind is much agitated & the spirit of party has taken deep root."[14] By the fall of 1795 Republicans had formed a solid political organization over the issue of the treaty. They wanted not only to defeat the Federalists in the fall elections, but to defeat, as John Beckley observed, the necessary appropriations in the House of Representatives to implement the treaty. Republicans, by their tactics, hoped to win the support of many Philadelphians who thought the treaty did not prevent the British from continuing their attacks on American commerce. They felt that the treaty could not be reconciled to the commercial interests of the country and that it threatened relations with France which, they believed, represented the only nation America could turn to in time of need. Other

Philadelphians viewed the treaty as a "Bill of Sale of our Liberties" and could not understand why both the Senate and the president had signed it.[15] Republican leaders wanted to use these various sentiments in an attempt to unite Philadelphians who opposed the treaty and the administration's policies into a broad-based urban coalition.

Republicans initiated their campaign for the legislature by holding a public meeting early in October. They drew up a slate of candidates to oppose the Federalists for Philadelphia's six assembly seats and the one state senate seat up for election. The ticket included men who had been active in opposing the excise taxes and the treaty, and who had supported the French Revolution. The ticket included Jacob Morgan for senator, Charles Pettit, Israel Israel, Henry Kammerer, Ferguson McIlwaine, Jacob Swyler, and William Barton for the assembly. Republicans called their slate the "Anti-Treaty" ticket. In Philadelphia County the Republicans also organized a slate for the county's six assembly seats. This ticket comprised men who had been leaders during the summer in organizing the anti-treaty meetings: Blair McClenachan, Michael Leib, Richard Tittermary, Isaac Worrel, Manuel Eyre, and William Leonard; for the senate they endorsed Jacob Morgan.[16]

The Federalists, at meetings held on the same day as the Republicans', nominated their six incumbents: George Latimer, Jacob Hiltzheimer, Lawrence Seckle, Francis Gurney, Benjamin Morgan, and Robert Waln for the assembly, and Robert Hare for the senate. The Federalist junto called their slate the "Treaty ticket," to indicate that they not only supported the treaty but were willing to stake their political fortunes on it. The junto ticket was also referred to as the Federalist ticket, a label it seemed willing to accept as it associated the party with support for the Washington administration. In the county the junto nominated three of its incumbents, Thomas Forrest, Thomas Britton, Thomas Paul, and three new faces, Peter Miercken, Jacob Servoss, and Richard Mosely; they also endorsed Robert Hare. The junto had its tickets from both the city and county published in the newspapers every day until election day, October 13, 1795.[17]

Immediately after their slate had reached the press, Republicans launched a vicious attack on the six junto assemblymen. They claimed that by their vote for William Bingham for United States Senator, assemblymen had, in effect, supported the treaty.[18] "W[illia]m Bingham was the man of their appointment, and his vote made up the ratification of the Treaty." Republicans also published a broadside, "The Philadelphia Jockey Club or Mercantile Influence Weighted," which listed forty-two men who, they claimed, supported the treaty for economic gain. The broadside included a brief sketch of each man and his reasons for supporting the treaty. The list included the leading members of the junto, such as Robert Morris,

Thomas Willing, Francis Gurney, George Latimer, and Matthew Clarkson.[19] This attack, Republicans assumed, would demonstrate to the voters that the friends of the treaty had a personal stake in it since it would allow them to continue their lucrative trade with England. It implied, moreover, that Federalists put their own self-interest over the honor and future of their country. It appeared the political effects of the Jay Treaty called into question the patriotism of each citizen and the future and stability of republican government.

Federalists adopted similar mud-slinging tactics, declaring that members of the condemned Democratic Societies, such as Israel Israel, Henry Kammerer and Blair McClenachan, had no right to run for election. It was universally known, the junto asserted, that the happiness of the country and the "Jacob Societies" were in direct opposition to each other.[20] Federalists told Philadelphians that the treaty would add to the city's prosperity. They tried to convince the voters that the treaty would expand economic opportunities, not restrict them. The treaty's supporters also used Washington's prestige, support of his administration, and the threat of war to win the electorate over to the treaty. The junto painted the attacks on the treaty and the administration as attempts to destroy "the great Washington" and weaken the "federal edifice." It also began to refer to the Republicans as "Democrats," thereby trying to associate them with the discredited Democratic Societies.[21]

Both sides, believing that a large voter turnout would bring success to their respective tickets, urged Philadelphians to the polls. The *Aurora* warned that for want of one vote the treaty would not have passed. "Let no man" then absent himself on the assumption that his vote would not count for much. One observer remarked that it would be a warm election caused by the "great stir among the Democrats." When the votes were counted that evening Federalists had won an impressive victory in Philadelphia while at the same time losing the county to the Republicans. A record 39 percent of the eligible voters went to the polls in this hotly contested affair, indicating the success both parties had in drumming up interest in the election. The returns in the city showed that all six of the junto's assembly candidates had won elections, and its candidate for the state senate, Robert Hare, had defeated Jacob Morgan. In fact, Federalist candidates for the assembly received 60.6 percent of the vote. The tallies showed a remarkable amount of party voting for both tickets. This was especially true of the Republicans where only 86 votes separated the top vote getter, Charles Pettit from the lowest, William Barton. Similarly, the Federalist ticket's most popular candidate, George Latimer, polled only 155 more votes than their lowest man, Robert Waln. The county returns showed a similar development, with only 36 votes separating Blair McClenachan from

William Leonard. The same held true for the Federalist ticket in the county, except that its six candidates for the assembly lost to their Republican opponents. In the senate race in the county the very popular Jacob Morgan trounced Robert Hare, getting 58.7 percent of the vote, but this majority could not offset the majorities that Hare amassed in Philadelphia and Delaware County.[22]

When the results of the election were announced in the late evening, the friends of the treaty responded with much drumming and parading through the streets. *The Gazette of the United States* cried that if the question of "Treaty or no Treaty" had not been the issue in the campaign, "the love of change might have obtained many more votes for" the Republicans, but as "it stood the question became too serious to trifle with." Mockingly, the paper added, "ha! ha! – *We the people* outvoted by the people!" After the election local Federalists revealed that they had little respect for men in the upper class, such as Swanwick and McKean, who had associated with Frenchmen and "the lower order of the people" to win political objectives. Many friends of government recognized that Republican leaders were not only using class appeals but were organizing the middle and lower classes as a means of winning political office. The treaty, they felt, was only a campaign issue to arouse popular support for the opposition ticket.[23] They were less cognizant of the fact that the treaty had allowed Republicans to form a united political organization that would continue to challenge them for every elective post in the city.

Despite their defeat Republicans took some comfort from the fact that they had swept the election in the county. Only the influence of wealth prevented a victory in the city, they argued. Bache asserted that the junto victory did not reflect the true sentiment of the voters on the issue of the treaty; rather, he indicated, the election proved the "dangerous monied influence that is every day gaining fresh strength among us." He then accused the junto of bringing in "gangs of sailors, draymen, and porters to the election grounds to pass of [f] their votes," which met with greater "success than such vile cause and vile means merited." But in the county, Bache added with glee, where mercantile and bank influences were unknown, the "triumph of liberty was complete, and the enemies of the treaty and British influence and politics carried their election by a majority of three to one."[24] The election results in the county demonstrated that among the artisans, unskilled laborers, and Irish immigrants, Republican campaign rhetoric had won a significant block of voters. These groups had been wooed to the Republican cause by the debate over the Jay Treaty and the emotions surrounding it in the class appeal used by Republicans.

In the city Republicans had failed to convince enough of the electorate that the treaty issue would have any effect on the men they elected to the state legislature. Federalists, on the other hand, had been able to label Republicans as men who opposed the government of the United States and who attacked and slandered the beloved George Washington. In view of the general support most Philadelphians had always given to the federal government, this point represented the most telling argument advanced by the junto. Moreover, Federalists used the threat of war with England and the disruption it would bring to the city commerce if the treaty had not been ratified. This obviously had some impact among much of the electorate in such a commercial city as Philadelphia. The issue of the Jay Treaty had aided the Republican party in strengthening their organization, but it had not convinced enough voters to come to the polls and vote Republican. Voters' traditional loyalty to the junto still played an important role in Philadelphia politics. Nonetheless, Republican strength in Philadelphia indicated the end of one-party domination and the beginning of two-party competition for political office.

The election of 1795 did not end the agitation caused by the Jay Treaty. The controversy spilled over into the presidential election of 1796. Republicans still thought that the treaty offered them the best opportunity of defeating the friends of government in Philadelphia. In 1796 Republicans realized that the Federalists could no longer rely on Washington to pull them through another election crisis. Most political observers believed that Washington would not seek another term, although Washington did not announce his decision until September. The political vacuum left both camps scurrying about for men of popular appeal to head their tickets.

During the winter and spring Republicans kept the treaty issue alive by their efforts to defeat the Jay Treaty appropriations. They pointed out that the treaty still had not stopped British seizures of American ships. "The British are so arbitrary," one merchant reported, acting as "they please toward us, that I am really afraid to do any sort of business–they are to us what the wolf was to the lamb." A few hours before the House of Representatives voted, local Republicans mounted a petition drive to convince wavering congressmen of the treaty's unpopularity among Philadelphians. Republicans gathered 2,300 signatures against the treaty. Philadelphians heard from Republican ward heelers how many of the country's ills, such as funding, cruel penal laws, harsh debtor laws, oppressive religious establishments, import and excise taxes instead of an equal land tax, came from England. Benjamin Rush, commenting on the passions engendered by the Jay Treaty, deplored the factions created in the country but believed that "all evil, is good in disguise." Which meant, of course, that Rush, like his fellow Republicans, hoped that the debate stirred by the Jay Treaty would result in their gaining political ascendency.[25]

Federalists at the same time organized an intense effort to gain support for the treaty among Philadelphians. Pro-Federalist merchants organized a meeting where they drafted a petition to Congress. Junto leaders Thomas Fitzsimons and Robert Waln headed the petition drive that saw Federalists canvass every home in Philadelphia to obtain signatures. Federalists emphasized that every Philadelphian's economic prosperity was at stake if the treaty was not implemented. To demonstrate this point Hamilton ordered insurance brokers to cease writing policies in order to scare the public and keep wavering merchants in line. But in spite of their efforts Federalists secured only 1,400 signatures to the petition.[26]

Nevertheless, the House by a vote of 49 to 48, approved the necessary funds to implement the Jay Treaty, with Muhlenberg voting for and Swanwick against, after which Philadelphia's Federalists breathed a sigh of relief. Federalists won the battle despite Republican opposition and the continued "daily abuses committed by the British cruising ships." Many merchants who supported the treaty sincerely believed that only by its approval could the United States prevent British raids against their shipping. There also appeared a strong resentment against the French, for many considered their extreme politics as the cause of the war with England.[27]

Republicans remarked bitterly that Federalists had carried the day only through the influence of British merchants and insurance companies, who had raised the prices of produce and sounded "the tocsin of foreign war and domestic convulsions." Although many Philadelphians may have disliked the treaty terms, there appeared little doubt that the threat of war influenced some of them to support the treaty.[28] Republicans had tried to use the wealth of the Federalist leaders as a means of arousing class bitterness and thus challenge the nature of Federalist appeals for the Treaty. In this regard the junto out-maneuvered the Republicans, but the emotions caused by these efforts would have their effect in the upcoming fall elections. The passage of the treaty represented one victory for the friends of government, with the major battles still to come.

In the spring the legislature passed an election law for Congress and for presidential electors. The law provided that the state's congressmen be elected from districts, with Philadelphia as one district and the county another. The electors would be elected on an at-large basis, similar to the way the state had elected its congressmen in 1792. As both parties in Philadelphia made preparations for the elections the development of two organized political parties appeared complete. John Adams wrote that the "accusal spirit which actuates a vast body of People partly from chirrup [*sic*] tools, will murder good men among us and destroy all the wisdom and virtue of the country." He feared, along with most Federalist leaders in Philadelphia, that the Republicans wanted to overthrow balanced government. To them the whole future of republican government seemed at stake.[29]

Washington lamented the growth of party spirit, which he found not only in Philadelphia but the rest of the nation. He asserted that two years before he had not anticipated the emotional excesses of parties. Nor did he believe he would be attacked for trying to establish a national character independent of foreign influence, or that "I would be accused of being an enemy of one Nation, and subject to the influence of another," or that the opposition would grossly misrepresent every act of the administration.[30] Washington expressed the views of many in Philadelphia's Federalist junto. They too believed that the best means Federalists had of weakening and defeating the Republicans was to characterize them as opposed to the United States government.

The opening salvo in the campaign began in August when Federalists met to name their candidate to oppose incumbent congressman John Swanwick for the city's congressional seat. At the meeting held in Dunwoody's tavern they selected Edward Tilghman, a wealthy lawyer whose clients included many of the merchants who comprised the leadership of the junto. The friends of government claimed that the administration had brought peace and plenty to the country. They noted that in spite of the attacks that Bache and his paper had launched against the government, the people of the city still supported it. Swanwick had indicated that he had thought the treaty essential to the interests of the nation, one writer stated, but yet he had voted against it. Federalists saw Swanwick and his supporters as hostile to the Constitution and to the peace and prosperity of the country.[31]

Republicans, with Bache and his *Aurora* leading the way, struck back at the junto and Tilghman. The paper printed a letter which followed established Republican rhetoric. The writer attacked the Federalists for conducting a closed meeting to name their congressional candidate and dared them to publish the names of those men in attendance. Republicans also called in question Tilghman's service during the Revolution, indicating that he had been a well-known Tory in Maryland.[32] This type of campaign effort was aimed at tying the city's Federalists to the support of Great Britain, thus further fanning the passions of Philadelphians to oppose the foreign policy of the federal government.

The fall elections for the first time brought both parties into competition for the offices in city government. The city's act of incorporation had been amended during the spring to separate the executive and judicial functions and to create a select council, which would take the place of the board of aldermen in the legislative branch of city government. All freemen in the city could, after the amendments, now vote for both the select and common councilmen. The terms for the city council had also been revised, calling for three-year terms for select councilmen, with one-third elected each year, and for annual elections for the twenty places on the common council.

Aldermen would be appointed by the governor to serve on good behavior. The mayor would be selected from among the aldermen by the city council.[33] Both parties had advocated these changes to bring the city charter into line with the federal and state constitutions.

After the passage of the amended city charter, Republicans intended to challenge the Federalists for control of the city council. The party held a meeting in September to form its council ticket, nominating twelve men for the select council and twenty men for the common council. In their campaign Republicans tried to arouse class antagonisms by charging that the Federalists ran city government for the benefit of the upper class. They cited, as an example, the ordinance which prevented the construction of inexpensive wooden buildings. This law worked an obvious handicap to middle- and lower-class citizens. Republicans failed to point out, however, that the ordinance had been passed only because of the severe threat of fire.[34] In the candidates named for the common council the party made an obvious effort to select artisans and tradesmen to strengthen the Republican's claim that they represented the interest of all classes, not a select few. The common council ticket included after each man's name his occupation, e.g., Andrew Guyer–bookbinder, and John Purdon–shopkeeper.[35] Republican efforts to construct a heterogeneous urban party are supported not only by the candidates' occupation (which in some instances could be misleading) but by their mean wealth. Republican candidates for the common council had a mean wealth of $4,891; while that of their Federalist opponents was $9,626. By emphasizing these facts Republicans hoped to demonstrate that they wanted to create a free and open setting where every man would have the opportunity to succeed in politics as well as business. Moreover, their choice of candidates reveals the lengths Republicans would go in order to build a wide-based urban political party.

Federalists also held a meeting to nominate their ticket for the city council. The thirty-two men named included such party stalwarts as Francis Gurney and Samuel Coates for select council and Samuel Hodgdon and Benjamin Chew for the common council. Both parties made a conscious effort to run two completely different tickets. Only two men appeared on both tickets, John Connelly and Isaac Pennington.[36] Federalists made little effort to mount a separate campaign explicitly for the city council. It appeared that they felt that the issues raised in the congressional campaign would adequately indicate the party's position, since they had given the voters a clear choice between the two parties.

Both Republicans and Federalists held public meetings to nominate their slates for the assembly. The Federalists, for example, held a meeting on September 21 to publicize their ticket for the assembly, selecting its incumbents with the exception of Joseph Ball, who replaced Benjamin Morgan.

Republicans nominated an assembly slate that included only Charles Pettit from the ticket than ran in 1795.[37]

In the county Republicans nominated Blair McClenachan for Congress and endorsed their incumbent assemblymen. Federalist leaders, aware of the unpopularity of Frederick Muhlenberg because of his vote for the Jay Treaty, nominated Robert Waln to run against McClenachan. Apparently, the friends of government realized that they had little chance to defeat the Republicans in the county, since Waln lived in Philadelphia and already represented the city in the assembly. The Federalists did make an effort to win the assembly seats from the county nominating their own slate and holding meetings to arouse support for that ticket.[38]

In assessing the parties' prospects, it can be observed that the Republicans hoped their position on the Jay Treaty would add supporters to the party's ranks. Moreover, the party continued to use class distinctions as one of its basic appeals to win the votes of the artisans, manufacturers, laborers, and ethnic minorities. On the other hand, Federalists hoped to continue their success by fastening the label of anti-federalists on the opposition. The junto also stressed that their support of the Jay Treaty had spared the country a war. Both parties conducted a lively campaign, using all the means available—newspapers, mass meetings, and broadsides, plus a well-organized party structure—to win the support of the electorate. As in the previous years, both parties had handwritten and printed tickets available to pass out to the voters, but this time the ticket distribution was done on a larger scale. This practice not only encouraged straight party voting but also made clear to the voter the choices he had between the two parties and gave rise to a growing practice of party loyalty among the electorate. This vast increase in party competition also aroused voter interest and increased voter turnout on election day.

The results of the election represented an overall victory for the Federalists. They captured the six seats in the assembly and all the seats in both the select and common council. But the party failed to defeat Congressman John Swanwick, with the Republicans winning 51.2 percent of the vote. The election brought a record turnout of 45 percent of the eligible voters to the polls. An examination of the ward returns (see table 10) indicates that Swanwick won the peripheral wards while losing all the core wards. In fact, in this election Swanwick managed to carry only five out of the twelve wards, but the majorities he polled in these wards more than offset those he lost in the center city. Swanwick's greatest percentage strength came from North and South Mulberry and Upper Delaware wards. He increased his percentage strength in New Market ward from the 1794 race, while he lost strength in Lower Delaware, North, and Middle wards. New Market ward, which ranked fourth in Republican voting strength,

TABLE 10
VOTES CAST IN CONGRESSIONAL ELECTION OF 1796

Ward	*Federalist (%)*	*Republican (%)*
New Market	44.6	55.4
Dock	59.0	41.0
South	66.7	33.3
Walnut	62.3	37.7
Middle	55.6	44.4
Chestnut	62.0	38.0
Lower Delaware	46.1	53.9
Upper Delaware	39.5	60.5
North	54.5	45.5
High	62.4	37.6
South Mulberry	36.3	63.7
North Mulberry	35.2	64.8
Totals	48.8	51.2

TABLE 11
COEFFICIENTS OF CORRELATION BETWEEN CONGRESSIONAL VOTING AND VARIABLES, 1796

Variables	*Federalist*	*Republican*
Property Assessment		
None	-.44	+.44
1-100	+.48	-.47
101-1,000	-.29	+.29
1,001-5,000	+.41	-.41
5,000-10,000	+.47	-.47
over 10,000	+.51	-.51
Occupations		
Public Officers	-.06	+.06
Professionals	+.17	-.17
Tradesmen	+.32	-.32
Merchants	+.50	-.50
Clerks	+.09	-.09
Building Trades	-.34	+.34
Cloth Trades	-.24	+.24
Food Trades	-.68	+.68
Marine Trades	-.54	+.54
Metal Trades	+.27	-.27
Wood Trades	-.24	+.24
Misc. Trades	+.19	-.19
Services	-.44	+.44
Mariners	-.09	+.09
Unskilled	-.01	+.01
Gentlemen	+.04	-.04

ranked second in percentage of unskilled laborers, seventh in percentage of artisans, and eleventh in percentage of eligible voters who owned property valued at over $1,000. On the other hand, Tilghman found his heaviest percentage strength in South, High, Walnut, and Chestnut wards. Federalists gained significant strength in North, Middle, and High wards, while losing some percentage strength in Dock ward. High Street ward, which ranked second in Tilghman's percentage strength, also ranked second in percentage of eligible voters who owned no real property. Moreover, Middle ward, which had supported Swanwick in 1794 and ranked sixth in Tilghman's percentage strength, ranked first in percentage of unskilled laborers. Finally, South ward, which gave Tilghman his heaviest percentage, ranked fourth in percentage of artisans and sixth in percentage of unskilled laborers.

The data in table 11 indicate that Swanwick had a relatively high negative correlation between his vote and voting units containing high percentages of property owners. Moreover, the data seem to show that Federalists gained ground in voting units that contained high percentages of merchants and tradesmen. The fact that the vote and socioeconomic variables did not have a significant correlation might in part be caused by the relatively high dispersion of the variables throughout Philadelphia.

Swanwick sought during the campaign to identify himself with the aspirations of the artisans and manufacturers. He had opposed the excise tax, was president of the Emigrant Aid Society, and his friends canvassed the homes of artisans and unskilled laborers asking their support. Undoubtedly, Swanwick's campaign effort to bring artisans and laborers to the polls in record numbers help account for his victory. In addition, his strong support in the peripheral wards indicates that his opposition to the Jay Treaty and his opponent's close association with British interests provided him with the issues to arouse a large following among those who harbored anti-British sentiments and from those who felt the nation's independence endangered by the Jay Treaty. The election demonstrates that Philadelphia's Republican leaders were attempting to build a party around the support of the middle- and lower-class citizens who owned little or no real property (see table 11).[39] In addition, by stressing a free and open society in their campaign, they securely fastened themselves to the ideal of upward mobility which had such great appeal to the mass of urban voters.

The races for the assembly seats, where ward returns were available for the first time, indicate that Republicans had little success in convincing the electorate to vote a straight ticket. In wards where Swanwick won by large majorities, Republican candidates for the assembly lost or carried by narrow margins. In the core wards Federalist majorities in the assembly elections were much larger than Tilghman's majority in the congressional race. In fact, Republican candidates carried just two wards, North and

TABLE 12
VOTES CAST IN THE ASSEMBLY ELECTION OF 1796

Ward	*Federalist (%)*	*Republican (%)*
New Market	58.2	41.8
Dock	73.7	26.3
South	72.1	27.9
Walnut	77.6	22.4
Middle	70.1	29.9
Chestnut	74.9	25.1
Lower Delaware	56.8	43.2
Upper Delaware	54.3	45.7
North	67.2	32.8
High	72.4	27.6
South Mulberry	44.1	55.9
North Mulberry	47.7	52.3
Totals	61.4	38.6

TABLE 13
COEFFICIENTS OF CORRELATION BETWEEN
ASSEMBLY VOTING AND VARIABLES, 1796

Variables		
Property	*Federalist*	*Republican*
None	-.50	+.50
1-100	+.55	-.55
101-1,000	-.29	+.29
1,001-5,000	+.46	-.46
5,001-10,000	+.49	-.49
10,000+	+.54	-.54
Occupations		
Public Officers	-.04	+.04
Professionals	+.22	-.22
Tradesmen	+.33	-.33
Merchants	+.67	-.67
Clerks	-.01	+.01
Building Trades	-.41	+.41
Cloth Trades	-.28	+.28
Food Trades	-.66	+.66
Marine Trades	-.48	+.48
Metal Trades	+.31	-.31
Wood Trades	-.29	+.29
Misc. Trades	+.15	-.15
Services	-.33	+.33
Mariners	-.07	+.07
Unskilled	-.15	+.15
Gentlemen	-.04	.04

South Mulberry (see table 12). Republicans lost significant percentage strength in Upper and Lower Delaware and New Market wards, wards that had gone heavily to them in the congressional race. Even in North and South Mulberry wards Republican percentages declined from 64.8 and 63.7 in the Swanwick-Tilghman contest to 52.3 and 55.9 respectively. On the other hand, Federalists received overwhelming percentages in Walnut, Chestnut, and Dock wards. Of the ten wards carried by Federalist assembly candidates, the party won six by percentages of over 70 percent.

Socioeconomic differences did not, it seems, significantly affect party divisions in this election. But relatively strong correlations did occur between Federalist votes and merchants and Republican votes and people engaged in the food trades, such as bakers and grocers. Both masses and elites agreed on whom they wanted to represent Philadelphia (see table 13). Voters had shown surprising party loyalty to the Federalist junto over the years, and Republicans had raised no issues or personalities that could alter that pattern. The fact that voter turnout declined to 40 percent might have had some impact, but even if more people had voted, Federalist majorities were so overwhelming that it is doubtful that the results would have changed.[40]

The results of the city council elections revealed a similar trend, with Federalists winning handily over the Republican slate. In these races for the common council and select council, Federalists received 60.2 and 56.2 percent of the vote respectively. In the council elections only 38 percent of the voters bothered to participate. Such Republicans as Benjamin Bache, Stephen Girard, and Matthew Carey were easily defeated. The strength of party voting was shown by Isaac Pennington's victory on the Federalist ticket for the common council and his defeat on the Republican ticket for select councilman.[41]

In the county Republicans repeated the party's victory of the previous year, electing Blair McClenachan over Robert Waln and winning the six assembly seats. The issues that had won for Republicans in the last election seemed to have won again. The election returns showed that in the more recently settled areas of Northern Liberties and Southwark, where artisans and unskilled laborers of German and Irish descent resided, the party polled the majorities necessary to win the county. In the more established areas, such as Germantown and Bussletown, Federalists won by a wide margin. The appeals to class, the rights of the individual to liberty, the future of republican government, along with the Jay Treaty and the anti-British sentiment carried the day for the Republican party in the county.[42]

Republicans viewed the election results as a great victory for the party's position on the treaty. This claim of victory was based entirely on Swanwick's success. "The barkers in favor of the government," the *Aurora* cried, "raised a most hideous yelp" against Swanwick. The British faction, "composed of apostate whigs, old tories, toad eaters of government, British raiders and runners, speculators, stockjobbers, bank directors, [and] mushroom merchants," made every effort to defeat him. The paper exaggerated that Swanwick was chosen by an immense majority, which seems to point up the Republicans' need to claim some success in the election in which Swanwick's victory was the only bright spot. John Beckley saw in Swanwick's election the seeds of a possible victory for the Jefferson ticket in the balloting for electors.[43]

The presidential campaign began in Philadelphia during the spring of 1796. Both parties held private meetings to form their respective tickets immediately after the legislature had passed a general election law. To kick off their campaign each party decided to hold a series of public meetings beginning in September. By that time the political picture would be clear regarding whether Washington would seek reelection. Political leaders in both camps thought that the president would not choose to run again, but Federalists wanted him to postpone his decision until at least the fall in order to place the Republicans in a situation where they could not really begin to campaign.[44] No one in the country doubted Washington's ability to have another term if he so desired.

When Washington announced on September 17, 1796 that he would not seek another term, Federalists accepted the decision with regret. Philadelphia's Republicans, on the other hand, felt that the way now appeared clear to carry the state for Jefferson. The city's Federalists found themselves supporting the candidacy of John Adams, who, they conceded, aroused little popular acclaim in Philadelphia. Nonetheless, the junto intended to make every effort to carry the city for the Federalist electoral ticket. For them, Adams, although no Washington, was much better than Jefferson.[45]

To publicize their party, Republicans planned a well-coordinated effort, which centered around distributing throughout the city, copies of their ticket, headed by the popular Thomas McKean and Jacob Morgan, and holding frequent public meetings. At meetings and in handbills they stressed themes that were intended to awaken fears of monarchy, aristocracy, and British influence, all associated with the name of John Adams. With the name of Jefferson, on the other hand, the party pictured the glories of republicanism, equality of man, and opposition to British influence. Republicans held meetings in wards that had consistently voted for Swanwick since 1794 in an attempt to add to the party's appeal and thus ensure the success of the ticket in Philadelphia.[46]

The campaign effort, led by John Beckley and Michael Leib, left little to chance. These men felt that the ticket they had prepared, which had received the endorsement of the other party leaders throughout the state, and the solid support of all those in Philadelphia who opposed the policies of the federal government. For the voters use on election day the party circulated both printed and handwritten tickets throughout Philadelphia. The electorate could not use printed tickets at the polls but could copy from them. This kept many party workers busy writing enough tickets so that if a voter appeared at the polls without a ticket one would be available for his use.[47]

The Federalists did not remain idle: they organized a campaign effort to acquaint Philadelphians with their ticket. The party's slate was headed by two Philadelphians, Israel Whelen and Samuel Miles, and called the "Federal and Republican" ticket. The junto held several meetings in the various wards and placed public appeals in the newspapers. Their advertisements emphasized that Federalists represented the friends of order, good government, peace, and support of Washington's policy towards Europe, which included the Jay Treaty.[48]

As election day neared, Republicans accused the junto of deceiving the people as to its choice for president. The *Aurora* asked, "are these federal republicans ashamed or afraid to avow that JOHN ADAMS is their man?" Many Republican leaders realized that the Federalist junto had not acknowledged that Adams was their choice for president because they wanted both Adams and Thomas Pinckney to receive the same number of electoral votes from Pennsylvania. This reluctance on the part of Philadelphia Federalists indicated that they were in full accord with Hamilton's plan of denying the presidency to Adams by having the New England and Middle states vote equally for Adams and Pinckney. South Carolina would vote unanimously for Pinckney and withhold a few votes from Adams, thus giving Pinckney the presidency. This scheme failed, however, to take into account the weakness of the Federalist ticket in Pennsylvania and the loyalty of the New England states to Adams.[49]

On election day Republicans in the city and county won an overwhelming victory over the Federalist junto. In fact, this majority enabled the Jeffersonian ticket to carry the state, although he lost the presidency to Adams by three electoral votes. In Philadelphia the Republican ticket captured 61.1 percent of the votes, carrying nine of the city's twelve wards. In the county the Republicans scored a complete rout, winning by over fourteen hundred votes. The voters had cast their votes on a party basis, with a difference in the city of only three votes among all fifteen candidates for electors on each ticket.[50]

The ward returns revealed that Republicans had forged their victory through a coalition of widely disparate socioeconomic groups. The magnitude of the Republican triumph can be seen in an examination of the wards.[51] Republicans gained significant percentage strength, from the fall elections, in North Mulberry (78.4), South Mulberry (76.4), Upper Delaware (69.2), New Market (65.9), and Lower Delaware (60.0) wards. The party won by large percentages in wards such as Dock (55.6) and Chestnut (55.4) that had voted heavily Federalist in previous elections. Moreover, Dock and Chestnut wards, which ranked sixth and seventh respectively in their Republican percentage also ranked first and second in the percentage of merchants. In addition, Republicans received heavy support from wards that contained high percentages of voters who owned no real property, and the party increased its percentage strength in wards that had heavy concentrations of property owners who owned over $1,000 in real property. Republicans also won in wards that ranked high in percentages of artisans and unskilled laborers. Federalists won only Walnut (63.2), South (54.6), and High (51.6) wards, wards that had traditionally voted for that party. Republicans achieved their victory in part because they presented their party as the vehicle that would create equality of opportunity in all phases of life. In so doing, they had begun to broaden the concepts of economic mobility to mean that the government must maintain a setting wherein each citizen had an equal chance to succeed in social and political life as well as a chance for economic improvement.

The key to the Republican victory in both the city and county was the well-organized campaign that the party conducted, featuring meetings and handbills, plus a steady attack on the monarchial views of John Adams and the Federalist ticket. This theme represented only a slight refinement of the appeal to class prejudice that Republicans had used increasingly since Swanwick's election in 1794. In addition, the party benefited from having its ticket headed by well-known state leaders such as Thomas McKean, Peter Muhlenberg, and William Irvine, while the Federalist ticket was headed by the little-known Israel Whelen. Moreover, Republicans propagandized the junto's endorsement of the administration's policy towards Europe and its approval of the Jay Treaty. Their campaign appeals fastened in many voters' minds the notion that Federalists were under British influence, which constituted a threat to republican government. These appeals, it seems, found support among many artisans and Irish and German voters who supported the Republicans' goal of taking a firm stand against England.

Some of the conclusions relating to the social and economic configuration of the voting returns seem borne out by William Smith, who assessed the reasons that the junto-supported ticket lost the election in Philadelphia. He reported that Republicans on election day had stirred up the crowd by shouting, "Jefferson and no King." When Republicans claimed that France would make war against the United States and that only Jefferson could prevent it, they had alarmed the Quakers. William Bingham added that the junto lost because of the efforts, accompanied by "some bribery, and a little chicane." John Adams complained that the Quakers of Philadelphia had abandoned him in favor of a ticket composed of "the lowest dreggs of the mob of Philadelphia."[52]

The junto had lost the election in spite of its organized campaign effort. The voters, the *Gazette of the United States* warned, had been taken in by false impressions to make a rash decision, but the junto was not routed nor was there any sign that the party feared for the future.[53] Republicans had demonstrated that they could win elections in Philadelphia for the major offices of congressman and president, although they had yet to win their first local office. But the victories offered the party hope that in the future they could win on all levels in Philadelphia. At the same time the junto's task was to recapture the support of the middle-class artisans, and in this task they would need issues, not tradition, on which to seek support.

Chapter Six

A QUESTION OF SURVIVAL

The dust from the debates over the Jay Treaty had hardly settled when Philadelphians found themselves faced with a new crisis—a threatened war with their former ally—France. Again Philadelphia found its economic life endangered from commerce raiders but this time they were French. A well-organized political response to the French threat by Philadelphia's Federalists set the tone for the rest of the nation and demonstrated how far the two-party system had come since the neutrality crisis of 1793. Both political parties in Philadelphia used yet another foreign policy issue in their attempts to achieve electoral success at the local level. As a result of this local party competition, many Philadelphians viewed the French crisis as a threat to America's independence and the achievements of the American Revolution. The French crisis, moreover, set off renewed fears of foreign influence in America's political life and caused some Philadelphians to question the future of republican government in the United States.

Immediately after the news of John Adams's election over Jefferson reached the French Directory, that body ordered the French navy to step up its seizures of American ships. At the same time it refused to accept the newly appointed American envoy to France, Charles Cotesworth Pinckney. The Directory believed these tactics would compel the Adams administration to redress the grievances between the two nations and force Great Britain to her knees by depriving her of the American markets.[1] The effects of the Directory's policy were immediately felt in Philadelphia, where much of the city's economy was based on trade and many of the city's political leaders had staked their political fortunes on the good intentions of the French nation.

When the news of French seizures began to reach Philadelphia, one

Federalist remarked that the eyes of a great many people were opened "to the real views of France, and the public mind is thereby become more open to receive impressions favorable to England." Meanwhile, Federalists took advantage of the public excitement caused by the French policy to introduce bills in Congress to increase the size of the regular army, to create a provisional army of 15,000 men, and to build three frigates. Some Philadelphians began to have second thoughts regarding their anti-British sentiment and felt that war between France and the United States was a distinct possibility.[2]

Republicans, as a result of the French policy, found themselves closely identified in the public's mind with support of a nation that was plundering American shipping and threatening the independence of the United States. Republicans responded by claiming that the Federalists had based their campaign upon the assertion that Adam's election would bring peace and that "the baseness and duplicity" of the Federalists could be heard in "the cry of, arms! arms! now that they had raised their favorite to the President's chair." Thomas McKean argued that Federalist efforts to take advantage of the French policy against America was directed primarily at weakening "our connection with the French Republic, not only in commerce but in every way." McKean seemed to speak for most Republicans in Philadelphia when he asserted that if a war resulted from Federalist policy, an offensive and defensive alliance would result with Great Britain. He added that no one who had opposed the "evil Treaty" had been appointed to office by Adams and that some had been displaced for opposing it, and that every person who held "an office under it, is active . . . in placing the French in an odious and the British in at least a favorable point of view." McKean did, however, see some hope for the future. The present friends "of Emergency, Aristocracy and British alliances will be disappointed, and in a few years they will be as much depressed as they have been inadvertently exalted." He noted that in spite of the losses to the party in terms of support those that defected would be sorry in the future.[3]

Other Philadelphia Republicans took pains to indicate that they did not support France but, rather, opposed any alliance with Great Britain. Benjamin Rush wrote, in a tone predictive of the policies that both Jefferson and Madison would use in later years, that the words "dignity" and "glory" when applied to the defense of governments and wars were nothing but dueling on a national scale. "Even the property we have lost by French spoiliation," he noted, is not sufficient or just cause for war. "A single life outweighs in value all the ships in the world, and yet thousands of these must be sacrificed to indemnify us for the loss of a few cargoes of sugar and rum."[4]

French seizures of American shipping, in addition to the threat of war, caused a serious economic depression. Although the French actions alone were not disastrous, when added to the losses inflicted by Great Britain, the results proved an economic disaster. The crisis affected the supply of money in Philadelphia, with many merchants unable to pay off their debts. In fact, 150 mercantile firms experienced economic ruin or were financially crippled. Many of the city's gentry lost much of their wealth during this period; for example, Robert Morris lost all his property to his creditors, and John Swanwick went bankrupt. Elizabeth Meredith observed that "Our city had exhibited such scenes of distress this winter" as she never could have imagined. William Bingham survived the crisis only by loans that he received from the Barings in London. Bingham noted that the present state of the country was critical and that a "great Stagnation has taken place in all pursuits of business." He added that the wages of labor and the value of property in Philadelphia were much diminished by the economic conditions.[5] Federalists obviously wanted to exploit the situation to their own political advantage. They again used the threat of war with France to convince the public that the causes of its miseries arose from the evil intentions of the French Directory, which was trying to provoke a war with the United States. With much of Philadelphia's commerce tied up in port, the city's money supply below its needs, and the ability of Philadelphia's entrepreneurs to acquire wealth threatened, it was a simple task for the junto to take advantage of the situation.

Accordingly, Federalists found the opportunity ripe to attack the Republicans, not only for that party's close attachment to France but for what Federalists claimed was the Republicans' desire to draw the United States into a war with England in order to aid the French.[6] The friends of government claimed they wanted peace with both countries and sought to prove this by sending a peace mission to France to settle any disputes that arose between the two countries. Federalist leaders believed that their actions would place the Republicans in an untenable position. Moreover, the correspondence of many Federalists revealed that they sincerely believed that Republican leaders were under undue influence from France and would allow that country to play a predominant role in the internal affairs of the United States.[7]

In this crisis-laden atmosphere, Federalists began to prepare for the fall elections in Philadelphia. The party's organization had been aided by the addition of another newspaper, *Porcupine's Gazette,* edited by the pro-British writer William Cobbett. Cobbett set the tone for the coming elections by viciously attacking the French and the Republicans. One Federalist observed that the paper had a great effect and was widely circulated among "the middle and town classes": its blunt, vulgar language, he noted, "suits them and has a great effect."[8] The paper, with its steady barrage of attacks against the French and their supporters, took the initiative away from Republicans and nullified Republican efforts to use any outrages that the British committed against American commerce.

During the late summer, yellow fever again struck Philadelphia, causing many of its citizens to move to surrounding towns. Federalist leaders did not want the fever to cost them any votes which could result in the city's being represented by "Yellow Whigs." One Federalist asserted that all means must be used to keep Republicans out of the legislative bodies. The party, before it held its public meeting to endorse its candidates, had tickets printed for the city council and handwritten tickets made for the assembly and senate. Federalists worked on the premise that it was easier to elect tickets that contained men "who have been tried and found faithful than new men." The junto did not overlook the importance of the councilmanic election, for these posts represented the power base on which the junto's continued political control of Philadelphia depended. To that end an election committee was named to have enough printed tickets available on election day for the city council and also to assure that the ticket received publication in the newspapers.[9]

Federalists held public meetings to gain popular endorsement of the ticket already nominated by the party's leaders. The junto ticket contained the names of all the incumbents who wished reelection: it included Benjamin Morgan for state senator, the same assembly slate of the year before, and the city council ticket, with a few exceptions, that had won overwhelmingly the previous year. The *Gazette of the United States* warned Philadelphians not to let cabals get possession "of the seat of election and overturn the house with Jacobins, Democrats, French, and pretended Republicans."[10]

Republicans approached the elections with guarded optimism, realizing that they had been hurt by their close association with France. Party leaders decided to underplay their friendship for France and attack the Federalists as representing the interest of a small minority of wealthy merchants. By this appeal Republicans wanted to associate Federalists with favoring the restriction of socioeconomic mobility to a privileged few. With that in mind, Republican leaders in their meetings framed a slate that contained many candidates the party had not previously employed. Of the twenty candidates for the common council, twelve were artisans, indicating the party's desire to win support from the middle and lower classes. This is in sharp contrast to the Federalists, who ran only four artisans, the other sixteen being merchants and lawyers. For the state senate Republicans went to one of their stalwarts, Israel Israel, to oppose incumbent Federalist Benjamin Morgan. Israel had built a solid reputation among the city's poor for his work in dispensing relief during yellow fever epidemics. By his nomination Republican leaders demonstrated their desire to recruit support from among Philadelphia's poor, who were in large part ethnocultural minorities. Party leaders decided to concentrate their chief efforts on this contest. Republicans no doubt felt that in order to maintain respect, the party had to continue its tradition of at least one major victory in Philadelphia at each election.[11] This did not mean that the party made no effort to elect the remainder of the slate, but the emphasis was placed on winning the election of the man at the head of the ticket. The party did not organize special committees for obtaining the election of its slate for either the legislature or the city council.

Republicans based their appeal chiefly on the claim that they wanted a government that would provide a setting where every citizen had an equal opportunity to achieve social and economic success. To prove this they pointed to Israel, a tavern keeper by occupation, and declared that although the "well-born" objected to him it was fortunate that the right of suffrage was "*not yet* confined to the *gentlemen* of the Learned professions." The *Aurora* added that the "useful classes . . . the artisans and mechanics have too much respect for themselves" to object to Israel. The party appealed to class prejudice when it attacked the gentry for oppressing the poor. Republicans asserted that the "gentlemen" only passed legislation that benefited the high born and paid little if any heed to the needs and wishes of the general voters of Philadelphia. The efforts to arouse class antagonisms indicated the lengths party leaders would go in building a broad-based urban party. Upper-class Republicans were attempting to revolutionize urban politics by courting the support of all socioeconomic groups. Federalists responded with the claims that Israel had no qualification for the Senate and that only their ticket contained experienced men of superior qualifications. The junto referred to its ticket as the "Federal-Republican" and the opposition as the "Democratic Ticket." In fact, both parties adopted names; Republicans began to refer to themselves as the "Democratic-Republicans."[12]

The election campaign brought a fair number of voters to the polls. Although the vote was down from the previous year (21 percent of the eligible voters in contrast to 45 percent in the congressional race of 1796) it was, considering the threat of yellow fever, surprisingly high. When the votes were tabulated the results proved a victory for the Federalists. The only loss suffered by the junto, although a bitter one, was the victory of Israel Israel over Benjamin Morgan by thirty-eight votes. In the contests for the select council, common council, and assembly, Federalists won, receiving 61.3, 59.5 and 61.1 percent respectively. The returns also demonstrated a consistent pattern of party voting. This was especially true in Republican voting, where the difference between candidates was not more than about ten votes for any of the offices. In fact, the four candidates for the select council all received the same number of tallies. For the Federalist party voting was not nearly as pronounced, but it could be seen in the returns for the assembly, where a difference of only thirty-two votes prevailed, while a greater degree of distribution was found in the voting for the common council.[13]

TABLE 14
VOTES CAST IN THE SENATE ELECTION OF 1797

Ward	*Federalist (%)*	*Republican (%)*
New Market	59.1	40.9
Dock	69.2	30.8
South	72.4	27.6
Walnut	63.6	36.4
Middle	76.1	23.9
Chestnut	73.5	26.5
Lower Delaware	74.0	26.0
Upper Delaware	52.6	47.4
North	65.9	34.1
High	86.0	14.0
South Mulberry	45.7	54.3
North Mulberry	47.2	52.8
Totals	60.6	39.4

The lone Republican victory had been forged on the huge majority (66.8 percent) Israel ran up in the county. In Philadelphia Morgan received 60.6 percent of the vote. An examination of the wards returns (table 14) reveals that Morgan carried ten of the twelve wards. With the exception of North and South Mulberry, Israel lost all the wards that Swanwick and the Jefferson ticket had carried in past elections.[14] The data in table 14 indicate that the Federalist vote represented almost a complete duplication of the assembly vote in 1796. The only change occurred in the percentage strength of some of the wards. Morgan received his heaviest percentages in High, Middle, Lower Delaware, Chestnut, and South wards. These voting units provided him with over 70 percent of their vote. Moreover, Lower Delaware ward, which ranked third in Federalist percentage and had in the past voted heavily Republican, contained the highest percentage of eligible voters who owned no real property, ranked first in its percentage of artisans and twelfth in its percentage of unskilled laborers. In addition, High Street ward, which ranked first in Federalist voting, ranked fourth both in percentage of voters who owned no real property and percentage of unskilled laborers. Middle ward, which ranked second in Federalist voting, had similar demographic characteristics, ranking first in percentage of eligible voters who were unskilled laborers.

Many Philadelphia voters, it appeared, blamed the Republicans for the economic stagnation and the actions of the French against American commerce. Moreover, Republican appeals to class antagonisms failed to convince enough city voters to break their support of the Federalist junto. Republicans, it seemed, could not snap the traditional apathy of Philadelphians with regard to city elections. If Republicans were to have any prospects of success, they would have to raise issues that voters could perceive had some direct bearing on their lives.

In the county Republicans won the districts of Northern Liberties and Southwark by 82.5 and 86.9 percent respectively. These heavy percentages enabled Israel to more than offset the traditional Federalist majorities compiled by Morgan in Germantown, Blockley, and Bussletown. Moreover, Northern Liberties and Southwark had a much greater voting population than the other districts of the county. The district of Southwark, which ranked first in Republican percentage strength, contained high percentages of artisans and unskilled laborers who owned little or no real property. In addition, Southwark also ranked first in the Philadelphia area in having the heaviest percentages of Irish immigrants. Northern Liberties, which ranked second in Republican voting strength, also had a great percentage of unskilled laborers, artisans and Germans among its eligible voters. Support for the Republican party from this widely diverse population grew out of four factors: one, Republican rhetoric about wanting to construct a society where it would be possible to improve one's station in life; two, Great Britain's Irish policy, which caused many to flee that country; three, anti-British sentiment engendered by the Revolution; and four, the party's organization, which solicited support from and provided aid for the middle and lower classes.

In reviewing the election results, Republicans claimed to have won a victory under very difficult circumstances. The yellow fever, the *Aurora* asserted, had driven many of the "aristocratics" out of Philadelphia but only as far as the nearby towns. But the great majority of the "industrious class" had been driven from the city because of the poor employment opportunities. Yet, the paper noted, the assembly races were closer than they had been in years and the "republicans carried their senator, a circumstance" which was unprecedented.[15] There appears little doubt that the yellow fever hurt Republican chances among middle- and lower-class voters and was reflected in the relatively low turnout in the peripheral wards. For Republicans to win in Philadelphia they had to get at least thirty percent of the voters to the polls. Republicans had to build a broad-based coalition that could appeal to voters in wards which contained large percentages of the city's eligible voters. Wards such as New Market, North, Middle, and Dock could provide the party with the needed majorities to offset traditional Federalist strength in the core wards. Federalists, on the other hand, could always rely on a solid majority of wards in the core and southern peripheral areas. These wards generally voted with the junto and seemed to support the notion that only the city's elite should be elected to public office.

Federalists saw Israel's election in a much different light. Cobbett remarked bitterly that the victory was a complete triumph of the "Jews over the Gentiles." Israel's ownership of a public house, Cobbett observed, gave him "a most excellent stand for collecting sentiments of the *sovereign people,* who never speaks [*sic*] mind freely, excepts when he's half dun." Other Federalists viewed Israel's election with equal horror and vowed to reverse it.[16]

Federalists were not long in making good their promise and redeeming the party's only loss of the election. On December 13, 1797, the Federalists presented a petition to the state senate demanding an investigation of Israel's election on the grounds that it was unconstitutional and void. As a result the senate appointed a committee to look into the charges as set forth in the petition. The committee immediately launched into an investigation which lasted several weeks. The Federalists' rather obvious political move rested on two contentions: one, that the elections in Southwark were not held in the proper place; and two, that fifty-three persons voted illegally in the Northern Liberties and Southwark districts of the county. Federalists even went so far as to produce the names of each of the alleged fifty-three illegal voters. Alexander J. Dallas, the counsel for Israel, argued that the attempt to oust Israel was prompted solely by partisan politics. He sought to prove his charge by demonstrating that Federalists had made no effort to dispute the election of the assembly members from the county. Did not, he asked, the voters usually vote for all public offices? Dallas also claimed that three of the alleged illegal voters had not even been to the polls. But the speech fell on deaf ears. As Cobbett remarked, the speech "was the most insipid stuff that ever found its way from the lips of any human being. Mere froth . . . the dull muddy overflowing from the bunghole of half brewed small beer."[17]

The committee agreed with the Federalist argument and reported that many unqualified men had voted and that the number exceeded the difference in votes between Israel and Morgan. This made it impossible to determine the man who was duly elected by the voters of the county. The senate later accepted the report, ruled Israel's election void, and called for a special election to be held on February 22, 1798, to fill the vacancy.[18]

Both parties immediately began an intensive campaign, and this effort demonstrated the extent of party development in Philadelphia. Both parties used national issues, each claiming threats of foreign influence and war if the other party was elected. Moreover, both sides used class appeals and cries of foul play in their campaigns. Federalists held several meetings immediately after the call for a special election, at which time it named two campaign committees to work for the election of Benjamin Morgan. Both committees sought to secure the right of suffrage from "Foreign influence by confining the exercise of it to 'citizens' born in the United States." The two Federalist committees saw to it that several public meetings were held throughout Philadelphia in support of Morgan.[19]

Federalist newspapers printed appeals to the voters to get out and vote as it was necessary for the friends of government and security of property to bring their influence to bear at the election. Cobbett made a special appeal to Quakers, claiming that "peace, order, morality, and religion" were at stake. Morgan supporters warned that "the lawless sons of anarchy and misrule" would steal the people's property. Federalists also issued broadsides which warned the electorate against French influence and a war if Israel should be elected. The friends of government appealed directly to German voters, warning them that their tax money would be used to support France.[20]

Republicans also held several meetings throughout Philadelphia to arouse public support for Israel. At each meeting the party based its campaign on its familiar theme that the select few in the city had violated the rights of the people by declaring the election of Israel void. In all its appeals the party warned voters that Federalists wanted to exclude others from the opportunity to reach the top of the socioeconomic ladder. They stressed Israel's work for the poor and his opposition to excise taxes, but Republicans made no attempt to answer the charges of French influence or their support of that nation's cause. In fact, the Republican campaign never really got off the ground. The party seemed almost apathetic to Federalist charges that they represented the French nation and not the interests of the American people. The party's campaign efforts to rally public support through the media of newspapers and broadsides seemed meager in comparison with their opponents' efforts. Every day for over a week Federalist newspapers denounced the Republicans. They denied the Republicans' claim of representing the people by arguing that Republican meetings attracted small numbers. Federalists also disputed the charge that they represented only the interest of one class, arguing that all classes depended on one another. "The enemies of the rich are the enemies of the poor; elect to office the enemies of men of property and public confidence is shaken to its foundation."[21]

When the polls at the State House opened on February 22, a huge crowd had gathered to vote in what many considered a very special election. Men from both parties had come to the polls expecting to find that the other side had armed itself for the occasion. Many reports had circulated throughout the city the last days before the election that riots would occur on election day.[22] But the rumors proved unfounded and the balloting, at least in Philadelphia, proceeded with calm and decorum. The results of the election reversed the decision of the previous fall. The data in table 15 demonstrate that Morgan again carried ten of the twelve wards, but his total percentage strength declined from 60.6 to 57.7 percent. In fact Morgan's percentage declined in eight of ten wards, with

TABLE 15
VOTES CAST IN THE SENATE ELECTION OF 1798

Ward	*Federalist (%)*	*Republican (%)*
New Market	56.0	44.0
Dock	67.6	32.4
South	63.8	36.2
Walnut	64.8	35.2
Middle	64.6	35.4
Chestnut	67.0	33.0
Lower Delaware	59.4	40.6
Upper Delaware	55.0	45.0
North	69.4	30.6
High	68.2	31.8
South Mulberry	42.3	57.7
North Mulberry	40.0	60.0
Totals	57.7	42.3

North and Upper Delaware wards the only exceptions. Morgan received his heaviest percentage strength in North, High, Dock, and Walnut wards. On the other hand, Israel's majorities in North and South Mulberry wards increased. The data in table 16 suggest that merchants tended to support Morgan, while Israel's votes had a relatively high correlation with many of the artisans. Morgan's vote also had a positive correlation among voters who owned real property valued at over $1,000. But Republican efforts to appeal to middle- and lower-class voters by arousing class antagonisms seems in large part to have failed. Of the five peripheral wards, where a majority of the city's middle- and lower-class voters lived, Israel carried but two and lost the other three by wide majorities. Philadelphians followed their traditional pattern of voting for Federalist candidates for state and local offices. Republicans could offer no compelling issues or personalities to alter that pattern.

In the county Israel again proved victorious, winning 60.9 percent of the vote. County voters again displayed their loyalty to the Republican party with Israel compiling large majorities of 72.0 and 69.9 percent respectively in the districts of Northern Liberties and Southwark, which

TABLE 16
COEFFICIENTS OF CORRELATION BETWEEN STATE SENATE VOTING AND VARIABLES 1798

Variables	*Federalist*	*Republican*
Property Assessment		
None	-.43	+.43
100	+.45	-.45
101-1,000	-.21	+.21
1,001-5,000	+.45	-.45
5,001-10,000	+.38	-.38
10,000+	+.56	-.56
Occupations		
Public Officers	-.05	+.05
Professionals	-.01	+.01
Tradesmen	+.36	-.36
Merchants	+.71	-.71
Clerks	-.11	+.11
Building Trades	-.47	+.47
Cloth Trades	-.10	+.10
Food Trades	-.58	+.58
Metal Trades	-.35	+.35
Marine Trades	+.18	-.18
Wood Trades	-.23	+.23
Misc. Trades	+.03	-.03
Services	-.24	+.24
Mariners	+.04	-.04
Unskilled	-.19	+.19
Gentlemen	+.00	-.00

more than offset Morgan's victories in Germantown and Bussletown. The deciding factor in Morgan's victory proved to be Delaware county, where he captured 73.7 percent of the votes.[23]

But the election results offered little in the way of surprises. The most remarkable aspect was the large number of voters who went to the polls in a special election.[24] When the voter turnout of almost 50 percent is compared with that of the 1794 and 1796 congressional races (34 percent and 45 percent respectively) and 41 percent for president, the interest generated by the two political parties is obvious. One decided factor in the huge turnout was the lack of yellow fever, which had tended in all the fall elections since 1793 to keep the number of voters down. But this only partially explains the increase. Another more important factor was the effort made by Federalists to arouse voter interest and to see to it that the electorate went to the polls.

Federalists saw their party's victory as an endorsement of their policies and the support they had given to the federal government. One paper remarked sarcastically that in spite of lawless mobs that threatened peaceful Federalists with "French code and club law," the friends of government stood victorious. A well-organized and determined Federalist party exploited the fear that the French had evoked during 1797 by seizing American ships and threatening war.[25] These efforts proved more than enough to thwart Republican attempts to continue their earlier successes in Philadelphia elections.

Republicans tried to shrug off their defeat by claiming the voters had been duped by moneyed interests. The *Aurora* charged that the members of the junto had threatened to deprive those in their employment of bread if they did not vote for Morgan, in addition to turning away from the polls men born in the country who could not prove their citizenship. This assertion was indeed accurate, for Federalists since 1796 had sought to eliminate as many Irish as possible by demanding that they prove to the judge of elections they had been naturalized.[26] But the election proved a severe blow to the party's efforts to construct a broad-based urban coalition. In this election, where a record number of voters went to the polls, Republicans lost votes from the very groups they had won in the past. The French war threat and the pressures exerted by some Federalist employers on their employees proved more than Republicans could offset by their campaign efforts among the middle and lower classes.

While Philadelphians seemed preoccupied with the special election of 1798, rumors circulated through the city that the peace mission sent to France in 1797 had met with failure. Philadelphia's Federalists believed that the French could not be trusted and that it was impossible to negotiate with that country. Republicans, on the other hand, thought that the administration had not made a sincere effort to negotiate the differences between the two countries. These feelings of mistrust intensified the party spirit that was tearing the city apart during the winter of 1797-1798. Many Republicans believed that Federalists were circulating the news that a failure of the peace mission would bring about a war between the two countries. Some merchants, such as Stephen Girard, pointed to the actions that Britain was still taking against American shipping, a fact, he observed, that no one in Philadelphia seemed to notice. Republicans were also annoyed that men suspected of Republican leanings were being driven from office. The comptroller of the treasury, Tench Coxe, a man who had been moving toward Republicanism since 1795, was fired by Adams.[27] Coxe did in fact become a strong advocate of the Republican party in Philadelphia, but had not up to that moment showed any strong manifestations of party feeling.

When President Adams submitted to Congress the details of the XYZ bribe offer to the American peace mission then in France and with it his request to increase the strength of the army and navy, Philadelphia and the Republican party were thunderstruck. One shocked Republican cried that he would not be surprised if the Directory should consider the president's message as a declaration of war. "It is vain," he declared, for the administration and its supporters to speak of their pacific intentions. "Their acts, their words, and the different newspapers under their direction and patronage speak a different language."[28]

Immediately after the president's message to Congress, Federalists began a public campaign for increased military expenditures to ward off the supposed threat of a French invasion. Merchants who supported the Federalist cause held a meeting and declared their intentions to rally around the government and "to support the constituted authorities in every measure proposed for the protection and defense of the rights and independence of the United States." The meeting, under the leadership of Francis Gurney, appointed a committee to draw up an address to the president indicating support for measures that would aid the United States in regaining its honor. The city council, in an address to the president, declared that they were satisfied that nothing had been wanting on "your part to preserve to us the blessings of peace and safety, we are prepared to meet with fortitude the consequences that may follow the failure of your exertions."[29] Adams no doubt received these expressions of support from his Federalist supporters with gratification, realizing that his party had an issue that could destroy or seriously weaken the Republican opposition.

Philadelphia's Republicans, stung by the disclosures of the XYZ affair, made a feeble effort to counter the Federalists' preparedness plans by shifting public opinion toward the actions of Great Britain and the influence they believed that country had in Federalist circles. Republicans thought that the United States should support France in her efforts to "set things with England and knock down Tyranny and establish liberty throughout nations, for their good, and for the good of the *Democratic* few in the world." One Republican scorned the efforts of Cobbett to weaken the country's attachment to France. James Douglas claimed that he would not read the papers of "Scunks, [*sic*] Porcupines . . . employed by the British Court . . . to dart their Quills into the bodies of Democrats."[30] But these efforts appeared to have little effect in quelling the fever set in motion by the French bribe offer.

Quakers of Philadelphia, and even some Federalists, expressed fear that the excitement generated against France could end in war. Some of the leading members of that sect, headed by James Pemberton, petitioned Congress that peace with the entire world was essential to promote the happiness of the country. How strongly this petition was motivated by the Quaker merchants' desire to maintain their trade with both belligerents can remain only a matter of speculation. Federalists reacted quickly. Cobbett urged the Quakers not to sign the petition, warning them that it had originated with the "worst enemies of your country," that its object was extremely "malignant and Wicked," and that if it was successful its consequence would prove dangerous and destructive to the people. "Mortified as you feel at being thus ranked with Democrats, with disorganizers and atheists; yet that mortification will be nothing compared to the odium . . . that this petition must bring you from the friends of government." This warning, published as an extra of Cobbett's paper and appearing for three consecutive days in the paper's regular edition, caused two members of the junto, James Pemberton and David Bacon, to withdraw their names from the petition.[31]

Philadelphia Federalists seized the opportunity to win future public support for their party and the administration by organizing a rally of the young men from the city and the districts of Southwark and the Northern Liberties. At the rally the young men adopted an address to the president which approved of the measures he had advocated against the French and declared that they would obey the first summons of the government if threatened by a foreign enemy. The address then was carried through the city and the county for signatures and later presented to the president. When the young men appeared before Adams they all wore black cockades on their hats as an indication of their opposition to France. Later in the same evening, stirred by liquor and the oratory of the occasion, some attacked the home of Republican editor Benjamin Bache and threw rocks through the windows.[32]

Federalists appeared delighted with the public's demonstration of support. Abigail Adams declared that the effects produced "upon the minds of the people by the publication of the dispatch is wonderful considering what a blind attachment they had towards France" before the publication of the XYZ affair. She noted that in Philadelphia before the publication many of the merchants had opposed the arming of merchant ships. Now that merchants had been made aware of the views and designs of France, the president had received from Philadelphia five different addresses concerning the conduct of the French. This show of support, organized and led by the city's Federalists, seemed particularly pleasing to Adams because Philadelphia had been "the center of Jacobinism and foreign Faction." Other Philadelphia Federalists were relieved that the federal government had taken action to protect their shipping and hoped the results would weaken the partisan activities that had so pervaded the city.[33]

The rallies and parades supporting the administration brought anti-French feeling in Philadelphia to a fever pitch. After the president had met with the young men on May 7, violence erupted almost every night for a week. The more radical Republicans, after Bache's home was attacked, took to the streets wearing the French cockades. One evening bands of roving men, some wearing the black cockade and the others the French, broke into open violence; and the militia had to be called out to put down the disorders. Jefferson claimed that the Federalist junto, which controlled the militia, had called it out to create further violence against Republicans. Bache asserted that the passions of the people were aroused by war speeches as well as threats and denunciations against Republicans. He warned Republicans not to wear any cockades which might be liable to misconstruction.[34] Violence and mob action demonstrate the tensions abroad in Philadelphia surrounding the XYZ affair. Philadelphians were gravely concerned that war would soon come between the United States and France. They realized that the Federalist party could use these violent demonstrations as propaganda to further fan the fires of passion among the electorate.

Federalists made little comment on the riots. Many thought that they could now win passage of strong military measures directed against the alleged French threat and that public sentiment was running decidedly in their favor for the coming congressional election.[35] Violence and mob action had become part of the political weapons available in urban centers to both parties, and both had made use of them.

As the war fever spread, Congress passed acts increasing the size of the navy and providing for a provisional army. Soon afterwards the militia of Philadelphia met at the State House and assured the government of its cordial and hearty support. The junto merchants, led by Thomas Willing and Thomas Fitzsimons, also met in June and announced that they had agreed to loan the federal government $64,000 for the building of ships. Federalists called other town meetings which pledged that Philadelphia's citizens would do all that was necessary to prepare the city for the expected war with France. But even the most zealous of the Federalists still hoped that peace would come between the two countries. Philadelphians seemed more than willing to prepare for a defensive war with

France, but had little inclination for an offensive war.[36]

The high Federalists in Congress, encouraged by their success in winning approval to enlarge the army and navy and aided by the absence of many Republicans who had gone back to their home states, passed what became known as the Alien and Sedition Acts in June and July of 1798. The intent of these laws was purely political–designed to weaken and suppress the Republican opposition. The laws provided for an increased residency period for immigrants before they could become citizens. Thus the Naturalization Act would deprive Republican candidates, especially in urban centers such as Philadelphia, of many immigrant votes. These acts particularly affected the Irish, who had been immigrating in increasing numbers in the 1790s to the Quaker city. The Sedition Law provided heavy fines and imprisonment for those found guilty of writing, publishing, or speaking anything of "a false, scandalous and malicious" nature against the government or any official of the government. Federalists, although they rationalized the bill as a war measure, intended it to stop or weaken the attacks that Bache and other Republican editors were making against Adams and the federal government. The acts, although mildly enforced by Adams, who never really favored them, aroused bitter resentment from Republicans.[37]

Republicans, although opposed to the enlargement of the army and navy, felt themselves powerless to prevent these measures from becoming law in the face of the public support Federalists had aroused. In addition to the bills increasing the army and navy, Federalists secured passage of a direct land tax they claimed was needed to pay the added expenditures. This land tax, many Republicans believed, would prove the eventual undoing of the public support Federalists had achieved. But for the moment Federalists rode the popular tide of anti-French resentment. The president's wife declared that she was delighted to find "what a martial spirit" had been raised in Philadelphia. She noted that even the Quakers were serving as volunteers, "as the *only way* to prevent war." As the fall elections approached, Republicans realized that the party appeared weaker and more disspirited than at any other time in its brief history.[38]

Federalists, expecting victory in October, held their nominating meeting in late August to take full advantage of the public favor the party found itself enjoying. They named wealthy Quaker merchant Robert Waln to run for Congress and Anglican merchant Francis Gurney for the state senate, with the assembly ticket headed by Lawrence Seckle. In the county Federalists selected Governor Mifflin to run for Congress. Mifflin had earlier declined to run for Congress in Philadelphia because of ill health, but after his nomination in the county he remained silent about his intentions. The *Aurora* branded the junto slate the "Tory" ticket and charged that Federalists were trying to run Republicans against Republicans by naming Mifflin to their ticket. Bache, along with other Republicans, had hoped that Mifflin would join with them, although he at no time indicated which party he preferred. Mifflin's nomination also drew opposition from some Federalists who were against running anyone who was not a tested supporter of the "Federal Cause." After the uproar, Mifflin, in late September, withdrew his name and the Federalists chose Anthony Morris, a wealthy Quaker merchant and a former state senator, to run in his stead.[39]

In organizing their campaign effort, Federalists decided to use all available means to discredit their Republican opponents. Richard Peters led the drive to bring Benjamin Bache to trial under the Sedition Law. Peters also directed the junto's efforts to use the Alien Laws against the "United Irishmen" of the city. Peters wrote that he and William Rawle, the United States Attorney for Philadelphia, closely watched "the internal Foes, who are plotting Mischief." Although they found no evidence which would allow them to bring the "Villians" to trial, they thought something would "turn up and we will not fail" to take advantage of it.[40] Federalists obviously intended to leave nothing to chance in their campaign to rout the Republicans from Philadelphia.

The Republicans, weakened by public reaction to the XYZ affair and the French seizures of American shipping, received a further shock to their hopes for success in the fall elections by the death of John Swanwick during the summer. The party's immediate task was to find a suitable candidate to run as his replacement in Congress. Fortunately for them, Alexander Dallas returned to active participation in party affairs. Differences between him and other party leaders were submerged in their efforts to head off a defeat at the polls. Republican party leaders, during that fatal summer, selected Samuel Miles as their choice for Congress. Miles in 1796 was one of only two electors elected on the Federalist ticket, but he had forsaken that party and voted for Jefferson.[41] He had also served as a junto-elected alderman in 1789. The reasons for his leaving the Federalist party are unclear, but it appears from his vote for Jefferson and his acceptance of the Republican nomination for Congress that he was not satisfied with the policies of the administration and the opportunities for public office within the Federalist junto.

Republicans feared that the laws and policies pursued by the federal government during the previous year would be damaging not only to the party but to the country as well. Jefferson remarked that Federalists intended to weaken the "republican parts of the constitution" by their efforts to strengthen the executive branch of government.[42] Republicans feared that the policies pursued by the Federalists would destroy balanced government and bring down the constitution. What policies the party wanted to pursue in the election campaign never became very clear beyond the mere token attacks that Rush and Jefferson alluded to in their correspondence.

Republicans did go through the motions of a campaign by holding public meetings to ratify the selections the party leaders had made during the summer. The meetings, held during September and early October, ratified Samuel Miles for Congress and the party's old warhorse Israel Israel for the state senate. In their ticket for Philadelphia's assembly seats, Republicans nominated former Federalist Tench Coxe for one seat. In the county the party selected Michael Leib to run for Congress. The party's campaign efforts were dealt another severe blow in September when the leading Republican editor of the state, Benjamin Bache, died of yellow fever.[43] This event robbed the party of its chief organ and further diminished their prospects in the elections.

In contrast the Federalists' campaign showed the energy and spirit that envelope men when they know they are on the winning side. They held meetings throughout the city and organized a campaign committee. The committee organized the party faithful and had the necessary handwritten tickets prepared for distribution before and on election day. The junto warned its workers that they had to prepare two separate tickets for Congress, since the election also served to fill the vacancy left by the death of Swanwick. Federalist leaders told their ward heelers to explain to every voter that it was necessary for them to vote twice for congressmen—once for the present Congress, and once for the next Congress. Federalists used the XYZ affair as their central campaign theme and pointed out to the electorate that they had always supported the policies of the federal government and wholeheartedly approved of the measures adopted by the administration to meet the French crisis.[44]

The election results revealed a complete Federalist rout of the Republican opposition. In the congressional race Robert Waln easily defeated Samuel Miles by almost five hundred votes out of a total of only 1,146 votes cast. Waln carried all twelve of the city's wards, compiling large majorities in those wards that had since 1794 voted Republican. For example, Waln carried North and South Mulberry wards by 56.1 and 55.0 percent respectively. In the state senate race Francis Gurney defeated Israel by about the same majority Waln compiled. Socioeconomic differences did not significantly affect voter behavior. Waln, it appeared, received votes from a wide spectrum of the community. The campaign played upon passions aroused over national issues which did not originate in class antagonisms. More importantly, Federalists benefited from a severe outbreak of yellow fever that reduced voter participation to eighteen percent of those eligible. Another factor that might have gained Federalist votes among middle- and lower-class voters was the sharp economic downturn in Philadelphia during much of 1798. In their campaign Federalists had associated this economic slump with the French raids on American commerce, a charge which added to the already strong anti-French sentiment abroad in Philadelphia. Those Philadelphians that bothered to vote again demonstrated that they were voting for the party and not the popularity of the candidates, as the margin between the candidates on each ticket amounted to only a few votes. In Philadelphia the Republican party's association with France proved its undoing, with many voters voicing their displeasure over the conduct of the French and the resulting commerce losses.[45]

TABLE 17
VOTES CAST IN THE CONGRESSIONAL ELECTION OF 1798

Wards	*Federalist (%)*	*Republican (%)*
New Market	73.0	27.0
Dock	79.5	20.5
South	75.7	24.3
Walnut	80.0	20.0
Middle	79.1	20.9
Chestnut	74.2	25.8
Lower Delaware	75.0	25.0
Upper Delaware	64.1	35.9
North	74.2	25.8
High	85.7	14.3
South Mulberry	55.0	45.0
North Mulberry	56.1	43.9
Totals	69.2	30.8

However in the county election returns, in contrast to those of the city, Republicans easily won every contest, but their percentage strength declined to 58.8, 56.7 and 55.2 in the assembly, congressional and senate races respectively. In fact, the loyalty of county voters to the Republican cause demonstrated itself when the former Speaker of the House of Representatives, Frederick Muhlenberg, running as a Federalist, was defeated for an assembly seat.[46] The county remained a Republican stronghold, but the Southwark district voted Federalist in all three contests. Only in the Northern Liberties did Republican percentage strength stay above seventy percent. In addition, the absence of yellow fever in the county, as opposed to Philadelphia, enabled voters to cast ballots for Republicans, whom they associated with favoring the right of every man to strive for economic wealth.

The years 1797 and 1798 saw the foundations of both political parties firmly established. The allegiance of politicians and voters to a party became more secure. Men who had not chosen a party even after the debate over the Jay Treaty had done so by the close of 1798. Loyalty to a political party had become the only effective way to win political office. Men who sought leadership in the community were forced to select a party affiliation and to stand by that decision even at the cost of losing public support. The ideal of loyalty to a political party seemed rather novel to politicians who in the past had shifted sides or taken new positions as public opinion or their own outlook changed on given issues. But by 1798, many of these practices had changed as men sought to influence public sentiment on a variety of national issues. The political party, then, had become the vehicle which gave expression to the way in which men wanted their governments, both local and national, to be run. Parties had become clearly defined, and the voters made their determinations on the positions each party took on the issues brought before the public.

Chapter Seven

THE CREST OF FEDERALISM

In 1799 Philadelphia became the focal point for the bitter struggle over the war measures Federalists had rammed through Congress to arm and secure the country from the expected war with France. The enlargement of the army and navy, the direct land tax, the Alien and Sedition laws, charges of foreign influence, and the future of republican government gave Federalists and Republicans issues that could arouse strong passions among the voters in their clash over Pennsylvania's gubernatorial election. The manner in which Philadelphians responded to these issues provided a critical test as to what party would control political institutions in both Pennsylvania and Philadelphia in the years to come. Moreover, the drama served as a prelude to the classic struggle between John Adams and Thomas Jefferson for the presidency in 1800.

The election of a governor in Pennsylvania proved a severe test of party strength and orgánization. The governor controlled a vast patronage army enabling the party that held that post to be in a superior position for the national and local contests in 1800. Under the state's constitution the incumbent governor Thomas Mifflin could not run for another term. Mifflin represented the last of those "independent" gentlemen politicians of the late eighteenth century whose personal influence and character was such that he could win and hold office without the necessity of party identification. By 1799 all this had changed. The two previous contests for governor had been held without any party opposition, but in 1799, with Mifflin's departure, both political parties saw the election as the supreme test for future political control of the state.

Immediately after the elections of 1798, political leaders of both parties in Philadelphia turned their attention to the coming race for governor. Republicans realized that their only hope in the race would turn upon whether peace would remain between the United States and France. If the war fever subsided then they could make an issue of the war measures adopted by the Federalists, especially the land tax. Party leaders also realized that peace would heighten their prospects for ousting Federalists from political domination of Philadelphia. Federalists, having regained complete political control in Philadelphia in 1798, wanted to continue associating the Republicans with France. But this strategy had one fatal weakness: it depended absolutely upon the continued hostile action of the French Directory and upon President Adams's support of a possible war with the French. If any of these elements changed the Federalists would be placed on the defensive.

A preview of the gubernatorial election came in Philadelphia county in December 1798, in a contest for a vacancy in the state assembly. The Republican candidate was George Logan, who had just returned from his well-publicized peace mission to France. Logan had gone to France upon the urging of Jefferson and other party leaders. He made the peace effort because he felt, as did many in the party, that the Adams administration had not done enough to preserve peace between the two countries. In addition, of course, Republicans felt the need to offset Federalists' use of the war fever as a political issue. Logan had returned home feeling assured that the French government wanted peace. The French, Logan said, had released all American ships and prisoners and were ready to settle the outstanding differences between the two nations. Federalists had scorned his efforts as interference in the conduct of government.[1] But Logan's message was what the majority of Philadelphians wanted to hear, and the campaign for the assembly seat was based upon that issue.

Logan had been nominated by party leaders without his knowledge, and the campaign was carried on without any effort by Logan in his own behalf. Republicans failed to realize the full potential of the peace issue. Instead they attacked Federalists and their candidate, Frederick Muhlenberg, for passing the Alien and Sedition Laws, arguing that the legislation was contrary to the Constitution and destructive to the rights of the people. The *Aurora*, now under the editorship of William Duane, did point out that Logan was a man of peace and that due to his mission to France "misery and Blood have been averted." Federalists made no real effort to campaign against Logan. They assumed that his mission, which had been strongly denounced by the Federalist press, would ensure his defeat. The electorate, however, endorsed Logan and his peace mission by voting him into office by an overwhelming margin. The victory instilled Philadelphia Republicans with the hope that public sentiment was swinging away from the Federalists' position and buoyed their spirits for the coming gubernatorial race. Federalist leaders made little comment on the election except to say that they wondered what the Directory would think of Logan's election.[2]

Meanwhile, as early as the fall of 1797, the selection of candidates to run for governor had become a matter of speculation. Philadelphia's Federalist junto and the other party leaders in the state had very early centered their attention on Senator James Ross of Pittsburgh. Ross, twice elected United States Senator, was considered by the junto as a firm party man; he had voted for the Jay Treaty and had strongly advocated all the Federalist war measures. The Republicans had many prominent men who wanted to run, but most attention, before the leaders met to select a candidate, centered around Thomas McKean, chief justice of the state supreme court. As early as 1790 McKean had taken a strong position that peace would have to be insured between France and America. Other Republicans considered as possible candidates were William Irvine and Peter Muhlenberg, both of whom were well known in Pennsylvania and had excellent records as patriots during the Revolution.[3]

To select their candidate, Pennsylvania's Republican leaders held several meetings climaxing with a large gathering held in Philadelphia on March 1, 1799. At this meeting party chieftains chose Thomas McKean as the party's choice for governor. Dallas had led the campaign for McKean's nomination, overcoming the initial opposition of Michael Leib and William Duane, who had favored Peter Muhlenberg. Leib and Duane were suspicious of McKean's democracy but were unwilling to split the party over the nomination. McKean had received the support of party leaders because he had the best prospects of winning in October. His service as chief justice, his many travels throughout the state, and his victory as head of the Jeffersonian ticket in 1796 made him the ideal choice for the Republicans. Immediately after Republicans had agreed to their nominee, they appointed a campaign committee consisting of Peter Muhlenberg, William Irvine, Samuel Miles, Michael Leib, Tench Coxe, and William Penrose. The composition of the committee represented a unifying theme, since Muhlenberg and Irvine had both been considered candidates and Michael Leib had originally opposed McKean as the party's choice.[4]

McKean, a patriot in 1776, had opposed the 1776 state's democratic constitution, had strongly advocated the adoption of the federal constitution in 1787, and had served as a delegate to the constitutional convention. He had always shown a tendency to distrust unlimited democracy and favored restrictions on voting privileges. Since 1792 McKean had actively sought to broaden the base of Republican support in Philadelphia by his service as president of the Hibernian Society, which assisted Irish immigrants in finding employment and places to live. Such aid provided Republicans with strong links to the Irish community, links that could be translated into votes at election time. McKean had first broken with Philadelphia's junto in 1790 when they had not backed him for a position in the federal government. By 1792 McKean's disaffection with the junto appeared completed when he supported candidates opposed to the Federalists and the policies pursued by the federal government.[5]

While Republicans picked their candidate, Federalists had not remained idle in their efforts to keep alive the fears Philadelphians had of the war with France. War fever offered the most effective means, many Federalists believed, to keep the Republicans on the defensive. Even before McKean had become the official candidate of the opposition party, the junto had charged that he would receive the support of the French government. In this vein the *Gazette of the United States* defended the policies of the government and explained that they were necessary because the "Jacobins" were always railing against establishments, "which their own vices and misconduct alone renders indispensable to the security of the government." Thus, the paper concluded, the expansion of the army and navy were necessary because of the "diabolical projects" which were intended to subvert the laws of the land. The Pennsylvania Legislature, controlled by the Federalists, passed resolutions to the president designed to keep alive the war fever. It claimed that France intended to invade America and that only by remaining strong could America stop this French threat and maintain peace. Federalists also arranged frequent parades and meetings to demonstrate the enthusiasm of the militia and the youth for the policies of the federal government.[6]

A feeling of distrust pervaded the conversation of Philadelphians concerning the real intentions of the French. Many people did not know whom to believe: supporters of the administration, who looked upon France as an enemy, or Republicans, who claimed that France wanted only peace. These doubts had not occurred a few months before, but the expected war or invasion from France had not materialized and by now the people did not know which way to turn.[7]

Republican leaders, sensing that the feverish conditions in Philadelphia were beginning to wane, organized meetings in opposition to the Alien and Sedition acts and to the laws increasing the size of the army and navy. At one meeting held in February, Republican leaders won the adoption of a petition and had it sent through the city to indicate that Philadelphians opposed both the Alien and Sedition laws and a standing army as unconstitutional. The meeting, of course, was highlighted by bitter speeches denouncing the acts as threats to the rights of the people and a danger to their liberties.[8]

The day following the Republican meeting violence between the two political parties erupted in Philadelphia. On February 9, William Duane, Dr. James Reynolds, and two other men went into the yard of St. Mary's Catholic Church to post handbills. The handbills asked Irishmen to sign the petition declaring their opposition to the Alien and Sedition laws. These posters were placed on the church wall and in parts of the yard. As the congregation left the church Duane and the others had the petition spread out over one of the tombs in the yard. After a few men had signed the petition some Federalists in the congregation tried to force Duane and the others from the premises. In the struggle that ensued Reynolds was knocked down and kicked by the Federalist crowd, causing the doctor to draw a pistol and point it at one of his assailants. At this moment constables arrived and hustled the four men to jail. Cobbett branded the incident as the "United Irish Revolt" and warned the people of Philadelphia "that the day has now come" when the Irish constituted a threat to the American republic. Other Federalist editors also exploited the incident as an illustration of foreign influence in American affairs and cautioned the people not to allow any foreign "renegades" influence or voice in American affairs.[9]

William Bingham had warned earlier that something had to be done to prevent the immigration of Irish insurgents into the country: "They will join the party in opposition to the government" and would attack those supporters of the government who were on friendly terms with Great Britain. Later the editor of the *Gazette of the United States* asserted that the absurd principles of universal suffrage and unrestricted admission of "foreign barbarians to share in the government would ruin any idea" that the former would work while the latter was practiced. "We are actually becoming *Helots*, and a host of uncouth outlandish barbarians are rising on the decaying spirit we inherited from our forefathers."[10]

In fact, Federalists did have reason to fear from the great influx of Irish that poured into Philadelphia. In just two years, 1798–1799, 910 immigrants were naturalized within the city boundaries. This figure far exceeded the 145 who were naturalized from 1789 to 1797. When these figures are considered with the number of other immigrants who never bothered to become naturalized but nonetheless participated in elections, Federalists fears are seen to have been well founded. The Irish and Germans tended to settle in North and South Mulberry and New Market wards, the Northern Liberties and Southwark district of the county. In the congressional election of 1796 the city's North and South Mulberry wards gave the Republican candidate 64.8 percent and 63.7 percent respectively, and in the 1798 county congressional election the Northern Liberties district gave Michael Leib, the Republican candidate, 76.7 percent of the votes. As early as 1796 Federalists had made efforts to restrict immigration and prevent those immigrants who did not have naturalization papers from voting.[11] Federalists realized that the German and Irish voter represented an essential block in Republican effort to build a broad-based urban coalition.

Nevertheless, Philadelphia's Federalists, seemingly inspired by the violent reactions their supporters had aroused among the electorate, plunged headlong into one of the most vicious campaigns conducted anywhere in the country. Federalists organized a campaign that assailed Republicans as vassals of the French and leveled personal attacks upon the character and qualifications of Thomas McKean. The hatred, bitterness and fear that Federalists felt toward their opponents highlighted almost every page of correspondence and newspaper reports. Still, Federalists did not rely solely on denouncing their opponents. To advance the candidacy of James Ross, they organized a system of committees throughout the state. The purpose of these committees, in addition to publishing attacks on McKean, was to circulate material that presented their candidate in a favorable light. Moreover, the Federalists' committees organized an effort by party workers to reach every voter in Philadelphia before the election.[12]

The *Gazette of the United States* opened the Federalist assault by painting the supporters of McKean as representatives of the French faction who wanted to destroy the government and those who had toiled so long to lay its foundations. One Federalist remarked that the efforts by McKean's supporters to discredit the laws passed by the federal government could only lead to civil war if he was elected.[13] Federalists stressed the theme that their party represented stability and order while Republicans represented disorder and confusion. Moreover, Federalists believed that Republican leaders were under foreign influence which threatened the future of republican government.

At the same time, Republicans opened their campaign in a letter published in the newspapers from the party campaign committee. The committee attacked the Federalists on two points: one, that Federalists wanted to replace the present republican form of government with a monarchy; and two, that a review of the conduct of the men in power would find that "the honors and emoluments of public offices" went only to the partisans of the administration. The committee went on to say that Federalists held in contempt the ideal of universal suffrage, which the Republicans implied they supported. The only effective means, they added, to safeguard the Constitution from the "violation of secret machinations or open force" was to support McKean for governor. Republicans seemed confident that their appeal would bring them victory in October. But Tench Coxe warned his fellow party members that every vote counted and the party should not overlook an opportunity to win votes from any source. Accordingly, the Republican campaign committee published a circular letter which was sent throughout the state stressing the issues the committee felt would weaken Ross's appeal. The committee pointed to the evil measures that Ross had supported while a United States Senator: an increase in the public debt, an increase in taxes, the danger of foreign war, establishment of a standing army and navy, and decline of the militia.[14] A review of the issues raised by Republicans will find little mention of the Alien and Sedition laws, a point the Republican leaders obviously believed lacked the appeal that the issues of taxes and war would have among the voters.

Republicans were also much encouraged by the success of the French armies in Europe and the removal in March of the state capital from Philadelphia to Lancaster. The latter event had been advocated for many years by the out-state Republicans, who claimed that once the capital was removed from Philadelphia the influence of Federalists in state affairs would diminish. Many Republicans from Philadelphia, such as Tench Coxe and John Beckley, were inclined to agree. The move, when it occurred in March, had been bitterly opposed by the Federalists, but Republicans had convinced even some out-state Federalists that Pennsylvania would be better served if the capital went to Lancaster.[15]

The intensity of the campaign and the fears both sides had of foreign influence on the other again generated into an outbreak of violence. In May, fifteen officers of the militia went to Duane's print shop and beat him with a "cow-skin." Some Federalists, although they disliked the means used on Duane, found it "difficult to devise other methods of detering such fellows" from scandalous abuse. Beckley called the incident the beginning of "club law" in Philadelphia and announced that Republicans had joined together to prevent any more attacks on Duane. After Republicans had collected their forces, Beckley reported, the "Macedonian leaves vanished in the shade, after having collected, avowedly to tar and feather Duane." In a similar affair the son of Thomas McKean scuffled with Fenno, the editor of the *Gazette of the United States*, because of attacks the latter had made against his father.[16] These incidents demonstrated the passions that supporters of both parties felt about the issues and the personalities involved and the length that they would go to silence and defeat the opposing side.

Throughout the campaign Republicans constantly stressed the peace issue, attacking Federalist war measures in an attempt to show that the other party wanted not peace but war. In every handbill, broadside, and published tract issued by the party, Republicans hammered at Ross as a supporter of war, and taxes, standing armies, the Alien and Sedition laws, and as a British partisan. At the same time the party pictured McKean as a lover of peace, an admirer of the militia, an enemy of oppressive taxation, "a steady Patriot of 1776," and a republican. By the use of the peace theme Republicans also accused Federalists of opposing republican forms of government. [17] As the campaign progressed Republican leaders realized that most Philadelphians wanted peace, and by the use of that issue the party had placed the Federalists on the defensive.

The Republican campaign received a big lift in February, 1799, when President Adams sent another peace mission to France. Adams, along with many Republicans, realized that the martial spirit of the people was quickly dying. The nomination of another peace mission to France placed Philadelphia Federalists on the horns of a dilemma. On the one hand, Federalists had been forced to defend the war measures adopted by their party, and on the other many wanted to support the position of the president. Their solution, if it could be called one, was to continue attacking Republicans as the agents of foreign influence and a threat to the constitutional government of the United States. After Adams sent the second peace mission to France, they resorted to highly personalized attacks on McKean and two of his chief supporters, Tench Coxe and Alexander J. Dallas. The split in the Federalists' ranks that many historians saw on the national level did not occur among Philadelphia Federalists. [18] Many probably had not agreed with Adams, but they were sagacious enough to realize that the party was in a life and death struggle with the Republicans for political control of Pennsylvania and could not afford the luxury of a public split.

As the campaign progressed the junto seemed confident that its attacks would bring victory in October. Alexander Addison told Washington of his confidence that Ross would be chosen over McKean. But he cautioned that the whole "spirit of party will be exerted against him and they [Republicans] speak also with confidence." He observed how important Ross's victory would be to the state of the union. The governor's influence in the important state of Pennsylvania, through his appointive power could prevent "mischievous printers, and the great importation of Irish" who were the "bane of the political" and moral character of the state. This antagonism that Federalists felt toward the Irish immigrants reveals the conflict that had been smoldering for ten years between native Protestants and the Irish Catholics. This clash grew out of the support the Irish usually gave Republican candidates, and the fact that some Philadelphians viewed the increasing number of Irish immigrants as an economic and social threat. They feared that the Irish might cause a labor surplus which would tend to lessen the opportunities available to native born men who sought economic prosperity in a free and open market. In addition, some Philadelphians disliked the general unruly manner of the Irish who did not practice the traditional ways of Philadelphia life.[19] Federalists, therefore, sought to translate these fears into support for the Alien Law that restricted immigration.

Federalists did not let their confidence in the final outcome prevent them from maintaining a vigorous campaign effort. They appeared certain that the electorate would see through the lies that Republicans had spread representing Ross as the author of the Alien and Sedition laws, the standing army, and the "Tax upon Widows." The junto assumed that its continued publication of the conduct of the French and the threat they believed the French represented to "the rights of man and every republic on earth" would more than offset Republican charges. The voters, the junto reasoned, wanted to fill the offices of government with men who had shown an exclusive attachment to the country, and since the people felt that way Ross was their only choice.[20]

Clearly, the junto expected victory in Philadelphia and the remainder of the state. Thomas Adams, a resident of Philadelphia, wrote his mother that he thought McKean would draw some votes from the city but he would not win because of the campaign in Ross's behalf. Bingham observed that he had little doubt of the result, "as the federal party had gained a great Accession of Strength, by the misconduct of the French." Washington also noted that the lines between the parties in the state were clearly drawn. But he warned that if "principle instead of men, are the steady pursuit of the Federalists, their cause will be at an end." Washington affirmed what to the junto had become political creed, namely, equating the policies of those who administered the Constitution with the Constitution itself.[21] This point was used repeatedly in the junto's campaign against McKean—that he favored, and was influenced by, those who wanted to destroy the constitutional government of the United States.

As the campaign drew to a close, both parties distributed handbills and held meetings throughout the city and county. At one such meeting Federalists adopted resolutions which declared the "judicial tyranny and intolerance of McKean," and declared its intention to make public the "illiberal" statement the Republicans had used in attacking Ross. Federalists further promised to expose the subversive intentions of McKean and his partisans. These public declarations showed the extent Federalists were willing to go to discredit the Republican's attack on Ross and the Federalist war measures. They apparently felt that the Republican attack was having an influence on public sentiment. Duane immediately responded that the Republicans had spoken only the truth in their attacks on the Federalists and their candidate. Was it a stigma, Duane asked, "to say that many enemies of our revolution are the warmest supporters of Mr. Ross? Was it wrong to point out that many" on the Federalists' campaign committee had deserted when the British were in possession of the city?[22]

Meanwhile, both political parties added a new dimension to politics by conducting polls and forecasting the number of votes their candidates would receive. These polls at best were crude and probably only intended to spur on the party faithful to a greater effort in the closing weeks of the campaign. Both parties, needless to say, predicted victory for their candidate. Federalists claimed that Ross would win in the state by fifty-five hundred votes, while Republicans claimed McKean would receive a majority of fifty-seven hundred votes.[23]

Near the end of the campaign both parties selected their ticket for the state senate, assembly, and the city council. A mixture of old and new names highlighted the Republican ticket: for the senate races they named Benjamin Say and Edward Heston; for the assembly, William Adcock headed the ticket; while for the select council party stalwarts such as Tench Coxe, Stephen Girard, Joseph Wetherell, and James Pearson were nominated. The Federalists placed some new names on their tickets for the other elective posts, while at the same time rewarding others, such as Joseph Ball, with the opportunity to run for higher office, which in Ball's case was the state senate. William Hall led the junto assembly ticket, and Samuel Coates led the ticket for the select council.[24] Neither party conducted an active campaign for the other offices but rather concentrated their entire effort on the race for governor. Party leaders no doubt expected that the battle for the top position would draw interest to each party's entire ticket, and with the growth of party voting this assumption did not appear unreasonable.

As the day of election approached, many people who had deserted the city for fear of yellow fever came back in large numbers to vote. One Federalist remarked the day before the election that the large crowds in Philadelphia would make the election of Ross almost a certainty. Governor Mifflin, seeing the large numbers of people who crowded back into the city, had the election sites moved from the State House to Center-House tavern. He feared that many people would be exposed to the threat of yellow fever, although in 1799 the outbreak of the dread disease was markedly lighter than in previous years.[25]

As the people gathered for the election an air of excitement and anticipation swept over the large crowds who congregated in the taverns of Philadelphia to discuss the probable winner. This race for governor had stirred the voters to great heights of interest, for many believed that the winner of the contest in Philadelphia would determine the political destinies of both political parties in the state as a whole. Most men who thought at all about the outcome realized that for the Federalists to win they had to carry Philadelphia by a large majority. Republicans, on the other hand, with the expected McKean victory in the county, had only to hold down the Federalists' majority in Philadelphia to be on their way to winning the state. A Republican victory in Philadelphia, which the party had worked so hard to achieve, would spell certain defeat for the friends of the government.

Election day seemed quiescent after the fever of the campaign. Philadelphians went to the polls in an orderly fashion without any of the outbreaks of violence that had so marked the last two years of electioneering in the city. After the polls closed and the votes tallied, Philadelphians had given Ross 58.6 percent of the vote. Ross carried nine of the twelve wards and lost one other by only a small margin. The data in table 18 show that

TABLE 18
VOTES CAST IN THE GUBERNATORIAL ELECTION OF 1799

Wards	*Federalist (%)*	*Republican (%)*
New Market	57.7	42.3
Dock	66.2	33.8
South	65.3	34.7
Walnut	78.3	21.7
Middle	68.6	31.4
Chestnut	68.2	31.8
Lower Delaware	60.0	40.0
Upper Delaware	49.5	50.5
North	66.6	33.4
High	82.4	17.6
South Mulberry	45.7	54.3
North Mulberry	37.1	62.9
Totals	58.6	41.1

Ross carried most of the wards that Republicans had won in previous elections, winning New Market ward by 57.7 percent, North ward by 66.6 percent, and Lower Delaware by 60.0 percent. Ross received his heaviest percentage strength in High, Walnut, Middle, and Chestnut wards. In fact, eight out of the nine wards Ross carried he won by more than 60.0 percent of the vote. The core wards, usually junto strongholds, went heavily for Ross. For example, High Street ward and Walnut Street ward gave Ross 82.4 percent and 78.3 percent respectively. McKean, on the other hand, managed to win only the northern wards of North and South Mulberry and Upper Delaware. He carried those wards by majorities far off the pace set by Swanwick in his two election victories for Congress and by the

Jeffersonian electoral ticket in 1796.[26]

However, in the state Republicans scored a major victory with McKean's election over Ross by 38,036 to 32,643. McKean carried twelve counties while Ross won thirteen and the city of Philadelphia.[27] The voter turnout represented a record for the state gubernatorial election, but the vote in Philadelphia was only 41 percent of those eligible, down considerably from the record turnout set in the Morgan-Israel special election in February, 1798. No doubt the threat of yellow fever kept the vote down in Philadelphia, because the interest generated by the campaign was greater than in any other city election held in years.

Socioeconomic differences did not significantly affect voting behavior. Ross won support from voters who had traditionally supported Federalist candidates in previous elections. It appears that the Federalists convinced enough Philadelphians that McKean's close association to the French cause could be harmful to republican government. Moreover, it is likely that ethnocultural and other social cleavages might have had an impact among some artisans living in New Market and Lower Delaware wards. Artisans in these wards probably could see how the growing number of Irish immigrants competing with them for jobs directly affected their own self-interest, resulting in their support for Ross's position on the Alien Law. At the same time, the city's economy was under such severe strain from the French and British seizures of American commerce that job opportunities were few in number. Many artisans blamed this fact on the French, and as a result McKean tended to suffer.

Federalists won all the other posts in Philadelphia. The party won all six assembly seats by obtaining 59.9 percent of the vote. Party voting in the races for the assembly showed a variance of only three votes separating all six junto candidates and eleven for the losing Republican ticket. The races for the select and common council showed similar majorities for the junto, with their candidates compiling margins of 59.8 and 60.2 percent respectively. These contests saw the same degree of party voting evident in the assembly contests.[28]

Federalist defense of the enlargement of the army and navy undoubtedly won backing from some Philadelphians who would be directly affected by supplying and building these federal projects. This was especially true in New Market, Dock, and Lower Delaware wards, where most Philadelphians who engaged in the various marine trades resided. The friends of government won endorsement from their constituents in Philadelphia, but they could not translate this support to a state-wide basis, where voters could not directly perceive what benefits these measures would have on their lives. The election results demonstrate that voters at the local level generally respond only to issues that they can see have some direct relationship to their way of life. Thus the issues of peace with France and the land tax probably won the support of Quakers, Germans, Irish, and farmers, who saw their own vital interests directly affected and accordingly voted for McKean and the Republicans. This factor also in no small way held down the Federalist majority in Philadelphia and won for the Republicans statewide.

The returns from the county, on the other hand, showed a complete Republican victory, with the party winning all six assembly seats and giving McKean 67.9 percent of the vote.[29] The Republicans' highest percentages came from Northern Liberties, Germantown, and Southwark; 77.4, 65.1 and 64.7, respectively. The most surprising aspect of the county vote was that Germantown, usually a safe Federalist district, went heavy for McKean. Republican totals in the county also enabled the party to win one of the two state senate seats for the Philadelphia district, electing a Republican for the first time since the disputed election of Israel Israel in 1797. The Republican candidate Benjamin Say received 50.9 percent of the votes. Since Ball had carried Philadelphia, getting 59.4 percent of the vote, the margin of victory came from the Republican sweep of the county. In the county Say received his heaviest percentage strength from Northern Liberties and Southwark districts, getting 78.6 and 76.4 percent respectively. In the other contest for the state senate, junto candidate John Jones defeated Republican Edward Heston by getting 50.4 percent of the votes. Jones's victory resulted from his 61.5 percent majority in Philadelphia, where Republican voters did not vote a straight ticket, giving Heston 84 fewer votes. Moreover, in the county not as many voters cast ballots in this race, reducing the percentage strength Heston received.[30]

Philadelphia Federalists, in spite of their victory in the city, faced the future with a sense of foreboding. The party had retained its complete control of all the city's elective offices, but it saw in McKean's victory the seeds of defeat in the important elections for president and Congress the next year. The party had been hurt by the issues of the land tax, peace with France, the enlargement of the army and navy, and the Alien and Sedition laws, and had been forced to defend these increasingly unpopular measures. Federalists had managed to carry Philadelphia, but with McKean in the governor's chair Republicans gained advantage of the governor's vast patronage powers and the prestige of the office.

Federalists blamed Ross's defeat on the party's failure to receive the number of votes it expected from the Quakers and Germans in Philadelphia. One observer noted that the yellow fever had kept "many gentlemen" out of the city, while McKean had not lost " a single vote by his D[amn] uprooters consisting of the mob chiefly—poor miserable beings—possessing not a farthing to move out with." John Fenno, editor of the *Gazette of the United States*, more precisely placed the blame on Adams for sending another peace mission to France, which Fenno observed had been played off against Ross by the Republicans with great success. "The government it was said, is friendly to Peace–Mr.McKean's attachment to Peace is notorious eyo [*sic,* i.e.], he is a friend of government." Other Federalists noted that the land tax had hurt their candidate, as Republicans appeared successful in linking Ross and his party with the support of that issue. [31]

The junto saw the victory of McKean as a grave event that would make the Republicans confident and overbearing. Cobbett asserted that McKean's election would make "Pennsylvanians feel all the abundant blessings resulting from the 'Glorious Revolution' of 1775." Others feared that the victory might seriously threaten the junto's political ascendancy in Philadelphia. [32] Still other Federalists saw that some good effects might come of the party's defeat at the polls. Fisher Ames noted that all good men would be shocked at the results and roused to action "by so scandalous an event." Had Ross been chosen, they would have slept, expecting him to keep all the "wild Irish who voted for McKean in good order." Federalists, he asserted, had a stimulus for the next three years to work towards strengthening the party. Fenno, in his paper argued that McKean's victory should convince Federalists that they had to work harder in order to defeat the Republicans. If the party did not heed the warning it would lead to an oppression of the party and the country by "a brutal democracy." Fenno feared that the same voters that "lifted McKean . . . may rise a Duane, a Reynolds . . . or any other vulgar demagogues" to political office.[33]

While Federalists of Philadelphia appeared dejected by the election results, the Republicans were overjoyed. Although they had lost Philadelphia the party had elected one of its own as governor and had won the first state-wide contest between the two parties. To celebrate their victory Republicans organized a grand jubilee to proclaim the triumph of "republicanism over a foreign faction." A feast, held in honor of the victory, was followed by a parade through the city streets to the homes of the various Republican leaders, who were treated with songs. McKean, in response to an address from Republicans of Philadelphia congratulating him on his election, declared that he would base his administration on the wishes of the people and not on the foreign faction within the Quaker city. McKean thus hinted that he and his party would pursue in coming elections the same issues that had won this election. [34]

The election had demonstrated the well-organized efforts of both parties. The issues had centered on peace with France and on Federalist war measures. The success the Federalists achieved in Philadelphia resulted from their ability to pin the label of "anti-government" on Republicans in a city whose economic life depended on trade. The junto had stressed throughout the campaign that the Republicans had opposed the policies of the federal government while supporting France, who robbed American commerce, destroying each Philadelphian's chance to achieve economic prosperity. Success had come to the Federalists also because of a well-organized campaign effort that took advantage of the well-defined political organization which the junto had assembled over the years. Elections in urban areas, such as Philadelphia, were not left to chance nor to a county committee that might be miles from many of the voters. Rather, they were conducted in a skillful manner by canvassing every house for votes and using public meetings, broadsides, and newspapers to reach the electorate with their messages. Both parties utilized these methods but the junto had, as it proved in 1799, the superior organization.

Chapter Eight

A MINORITY NO LONGER

The election of 1800 found Philadelphia Federalists facing a real threat to their continued domination of city politics. Although the party had carried Philadelphia in 1799, it had lost the gubernatorial election to the Republican party, which appeared united and organized for the coming elections. Moreover, Federalists lost, during 1800, their central issue when they found that the French war threats no longer provoked fear in the hearts of Philadelphians. This issue had brought the party success since 1797, but with its passing Philadelphia's friends of government found themselves forced to defend unpopular measures passed during the war scare.

The Federalists realized that in addition to the presidential election they faced challenges to their hold on the city's congressional seat, state senate seats, six places in the assembly, and control of the city council. After their defeat in the last election, party leaders viewed with pessimism the approaching elections and seemed interested in merely stemming the Republican tide. Federalists also seemed disheartened and dispirited by the removal of the federal and state capitals.[1] The party had found assistance in the form of information and campaign support in having the nation's capital and the leaders of the federal government in Philadelphia. Moreover, it placed Philadelphia at the center of political activities, allowing Federalists to relate national issues to the needs and interests of Philadelphians. The removal of the capital was a psychological loss; it apparently left the Federalist junto aware that the city they had controlled for so many years and had taken so much pride in was no longer the center of political activity.

Republicans, unlike the Federalists, approached the election with the greatest optimism since the birth of their party. They were united and working to broaden their base of support, particularly among middle- and lower-class artisans and ethnocultural minorities. McKean's election had provided the party the patronage needed to begin to weaken the junto's hold over the loyalty of many Philadelphians. But Republicans also believed that they had the issues and candidates to lead the party to victory in the fall. They thought that Thomas Jefferson and the issues of peace and Federalist war measures would carry them to both national and local victories.[2]

The immediate concern of both parties, following McKean's election, was the need to pass an election law for presidential electors. Republicans, fresh from their success in a state-wide election, favored a general election law similar to that used in 1796. Federalists, on the other hand, who controlled only the state senate, wanted a district election law. This method, they thought, would offset Republican advantages in the county and western section of the state and give them the opportunity to elect some federal electors.[3] Thus, the campaign of 1800 really began in December 1799, when the legislature opened its session with both parties intent on the passage of their form of election law.

After the legislature opened, Federalist leaders reflected the pessimism that pervaded the party. Only by the passage of a district election law, they believed could they split the Republican vote and keep the state from going to Jefferson. The junto organized committees to have petitions signed by its supporters in Philadelphia and sent to the legislature requesting that the state be divided into election districts. The senate passed such a bill, while the Republican-controlled assembly passed a general election law.[4] By January the deadlock between the two houses over the issue seemed complete, with neither willing to compromise.

Meanwhile, Republicans under McKean's leadership began the removal of Federalist officeholders in Philadelphia. John Beckley and Alexander J. Dallas became the governor's chief patronage advisers for Philadelphia. The only criterion used was whether or not the men holding the offices had supported or opposed McKean.[5] The offices included prothonotaries, registrars, and recorders. In an urban situation with a relatively high population density these offices provided the means of building a broad-based urban political organization. The favors performed by these minor governmental officials resulted in debts which could be called in on election day.

Federalists reacted to McKean's removal with the expected outcry. "There is no doubt," wrote one Federalist, "but every person in his [McKean's] power to Remove from office will be turned out that was against him." On every question, cried the junto, Republicans expected to achieve some political gain from it. McKean's action, Fenno suggested, would tend to destroy republican government, for what man would accept a public office "if the mere will of a governor" could deprive him of it?[6] Of course, Federalists themselves had established the precedent with the removal of Tench Coxe and others from office. Moreover, Federalists knew that political support rested on elected officials' ability to get things accomplished; without political patronage, this task would be difficult.

McKean wrote to his friend John Dickinson that he was working very hard to place good party men in public offices in Philadelphia and the remainder of the state. "I have waded thro' a sea of trouble & surmounted my principal difficulties, tho' no Herculus, I have been obliged to cleanse the Augean stable, with little or no aid, for I am my own Minister and Amanuensis." James Monroe heartily approved McKean's action and felt that it would add to the party's prospects in the fall elections.[7]

While McKean began the removal of Federalist officeholders, Republicans began to prepare for the fall elections. Dallas expressed the opinion that since an election law appeared blocked in the legislature, the party should make a "great exertion" to win control of both houses of the legislature in October. By doing that, he claimed, Republicans could pass an election law and win the state for Jefferson. Philadelphia represented a principal target for the Republicans since all six of the city's assembly seats and its state senate seats were held by Federalists. If the Republicans could sweep the city elections it would place the party in an excellent position to control the legislature. To that end Republicans made a serious attempt to win support from all segments of the community by organizing ward committees in every ward. Republicans wanted to call on every voter to inform them of their ticket and insure that they went to the polls.[8] This type of ward politics was the forerunner of the later urban political machines. It also showed the ease with which political parties were organized in urban areas, where close contact with the voter was always available.

Thomas Adams wrote his brother of the massive Republican effort to win control of Philadelphia's six assembly seats. "Men of distinguished talents, great popularity," with some who had in the past declined to serve, "are now brought forward, by the Democratic interest, to fill all offices of Government." He observed that in almost every case they had succeeded in winning the office to which they aspired, and it was well understood that a "trial of strength between the two candidates for chief magistrate . . . is not to be in the choice of electors by the people, but in the complexion & character of the individual legislatures." Federalists in Philadelphia feared that McKean might try by proclamation to use the election law of 1796, which they thought would result in a complete Republican rout of the Federalists because the friends of government would not turn out to vote.[9]

The junto seemed unable even by the summer to unify the party organization sufficiently to find candidates to oppose the Republicans. The party still had not recovered from the shock of McKean's election and their subsequent losses of state patronage in Philadelphia. Thomas Fitzsimons observed that he could promise nothing for Pennsylvania, since, after several meetings, the party leaders had been unable to find a man in the city to run for Congress. The Federalist incumbent, Robert Waln had declined to run again. "The party appears" Fitzsimons noted, "To be either supine or deranged." He pointed out that Robert Wharton, the mayor of the city, had been asked but had not as yet accepted. Fitzsimons concluded that Federalists should not despair, as it often happens that "after a paroxysm of indolence we reverse and become zealous." It appeared that most Federalist leaders wanted their ticket headed by Wharton, but by late July it seemed that the mayor would not run. Fitzsimons lamented that in a city of sixty thousand "not a man is to be found who is fit for the station, who will accept the nomination for congress."[10]

Nevertheless, most friends of government wanted at least to unite their forces to prevent the election of Jefferson. William Bingham pleaded with his friends to make every effort to exclude Jefferson. Otherwise, he said, Jefferson's election would increase the hostility of Great Britain toward America and would prove fatal to the tranquility of the country. He failed, however, to spell out how the party could prevent Jefferson's election or what men or man they should run to oppose the Republicans. The friends of government also opposed the reelection of, or at least expressed resentment against, Adams for having sent the second peace mission to France and having removed the high Federalist Timothy Pickering as secretary of state. Fitzsimons, speaking for most Philadelphia Federalists, thought that Jefferson would prevail if the Eastern or New England states split, as he expected, since Pennsylvania would cast no votes. "I really know not," he said, "whether we shall be much worse off with him [Jefferson] than the present man; we fear from either the destruction of our government." He also emphasized that the government could not carry on without the support of one of the two parties, and it appeared that Adams had the support of neither.[11] This was an indication of the importance politicians attached, by 1800, to the two-party system.

While the junto seemed divided and unable to unite for the elections, Republicans appeared well organized and optimistic. Michael Leib observed that Republicans were "as much indebted to the violence and indiscretion" of the Federalists as "to the goodness of our cause. Let them go on and they will render us invulnerable in a short time." To insure that each candidate had the united support of party leaders, Republicans held several meetings to form their tickets. Republicans adopted procedures designed to make it appear that the party's candidates were selected by the general public in open meetings. The party allowed the meetings to choose the candidates from a list of men submitted to the meeting. In July Republicans in both the city and county held general meetings to nominate candidates for the election. In addition to candidate selection, Republicans adopted addresses, which followed the party's general theme that Federalists represented only the elite and wealthy, while Republicans spoke for the welfare of every citizen. In an effort to win control of the city council, Republicans attacked the junto for its management of Philadelphia. Republicans asserted that the "finances of the city should neither be enriched by oppressive taxes, nor be impoverished by expensive projects." The "council of our Metropolis," they continued, should consist of men "who have common interest, a common feeling, with every description of citizen," who refuse to pervert power or influence for "the purpose of party," and who would conduct the government with vigilance and economy.[12] Republicans, in order to win, had to convince large numbers of middle- and lower-class voters that they represented their interest and encourage them to cast their ballots.

To lead the ticket the party selected William Jones, an Anglican merchant and a close friend of Dallas, to run for Congress. Dallas also found a place on the ticket when the party named him to run for the common council, along with Matthew Carey and eighteen other party men. For the important state senate race the Republicans chose John Pearson, a Quaker who had party boss Michael Leib's support. Pearson's selection seemed an obvious attempt to win Quaker votes for the party. In the county the party nominated all its incumbents, headed by Leib. Republicans seemed by their selections to assume that the electorate was now voting for party and not for any one man. Every candidate supported the party's opposition to Federalist war measures and its desire to maintain peace with France, along with supporting Jefferson for the presidency, of course.[13]

Immediately after the Republican ticket appeared, Federalists brought out their old charge that the men nominated lacked the qualifications for public office. They appealed to the freemen, declaring that a "man may be honest in *trade*, but either through incapacity, or by the influence of his party, in politics might be a dangerous Knave." The men who make your coat may "either willfully or ignorantly, when elevated to a public shopboard, spoil the skirts of political happiness and prosperity."[14] This appeal was framed to keep alive the elitist tradition with which the Federalist junto had maintained its power, a tradition that only the wealthy, well born, and the leisured should be elected to political office. But Republicans, by appealing across class lines, sought the construction of a heterogeneous political organization, which they hoped could remove Philadelphia's Federalists.

Republicans wanted to convey the idea that they supported the concepts of democratic rule. In the county, for example, before the ticket was finally agreed upon, delegates from all the districts met to decide, as representatives of the people, on the composition of the ticket. These delegates had been chosen by meetings in the various districts and gave Republicans the grass roots support they needed to interest and later turn out the voters on election day. This delegate system also demonstrated the breadth of the Republican organization in the county, which in no small way accounted for the party's continued and overwhelming victories over the past five years. John Beckley, who directed the Republican campaign in Pennsylvania, and other leaders in the city and county decided to continue attacking the Federalists over the issues of the direct land tax and peace with France. Beckley believed that the party would continue to gain support from these issues and, considering the junto's disarray, that the issues would bring Republicans victory in the fall.[15]

Meanwhile, Federalists had met and appointed a committee to decide on the party's ticket for the fall elections. The committee selected the candidates and three days later reported them to a more general meeting, which tried to give the appearance of popular choice in the party's selections. State Senator Francis Gurney, an Anglican merchant, was chosen to oppose William Jones for the congressional seat, but it appeared that Gurney represented only an interim choice. Fitzsimons wrote after the meeting that the party "had been entirely at a loss for a proper character to send to Congress and at last have been under the necessity of following up one" whose chief claim was fitness for office rather than interest. Earlier Fitzsimons had written that the party had wanted Wharton to run, but by the time of the Gurney selection it appeared that he had declined. Fitzsimons had implied, however, that he and the other leaders had hopes of persuading Whatron. For the assembly seats the junto nominated four of its incumbents, William Hall, Godfrey Haga, George Fox, and Samuel Fisher, plus two new additions, John Blackley, and H. K. Helmuth.[16]

This split in Federalist ranks was quickly seized upon by Republicans as another example of the junto's efforts to exclude Philadelphians from having a voice in the selection of candidates. Duane claimed that the junto had solicited seven different men to run for Congress. Wharton, he asserted, had wanted to run, but "upon dcliberation at their *Caucuses*" it was agreed that since he had been head of the committee of "Slander against McKean he was not safe and so they set up poor *Francis Gurney.*"[17] This account, published and used by Republicans during the campaign, although untrue, went a long way in establishing the party's charges that Philadelphians had no power in the selection of the junto's candidates and that these candidates represented only the interests of the few.

Although Philadelphia's Federalist leaders tried to appear confident, many of them doubted that they could carry the state and felt bitter toward Adams for sending the second peace mission to France. Fitzsimons wrote that "all eyes had turned towards the French negotiations which [will] decide whether the Federal party keeps the present President." William Bingham resented what he termed the lack of energy of the administration in not pursuing the desires of the Hamiltonian wing of the party. He realized that Republicans were willing to encourage mass participatory democracy in order to oust the Federalist junto by appealing to the "lower class of people." He feared the results of the election for he knew that the once powerful Federalist junto seemed disorganized when compared with the Republicans.[18]

Federalists continued to rely upon the French war scare as a political issue but found that it aroused little excitement among Philadelphians. Bingham lamented that the people seemed "to have less National Pride & Affection than any other People." Many could not understand why Republican attacks on the direct land tax and the "Quiting laws" (Sedition laws) aroused so much support when they believed that such laws were necessary. Federalists seemed to flounder in their reach for an issue or issues which could win for them in the fall elections. Junto leaders appeared to feel sorry for themselves and lacked the initiative to find new issues. Fitzsimons moaned that since the removal of the federal capital Philadelphia Federalists had suffered a "very serious disadvantage." He contended that when the capital was in the city, it enabled "the friends of government to contradict certain misstatements, or by explanation to satisfy those with who [*sic*] reason would prevail," but now the party was uninformed of the actual state of affairs, "as if the seat of government was in Europe." Republicans, he claimed, seemed to have access to information that he and his party lacked, and he knew of no way of remedying the situation.[19] Consequently, the friends of government based their campaign appeals on the old issue that Republicans represented forces that wanted to bring down the Constitution by destroying balanced government.

The split within the ranks of the national party damaged the junto, but they did continue their efforts to retain their political position. They could not afford to allow the Republicans to win control of the political offices in Philadelphia. The moderate Federalists and those who supported Hamilton, which included Fitzsimons and Bingham, united by late summer to oppose the Republicans. In its efforts to maintain the status quo, the junto organized a campaign committee under the direction of William Rawle. In the months before the election the committee had the Federalist ticket for Congress, the legislature, and city council published in the newspapers every day. The party had agreed during August on the ticket for the city council. Before this ticket had been named it had caused party leaders many anxious moments. At a series of meetings to select candidates the party leadership appeared badly split over whether or not to renominate incumbent councilmen. Thomas Adams reported to his father that the party wanted to secure its continued control of the city council, but that a very unpopular measure of taxing the people for supplying the city's water had been enacted. "The labor is yet incomplete" and more money would probably be necessary to complete the project, creating a general outcry against the "present Councilors & in order to appease the wrath of the Sovereign people" Federalists had consented to replacing a large percentage of the city council.[20]

Thomas Adams later informed his father that the junto had solved the problem of the schism by agreeing to nominate a majority of the incumbent common councilmen. He explained that no notice of the differences reached the public and that everyone in the leadership appeared satisfied with the results. Adams's reports were verified when the party published a different ticket for the city council on September 20. The ticket the party finally agreed to run contained a majority of those men who had been elected the previous year. Evidently, Federalist leaders had decided that the Republicans were not going to make an issue of the water tax and felt safe in nominating their incumbents, thus avoiding what might have precipitated an open break within the junto.[21] The Republicans' failure to take advantage of public opinion against the water tax cannot really be understood, unless their motives could be attributed to a sense of public welfare, a realization that Philadelphia needed a fresh water supply to help prevent yellow fever.

While Federalists struggled to reach agreement on their tickets and unity in their ranks, Republicans continued their incessant attacks against them. The Jeffersonians accused the junto of supporting men who had led the nation to arm "without a foe, and divided without a cause." Duane echoed Republicans' fears that the friends of government had created a reign of terror and false alarms to promote domestic feuds and foreign war; in addition, he claimed, they had raised taxes and increased the public debt. Federalists, it seemed to Republicans, threatened the existence of republican government. They also campaigned against Federalists for their opposition to a general election law. "A willful handfull of men," the party claimed, thwarted the wishes of a majority in the state in holding out for a district plan of election, which if enacted would represent a minority viewpoint and take away the real desires of the people.[22]

Meanwhile, Federalists directed the brunt of their criticism at Israel. They argued that Israel had sought and had been rejected for almost every political office available and was now trying to become the sheriff of Philadelphia. Fenno wrote that one of Israel's supporters had claimed that the Unites States had become, under Federalist rule, as dirty as the "Augean stable," an allusion, Fenno ironically assumed, referring to the importation of Irishmen; he then ridiculed Israel for his claim that low birth gave him the ability to clean up the mess created by the junto. "This might be well enough, if we could see any connection between the business of sheriff, and cleaning the stable of its filth." Federalists also pointed out that Israel's candidacy had created a split within the Republican party between Dallas and Tench Coxe.[23] This charge, Federalists thought, would not only weaken Israel's support but also sow seeds of doubt and distrust among Republicans. Federalists also sought to widen their base of support by organizing a meeting of Roman Catholics. By such methods they wanted to demonstrate that the party had backing from all segments of the community and, at the same time, to woo Roman Catholic votes.

As election day approached, Federalists saw that Republican efforts to establish a broad-based urban political party had succeeded. They realized that Republicans, in their quest for political power, had aroused an interest in politics among those who had not participated in the past. Republican propaganda techniques, based on the premise that society should be open and fluid, had stimulated urban middle- and lower-class workers to come out and vote. This process spelled doom for the Federalists' hold on Philadelphia's political institutions. Thomas Adams observed pessimistically that Philadelphians appeared "so completely democratized that I have no confidence in the success of any measure which is advocated by the friends of the federal government." Other Federalist leaders believed that perhaps the party would win the city, but held out little hope for the county.[24]

After the polls closed and the ballots were tabulated, Philadelphia Federalists learned that the party had lost some major ground to the resurgent Republicans. The contests proved very close, with neither side winning by more than a few votes. In the congressional race William Jones defeated Francis Gurney by a margin of only fourteen tallies. The data in table 19 indicate that Jones carried only six of the fourteen wards. The number of wards had been increased from twelve to fourteen to accommodate the increase in the population (see fig. 2). Jones's margin of victory came from the northern wards, which had in the past given Republicans their victories. He also carried the two new wards, Cedar and Locust, added in the southwest section of the city. Jones's greatest percentage strength came from North and South Mulberry, Upper Delaware, and Cedar wards. Cedar ward, which ranked fourth in Republican voting strength, contained high percentages of artisans and unskilled laborers. In fact, when the division of New Market occurred the majority of the former ward artisans and

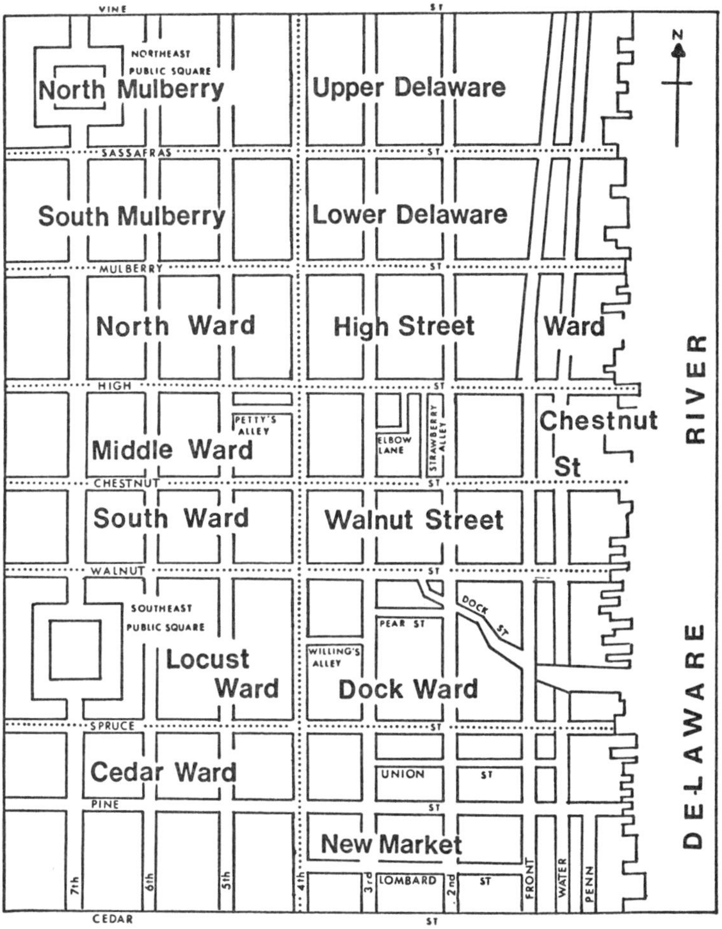

FIGURE 2
PHILADELPHIA'S 14 WARDS

unskilled laborers were thrown into Cedar ward. A similar occurrence took place in Locust ward, but not to the same extent. On the other hand, Gurney's heaviest percentage strength came from Dock, High, Middle, and Walnut wards, wards that had traditionally supported Federalist candidates.

TABLE 19
VOTES CAST IN THE CONGRESSIONAL ELECTION OF 1800

Wards	*Federalist (%)*	*Republican (%)*
New Market	54.7	45.3
Dock	69.1	30.9
South	54.2	45.8
Walnut	58.6	41.4
Middle	62.9	37.1
Chestnut	52.1	47.9
Lower Delaware	47.8	52.2
Upper Delaware	35.7	64.3
North	55.4	44.6
High	66.8	33.2
South Mulberry	31.3	68.7
North Mulberry	26.2	73.8
Locust	45.4	54.6
Cedar	38.9	61.1
Totals	49.8	50.2

Republicans had recaptured and enlarged their base of support in some of the peripheral wards. The issues of taxation and the Alien Laws might have played an important part in the way ethnic minorities and middle- and lower-class voters perceived the issues and candidates. Gurney continued what had become an established Federalist pattern by carrying the core wards and those areas closely connected with the maritime industry. The data suggest that Jones owed his success to the large voter turnout; for about fifty percent of the eligible voters went to the polls, demonstrating the strength of the Republican organization where large blocks of previously apathetic voters, chiefly from the middle and lower class, had been aroused by Republican ward heelers.[25] This portion of the electorate probably responded to Republican rhetoric that, when elected, that party would maintain a free and open society where every man had an equal opportunity to succeed. This ideal appealed to Philadelphians who were striving to attain upward socioeconomic mobility.

In the assembly races Republicans for the first time managed to win one seat in Philadelphia. The races were very close, with only a few votes separating the candidates. The top vote getter, Federalist Godfrey Haga, had 1,691, and the lowest Republican, John Barker, had 1,643. Republicans increased their share of the city-wide vote for assembly seats to 49.3 percent, up from 40.1 percent in 1799 and 27.1 percent in 1798. In these assembly races the electorate again demonstrated that it was in large degree voting for the party and not the man. Indeed, Benjamin Morgan, former Federalist who ran as a Republican in 1800, lost his bid for an assembly seat. Party voting further revealed itself in the fact that only fourteen votes separated Republican candidates and only fifteen votes separated the Federalists.[26] The lone Republican victory represented a real breakthrough for the development of the party's organization within Philadelphia. For the first time it had won an elective office not connected with the federal government.

The results of the city council races also showed a single Republican victory for a place on the common council, with Casper Wistar polling the same number as the top vote getter for the junto, Robert Ralston. Nevertheless, the junto won all the seats on the select council and nineteen places on the common council. Voting in the city council races showed the closeness of the returns, with only about twenty votes separating the two parties. The Republicans increased their percentage of the popular vote in the council elections to 49.7 percent in the common council, up from 39.8 percent in 1799 and 40.5 percent in 1797.[27] Wistar's personal popularity within the city accounted for the single Republican victory.

In the county Republicans again demonstrated the efficiency of their organization by winning all the offices up for election. Congressman Leib, who headed the ticket, won an overwhelming victory, getting 78.2 percent of the vote. In the contests for state senator and sheriff, which included both the city and county, the margins compiled by Republicans in the county carried the day for the party. In the senate race John Pearson, the Republican, defeated the incumbent Federalist Nathaniel Newlin, receiving 60.5 percent of the vote. Newlin's percentage strength in Philadelphia was only 50.9, while in the Northern Liberties and Southwark districts of the county Pearson carried by 74.5 and 80.9 percent respectively. The Republican majorities in the county also allowed Israel to win the office of sheriff by a comfortable margin, getting 62.5 percent of the vote. However, in Philadelphia the Federalists received 51.5 percent of the vote.[28]

Republicans viewed the election as a complete triumph. Andrew Elliot wrote to Jefferson that the elections went well for republicanism. He noted that this marked the beginnings of a new century which he hoped would be distinguished "as an epoch in which republicanism [is] not only triumphant" but would become too firmly established "ever again to be shaken by the advocates for monarchy."[29] The party had scored almost a complete reversal of the elections of two years before and had come within a hair of winning all the elective offices in Philadelphia.

Federalists lamented the party's reversals in the election, particularly their loss of the city's congressional seat. Fenno explained the defeat by asserting that a large number of Federalists had voted for Jones. He implied that this cowardly conduct was due to the pressure that the "French faction" had used during the campaign. He believed that Republicans had intimidated many Federalists before the election. Even one Republican noted that the party might not have won had not a number of "old Quakers" stayed away from the polls. But others more accurately blamed the loss on the efforts of the Republican organization and noted that Republicans would probably carry everything within a year or two.[30]

The Republican party owed its success to its ability to build a political organization that constantly searched for methods to strengthen and enlarge its base of support. The urban environment of Philadelphia provided Republicans with easy access to a large number of voters who could be easily contacted and made aware of issues and candidates. After the election Republicans were in such a position that if the party could capture the presidency it might provide the basis for completely overturning the junto. The party had enjoyed great success by attacking Federalists' actions during the French war scare and thus forcing the junto to defend what had become by 1800 very unpopular issues. The split within the junto and its indecisiveness in the selection of its candidate for Congress appeared to have little effect once the campaign began. The junto had used its traditional plea that only men of wealth and social position should be allowed to run for elective office. This had once been a powerful appeal, but with the development of the two parties and the competition for office, it had begun to crumble in the face of Republicans' rhetoric that all men, regardless of their station, should have equal access to political office. The closeness of the returns indicated that this rhetoric had begun to make its mark. While the junto lost some of its control of the city's assembly seats and the city council, it continued to survive by the strength of its organization and the traditional support it received from the more established residents of Philadelphia. The only Federalist issue that seemed to seduce any voters was their charge that Republicans lacked the qualified and experienced men to handle elective office; otherwise, Republicans would have won everything. Even this issue would prove fatal in the future, when the Republicans demonstrated that they could govern effectively.

The success of Republicans in establishing a two-party system in Philadelphia can be directly related to their efforts to broaden the concept of social mobility to mean that each person had the right to an equal chance, not only for economic success but for success in social and political life as well. By widening the meaning of social mobility, Republicans had broadened the social and political life of the Quaker city. Now men who had achieved economic success, no matter what their birth or occupation, could compete through the party system for political office.

Immediately following the fall elections both parties in Philadelphia set to the task of the presidential election. From the outset the Republicans seemed determined to do all they could to win the state's electoral votes for Jefferson and Burr. Republican leaders, under the direction of John Beckley, sought to convince state senators that Pennsylvanians demanded that the state not lose its votes in the presidential election. By October, it was too late to hold an election to choose electors; thus the task fell to the legislature to elect the state's electors. The Republicans' problem was that they controlled only the assembly, while the Federalists held a majority in the senate. McKean had issued a call for a special session of the legislature to convene on November 5, 1800. Since Philadelphia Republicans knew that electoral selection by joint ballot of the two houses would carry the state for Jefferson, they sought through petition to convince the senate that this method was the choice of most Philadelphians.[31]

Philadelphia's Republicans held a meeting at the State House, where they approved a petition to the senate. This petition called upon the legislature to put aside party differences and perform their duty to uphold the Constitution by drafting an election law. It asked the legislators to heed the voice of the majority, not party spirit. Republicans used the ward committees created for the fall election to pass the petition through each ward and every district of the county. A week later Beckley wrote to Dallas, indicating that the petition had received 2,448 signatures in the city, and that in the Northern Liberties, Southwark, and other parts of the county it "received upwards of 2700 signatures." The relative ease with which a vast number of people could be mustered to sign these petitions indicated the extent to which the Republican organization had developed within Philadelphia and the ease with which party machines could function within an urban environment. Beckley also told Dallas that John Jones, senator from the Philadelphia district, publicly declared that "if a majority of *his Constituents* demanded a joint vote, he would vote for it." He then instructed Dallas to put all the petitions together and demonstrate to Jones that a majority had indeed signed.[32]

Though lacking the determination to reelect president Adams, Federalists sought to insure that Pennsylvania's electoral votes would not go to Jefferson. The leaders in Philadelphia were badly divided as to whether to support Adams for another term or to follow Hamilton's desire to have Charles Cotesworth Pinckney elected in his place. Many could not forgive Adams for sending the second peace mission to France, thereby destroying the campaign issues that they had used so effectively against the Republicans. After the elections in October, many in the junto swallowed their pride and came out in support of Adams or at least declared that they would do all they could to prevent the election of Jefferson.[33] To accomplish their aims Federalist leaders decided to pursue a twofold course: one, attack Jefferson and his supporters; and, two, maintain in the state senate that it was unconstitutional to join with the assembly in a joint vote for electors. In this regard Federalists, in spite of their election setbacks, could still count on a thirteen-to-eleven majority in the state senate.

Accordingly, the junto led off its campaign by attacking Tench Coxe, who had been writing a series of articles against Adams in the *Aurora.* Many Federalists believed that if they could discredit Coxe they would undermine Jefferson's support. Federalist newspapers brought up the old charge that Coxe had aided the British when they had occupied Philadelphia during the Revolution. At the same time the friends of government attacked Jefferson for his seeming dislike for urban areas. The *Philadelphia Gazette* reprinted portions of Jefferson's *Notes on Virginia* wherein Jefferson claimed that farmers were the chosen people of the earth. This man, the paper charged, could not be a friend to the artisans, as his friends claimed, but would instead oppose and abuse the mechanics of Philadelphia. The paper also noted that Jefferson's own mechanics were his black slaves.[34]

Along with their newspaper campaign against Jefferson and his supporters, Federalists organized a meeting on November 5 which adopted an address to the senate. They declared that it was unconstitutional for the senate and assembly to unite to vote since only by concurrent voting could the sense of the people be obtained. Besides, they noted, the far more numerous assembly would always outvote the senate. In addition to the address, Federalist leaders formed a committee to help the senate maintain its constitutional rights. Of course, the primary purpose was to insure that the thirteen senators held firm against the Republican-controlled assembly. The committee immediately began writing letters to Lancaster to insure the firmness of the federal senators. It even sent some of its members to Lancaster to lobby and keep the spirit of the thirteen steady.[35]

Meanwhile, Philadelphia Republicans continued their campaign for Jefferson's election. They held additional meetings in which they attempted to arouse Philadelphians against the conduct of the thirteen Federalist senators. The meetings were large, with the party organization making every effort to insure that they were well attended. Such meetings enabled politicians not only to show support for a certain viewpoint but also to win support for the party. The meetings were relatively easy to arrange because of the high population density and the interest Philadelphians had in politics. The turnout for the meetings also reflected the ability of urban politicans to use the newspapers available to aid them in their organizing efforts.

At one such meeting Republicans adopted an address declaring that the Federalists were attempting to destroy the will of the people by treating with contempt the petitions sent from Philadelphia. The address added that in the last election voters had repudiated the "federal system of government" and that those thirteen men were blocking the wishes of the people. Federalists scorned the address, claiming that the men who prepared it could not write "good English."[36] This type of haughty response actually played into the hands of the Republicans by demonstrating the contempt Federalists held for the "lower classes" of people.

Indeed, by the end of November both sides had made their respective positions very clear. It now became a matter of whether Pennsylvania would cast its votes in the presidential election. At the outset of the struggle Republicans seemed confident that they could deliver the state's electoral votes to Jefferson, but when they saw the firm Federalist position and the results from the other states indicating that the election would be very close, party leaders decided they must work out a compromise. Republicans agreed to an arrangement whereby each house would nominate eight men with one being eliminated in the voting, thus giving the Republicans eight electoral votes and the Federalists seven. Federalists accepted the plan as the only means of avoiding the possible blame for Pennsylvania not casting its electoral votes. Republicans, on the other hand, felt that the importance of a single vote, if it could help elect Jefferson, was well worth the price.[37]

Federalists reacted to the choosing of electors by declaring their satisfaction with the results. Many now believed that Adams would be reelected. The junto obviously thought that they had struck a solid bargain, one that would assure, along with South Carolina's eight votes, the Federalist retention of power. For that reason, when the news reached Philadelphia that South Carolina had gone to Jefferson, insuring the defeat of Adams and Pinckney, they were "thunder struck." Richard Peters lamented that "Tis heavy with us poor *Feds,*" as the leaders of the junto slipped back into their homes after the defeat. Many realized that the end of a political era was at hand, and they simply did not know how to react.[38]

Republicans of Philadelphia greeted the news of their national victory with a great outpouring of joy and celebration. The tie between Jefferson and Burr appeared not to bother the leaders in Philadelphia. Their first thought after the news came was that they would now control the federal patronage in Philadelphia, which party stalwarts such as McKean, Dallas, and Leib believed would enable them to win complete control of the city's political institutions as well as to strip much of the social prestige from the Federalists. With the election over and the new year about to begin, Federalist officeholders learned that they would soon be removed from their posts. The subject of offices dominated conversations among Republicans, as the party at last would pick the sweet fruits of victory. This point Jefferson made clear after his election in 1801 by the House of Representatives, when he told William Barton that those Federalists who had opposed him would be removed. Jefferson kept his word. He appointed a number of local Republicans to federal posts, including Alexander J. Dallas as United States attorney for eastern Pennsylvania.[39]

The loss of federal patronage caused grave consternation among Philadelphia Federalists. They realized that because of the election results of 1800 coupled with the loss of federal and state positions, the Federalist party faced an uphill struggle in the local elections of 1801. In the coming contests they would meet an inspired Republican party awaiting the opportunity to finally crush their long standing foes. But the junto did not concede the election. They organized ward committees in each of the fourteen wards, which in turn would appoint workers to round up Federalist voters and get them to the polls. Federalists campaigned vigorously for their slate by attempting to arouse fears that a Republican victory would constitute a threat to republican government. They equated Republicans with favoring democracy, a concept Federalists assumed would be repugnant to Philadelphia voters.[40]

Republicans, on the other hand, armed with federal and state patronage, saw in the 1801 election an opportunity to win complete control of Philadelphia's elective offices. In planning their campaign they followed the successful practices of county Republicans by organizing ward meetings in each of the wards to nominate a slate of candidates. Each of the ward meetings would select delegates to a city-wide meeting which would finalize the Republican ticket. These procedures gave the appearance of widespread public participation in candidate selection and allowed party workers to build up enthusiasm for the elections. By such methods Republicans sought to demonstrate their commitment to broad-based participation in public affairs. Following that theme Republicans campaigned, stressing the need for an open society where all classes would have an equal opportunity to achieve success. Using this rhetoric and their organization at the ward level, Republicans felt they had a good chance to win political control of Philadelphia.[41]

The election results fulfilled Republican optimism. The party elected its entire ticket for the state senate, assembly, select council, and common council. Moreover, the victory gave the Republicans control of the common council for the first time. Republicans won 53.0, 52.1, 51.8, and 51.5 percent of the vote for the assembly, select council, common council, and senate respectively. The data in table 20 reveal that Republicans won large majorities in the peripheral wards while holding down the Federalist vote in the core wards. In fact, the election marked the first time Republicans won a majority of the city's wards, winning nine wards in the assembly and eight in the senate, select council, and common council races. Republicans compiled their greatest percentage strength in North and South Mulberry, Cedar, and Upper Delaware wards. Moreover, Republicans captured the wards that were undergoing the most rapid population growth, enabling them to increase their overall majorities. In addition, the party won New Market and South wards, wards which had voted Federalist in 1800. On the other hand, Federalist voting strength continued to come from High, Dock, North, and Chestnut wards, wards that had a smaller population base and were not growing at the same rate as the rest of Philadelphia. Republicans demonstrated the effectiveness of their ward organizations by turning out 50.4 percent of the eligible voters. Such voter participation in an off-year election indicates Republican success in constructing their party machinery at the ward level and their efforts to bring middle- and lower-class voters to the polls.

TABLE 20
VOTES CAST IN THE SELECT COUNCIL ELECTION OF 1801

Wards	*Federalist (%)*	*Republican (%)*
New Market	48.3	51.7
Dock	65.4	34.6
South	45.8	54.2
Walnut	53.9	46.1
Middle	55.9	44.1
Chestnut	58.6	41.4
Lower Delaware	43.1	56.9
Upper Delaware	38.8	61.2
North	59.0	41.0
High	70.4	29.6
South Mulberry	29.3	70.7
North Mulberry	17.3	82.7
Locust	48.4	51.6
Cedar	32.7	67.3
Totals	47.9	52.1

Over the years Republicans had generally won most of the peripheral wards in congressional and presidential elections, but in their election the party finally convinced enough eligible voters from the entire city to come out and vote. The ward returns show that Republican candidates sharply reduced traditional Federalist voting strength in the center city wards while at the same time winning by huge majorities in the outer wards.[42]

It appeared that Federalist appeals of foreign influence and unchecked democracy had little attraction to a majority of Philadelphia voters.

With the Republican victory in the local elections of 1801, the Federalist junto, which had dominated Philadelphia for most of its existence, passed into a minority position. The ground for this triumph had been broken with the party's victories in 1800 and Jefferson's elevation to the presidency. Republicans had achieved a goal that had taken almost ten years, and now the way appeared open to equality of opportunity in political and social life. Local Republicans won control of Philadelphia by building a broad-based urban coalition that attracted votes from all classes as well as ethnic minorities. The democratic liberalism that the party had preached for almost ten years would now have to stand the test of practice.

Chapter Nine

CONCLUSION

Historians have argued that the political parties formed in the 1790s developed out of conflicts on the national level and were later organized downward to the local level.[1] This was not true of political parties formed in Philadelphia. The party organizations that developed there were local in origin, using national issues where appropriate in order to win voter support. The fact that the local parties later allied themselves to a national movement in no way proves that party formation at the grass roots level arose out of conflicts in Congress. Local conditions provided the climate wherein men seeking political power could more readily organize a political movement. The colonial epoch and the state parties formed during the Revolutionary era furnished the experience necessary for a two-party system in Philadelphia. Philadelphians were accustomed to partisan strife and found little to fear from competition for political office. The parties that developed in Philadelphia owed little if anything to Jefferson, Hamilton, or Madison. In fact, political parties developed before them and would have developed without them.

The development of the Federalist and Republican parties in Philadelphia was an accomplished fact by the election of 1796. This rapid growth of two readily identifiable parties differed sharply from that in most other regions, where a largely rural environment hindered party development. In contrast an urban area with its high population density made the task of organizing political parties much easier. Politicians could achieve close contact with large numbers of voters within a short space of time, and could arouse passions almost overnight by simply posting notices throughout the city and bringing people together for meetings. In addition,

Philadelphia's politicians could use policies and decisions reached by the federal, state, and local governments to demonstrate how these decisions directly affected the lives of the city's inhabitants. Hence, urban politicians found a need to establish and perfect political organizations that could effectively exploit the issues of the day for their own political advantage.

As early as the 1790s urban politicians had refined the art of campaigning. They had developed the use of ward meetings that gave the appearance of involving the people in the selection of candidates while, at the same time, stirring interest in the elections. In addition, ward committees were formed, giving ambitious types the opportunity to canvass voters and make them aware of their party's position. These ward heelers were used extensively by both the Federalist and Republican parties to bring voters to the polls. Moreover, the use of patronage to reward the party faithful became a necessary tool for winning widespread support. This aggressive politicking by Federalists and Republicans stimulated voter interest. Republicans, for example, made an all-out effort to develop support among ethnocultural minorities by providing assistance in finding employment, relief, and housing. Republican leaders Michael Leib, John Swanwick, and Israel Israel built their political following from among the city's ethnocultural groups. In fact, the political machines attributed to the nineteenth-century urban experience had their antecedents in the urban political parties of the early national period.

Philadelphia's Federalist junto of wealthy families had organized itself into a well-defined political organization by 1786. They supported the Constitution of 1787 and the policies and personnel of the federal government after 1790. Moreover, the junto had established a pattern of support with Philadelphians that stretched back into the colonial period. People who were eligible to vote gave their ballots to men from the upper class. This differential society, where only the elite ran for and held political office, was the cornerstone of Federalist support. Philadelphia's Federalists did not believe in mass participatory democracy, and this elitism found itself in direct conflict with the ideals of the Revolution. Republicans, who established a political interest in Philadelphia, used the means of mass appeal and mass participation. Both political parties, from 1796 on, showed that they could marshal the forces necessary to use the issues and personalities of the day to win elections. Neither political group, in practice, feared the necessity of political organizations; in fact, both were constantly seeking means and techniques to improve their party's appeal.

The men who formed the Republican party were themselves members of the upper class who had been excluded socially and politically by the Federalist elite. Although not generally as wealthy as their Federalist counterparts (see table 5), Republicans had attained economic success and wanted a share of the spoils. The attraction that pulled Republicans together rested not with any ideology, but in their desire to participate in the distribution of the "loaves and fishes." Their exclusion compelled them to construct a political party that directed its appeal toward middle and lower-class voters and ethnic minorities. Republicans had to win support from these groups in order to achieve victory at the polls. The success of the Republicans in organizing a broad-based urban political party came through such issues as excise taxes and the Jay Treaty. The issues adopted by Republicans did not represent a distinct ideological difference with the Federalists, but merely propaganda devices designed to magnify their voter appeal. These issues provided the vehicle by which the coalitions that opposed the junto united and formed a distinct political party. But in no sense did foreign policy issues stimulate Republican success at the polls. In fact, the opposite holds true. Republicans achieved no election victories as a result of using foreign policies as issues in their campaigns. Instead such issues as British depredations and the Jay Treaty gave expression to an ideology that had begun to express itself in the ideals released by the American and French Revolution. This ideology demanded that the general class of people should have a strong voice in the political process and a government that would respond to the expressed wishes of the voters. Republicans used this type of appeal to encourage greater participation among the electorate and to demand that business, government, and society be open to all. This open society that the rhetoric called for enabled Republicans to champion the cause of socioeconomic groups who had been left out or overlooked by Federalist policies.

Philadelphia's population presented insurgent Republicans an ideal environment to test the appeal of their democratic rhetoric. The distribution of wealth in Philadelphia had become increasingly unequal, with only 10.5 percent of the taxpayers owning real property valued at over $1,000; while 58.4 percent of the taxpayers owned no real property at all (see table 1). This situation provided Republicans the opportunities to cultivate the middle- and lower-class voters. Republicans constantly stressed that government at all levels must maintain policies that would enable every man to have the chance to increase his own private wealth. Moreover, by working with the lower-class in times of economic need, Republican leaders demonstrated that they had the interest of the average citizen at heart. During the 1790s, Republicans awakened among middle- and lower-class voters an interest in politics by showing them that their own self-interest dictated that they become involved in city affairs. These voters responded to the Republican party. In fact, much of Jacksonian rhetoric had its origins in the partisan strife of the 1790s.

Republicans used this democratic ideology and gave it substance by their persistent attacks on the Federalist junto. They pictured the junto as representative of the wealthy, who supported policies that benefited only the few. Republican leaders, though members of the upper class themselves, sought to represent their party as the one which would create even greater equality of opportunity in all phases of life than currently existed. In so doing Republicans broadened the concept of economic mobility to mean that government must maintain a setting wherein each citizen had an equal chance to succeed in social and political life as well as to gain economic prosperity. By proclaiming themselves Republicans they implied that the junto favored monarchy and monopoly, an appeal that was particularly suited to Philadelphia, with its great contrast between the wealthy, who lived in the splendid homes in the center city and drove about in carriages, and the artisans and unskilled laborers, who lived in modest and poor conditions. Furthermore, Republican rhetoric found a very receptive audience after 1795 among the large numbers of immigrants from Ireland, Germany, and France who found their way to the city and its surrounding areas during the 1790s. These ethnocultural groups came with a long and deep-seated hatred of the British. Republicans used these anti-British sentiments, along with the lively remains of hatred engendered by the Revolution toward the British, to denounce supporters of the government's policy toward Great Britain.

Meanwhile, the junto continued their traditional appeal to patriotism and to elitist rule. In all their campaign appeals Federalists made no effort to disguise their belief that the "common man" lacked the ability to deal with the issues of the day. Instead, the junto argued, political decisions should be left in the hands of those fit to govern, and the general public should merely conform to what their betters had decided. The junto continued to stress that the leaders in society should be drawn from the traditional families who had always provided the core of Philadelphia's leadership. By using its political organization to turn out the vote, the junto actively campaigned in every election for its candidates, an indication that it was forced to solicit the support of the electorate. But the junto represented those in Philadelphia who favored an increasingly restricted brand of privatism, postulating a closed society where opportunity for advancement into the higher circles of social and political life should be limited to the very few. Consequently, the junto's exclusiveness was increasingly out of step with the democratic ideals and practices unleashed by the American Revolution.

The competition that these two opposing sides brought to the political life of Philadelphia caused a greater interest among the voters in the issues that affected their lives and well-being. More people came to the polls to vote and more came to feel a loyalty to one party rather than the other. So effective were their organizations, so persuasive their appeals, that voter participation increased from about twenty-four percent of the eligible voters in 1789 to over fifty percent in 1801.(see table 21). As party competition grew after 1795, the electorate came to vote more and more for the party rather than for the man. The voters became educated in what the parties stood for in terms of their position on any given issue and their basic ideology.

The demands by Republicans for an open and liberal society opened the door, after the party's victories in 1801 for steady erosion of the political position of the older gentry in Philadelphia. After the Federalist defeats, many of them returned entirely to the business of making money and stayed almost completely out of the political arena. Philadelphia shifted from the political capital of the country to a large city whose citizens continued the practice of increasing their own individual wealth. It was this spirit that encouraged the city toward the path of future industrialization. As a result of the clashes between Federalists and Republicans, the decade of the 1790s allowed Philadelphians to experience increasingly democratic political practices. These contests brought more people into the political process and demonstrated that change could be effected through elections. Republican rhetoric that demanded equal access to political and social decision-making for all men regardless of class opened the door later, in the 1820s, for the growth of a broader-based participatory democracy where officeholding was not restricted to the upper class.

TABLE 21
PERCENTAGE OF VOTER PARTICIPATION IN PHILADELPHIA ELECTIONS, 1789-1801

Year	*Election*	*Percentage*	*Year*	*Election*	*Percentage*
1789	City Council	24	1797	Assembly	21
1790	Governor	26	1798	Special Senate	50
1790	Assembly	25	1798	Congress	18
1792	Congress	30	1798	Assembly	17
1792	Electors	11	1799	Governor	41
1793	Governor	14	1799	Assembly	37
1794	Congress	34	1799	City Council	35
1795	Assembly	37	1800	Congress	50
1796	Congress	45	1800	Assembly	48
1796	Assembly	39	1801	Assembly	50
1796	President	41	1801	City Council	50

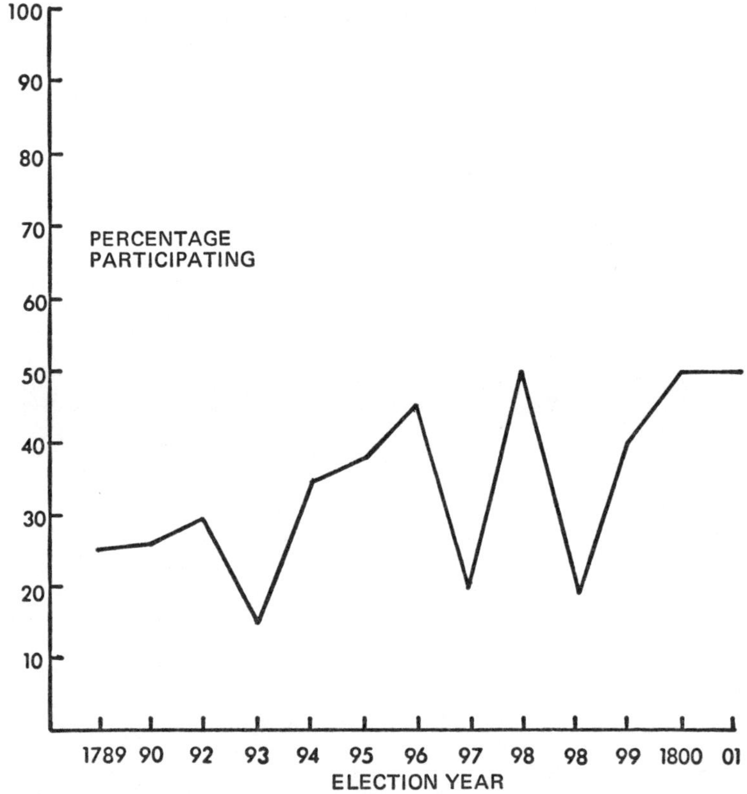

FIGURE 3
VOTER PARTICIPATION IN PHILADELPHIA

NOTES

1: Gentry and Entrepreneurs

1. James A. Henretta, "Economic Development and Social Structure in Colonial Boston," *William and Mary Quarterly*, Third Series XXII (Jan., 1965), 75-102; James T. Lemon and Gary B. Nash, "The Distribution of Wealth in Eighteenth-Century America: A Century of Change in Chester County, Pennsylvania, 1693-1802," *Journal of Social History*, II (Fall, 1968), 1-24; Allan Kulikoff, "The Progress of Inequality in Revolutionary Boston," *William and Mary Quarterly*, Third Series XXVIII (July, 1971), 375-413; Jackson Turner Main, *The Social Structure of Revolutionary America* (Princeton: 1965); Gary B. Nash, *Class and Society in Early America* (New York: 1970), 1-15.
2. See Main, *The Social Structure of Revolutionary America*, and Robert E. Brown, *Middle-Class Democracy and the Revolution in Massachusetts, 1691-1780* (Ithaca: 1955), for examples of this thesis.
3. Henretta, "Economic Development and Social Structure in Colonial Boston," 75-92; Kulikoff, "The Progress of Inequality in Revolutionary Boston," 375-413.
4. Nash, *Class and Society in Early America*, 10.
5. The statistical methods employed in this study are not unimpeachable. The federal census, state census, and federal and Philadelphia tax rolls contain many errors and are not precise; and the indices based on them are not completely accurate. Therefore, percentages relating to socioeconomic groups and political leaders show only general tendencies and are not exact. Observing these reservations, however, quantification methods cannot be dismissed as useless, nor can the conclusions be disregarded.
6. *First Census of the United States, 1790*, "Philadelphia;" (Washington, D.C.: 1907-1908); *Second Census of the United States, 1800, Population*, "Philadelphia." (Washington, D.C.: 1907-1908).
7. George Geib, "A History of Philadelphia, 1776-1790" (unpublished Ph.D. dissertation, University of Wisconsin, 1969); Regin F. Duvall, "Philadelphia's Maritime Commerce with the British Empire, 1783-1789" (unpublished Ph.D. dissertation, University of Pennsylvania, 1960); Carl and Jes-

sica Bridenbaugh, *Rebels and Gentlemen: Philadelphia in the Age of Franklin* (New York: 1942).

8. Samuel Hazard, (ed), *Register of Pennsylvania, Devoted to the Preservation of Facts and Documents, and Every Other Kind of Useful Information Respecting the State of Pennsylvania,* 16 vols. (Philadelphia: 1828-1836), 2: 22-24; Henry Wansey, *Journal of an Excursion to the United States of North America* (Salisbury, England, 1796), 184-186; *General Advertiser,* April 17, 1790.

9. Bridenbaugh, *Rebels and Gentlemen;* see also Carl Bridenbaugh, *Cities in Revolt: Urban Life in America, 1743-1776* (New York: 1955), for an excellent account of Philadelphia's growth through the American Revolution.

10. "Dr. Solomon Drowne," *PMHB,* XLVIII (April, 1924), 234.

11. Sam Bass Warner, Jr., *The Private City: Philadelphia in Three Periods of Its Growth* (Philadelphia: 1968), 6-7; Bridenbaugh, *Rebels and Gentlemen,* 9-11; Leonard Bernstein, "The Working People of Philadelphia from Colonial Times to the General Strike of 1835," *PMHB,* LXXII (July, 1950), 324-325.

12. Main, *The Social Structure of Revolutionary America,* 12-43; see the remarks of Thomas Paine that any "man with a chest of tools, a few implements of husbandry, a few spare clothes . . . a few articles for sale in a window" could prosper in Philadelphia before the Revolution. Philip Foner, ed., *The Complete Writings of Thomas Paine,* 2 vols. (New York: 1945), 2: 387-388.

13. Richard G. Miller, "Gentry and Entrepreneurs: A Socioeconomic Analysis of Philadelphia in the 1790s," *The Rocky Mountain Social Science Journal,* XII (Jan., 1975), 73-74; Abraham Ritter, *Philadelphia and Her Merchants, as Constituted Fifty @ Seventy Years Ago* (Philadelphia: 1860).

14. For a significant study of the poor of Philadelphia see John K. Alexander, "The City of Brotherly Fear: The Poor in Late Eighteenth-Century Philadelphia," in *Cities in American History,* ed. Kenneth T. Jackson and Stanley K. Schultz (New York: 1972), 79-99; John K. Alexander, "Poverty, Fear, and Continuity: An Analysis of the Poor in Late Eighteenth-Century Philadelphia," in *The Peoples of Philadelphia: A History of Ethnic Groups and Lower Class Life,* ed. Allen F. Davis and Mark H. Haller (Philadelphia: 1973), 13-36; Donald R. Adams, Jr., "Wage Rates in the Early National Period: Philadelphia, 1785-1830," *The Journal of Economic History,* XXVIII (Sept., 1968), 404-417; Erna Risch, "Immigrant Aid Societies Before 1829," *PMHB,* LX (Jan., 1936), 16-27; O.A. Pendleton, "Poor Relief in Philadelphia, 1790-1840," *PMHB,* LXX (April, 1946), 161-172.

15. Manuscript returns for Pennsylvania Septennial Census, 1800, PHMC. My figure of 6,818 is higher than the state census figure of 6,625. My calculations are based on both the state census and the city tax rolls for 1800.

16. Anthony N. B. Garvan, "Proprietary Philadelphia as Artifact," in *The Historian and the City,* ed. Oscar Handlin and John Burchard (Cambridge: 1964), 177-185; Warner, *The Private City,* 16.

17. J.H. Powell, *Bring Out Your Dead: The Great Plague of Yellow Fever in Philadelphia in 1793* (Philadelphia: 1949); see also Martin S. Pernick, "Politics, Parties and Pestilence: Epidemic Yellow Fever in Philadelphia and the Rise of the First Party System," *William and Mary Quarterly,* Third Series XXIX (Oct., 1972), 559-587; Matthew Carey, *A Short Account of the Malignant Fever Lately Prevalent in Philadelphia* (Philadelphia: 1794).

18. *A Century of Population Growth* (Washington, D.C.: 1909), 11--25;

David T. Gilchrist, (ed.) *The Growth of the Seaport Cities, 1790–1825* (Charlottesville: 1967), 25-47; Edward C. Carter II, "A 'Wild Irishman' Under Every Federalist's Bed: Naturalization in Philadelphia, 1789-1806," *PMHB*, XCIV (July, 1970), 341-342; Andreas Dorpalen, "The German Element in Early Pennsylvania Politics, 1789-1800," *Pennsylvania History*, IX (April, 1942), 176-190.

19. Professor Carter concludes that the Irish accounted for 56 percent of the immigrants entering Philadelphia during the era. In fact, he calculated that between 1790 and 1800, 7,415 Irish immigrants made their homes in Philadelphia and Southwark. See Carter, "Naturalization in Philadelphia," 341.

20. Manuscript returns for Pennsylvania Septennial Census, 1800, PHMC; additional data on occupational classification was obtained from the Philadelphia City Tax Assessment Books, 1799 and 1800, PCA.

21. For a detailed account of the shipbuilding industry in New Market ward and the suburb of Southwark see Joshua Humprey Papers, Humprey Correspondence, HSP. The collection contains an excellent account of the efforts by Joshua Humprey, a prominent Federalist, to locate a shipyard in the New Market-Southwark area in 1798-1799.

22. Carter, "Naturalization in Philadelphia," 341-342.

23. See Bernard Barber, *Social Stratification: A Comparative Analysis of Structure and Process* (New York: 1957); Robert Merton, *Social Theory and Social Structure* (New York: 1968), for analysis of occupational prestige.

24. Ethel Rasmusson, "Capital on the Delaware: A Study of Philadelphia's Upper Class, 1789-1800" (unpublished Ph.D. dissertation, Brown University, 1962), 55-56. See also Ferdinand M. Bayard, *Travels of a Frenchman in Maryland and Virginia with a Description of Philadelphia and Baltimore*, ed. and trans. Benjamin C. McCary (Ann Arbor: 1950), 128, 130; Bayard divides Philadelphia's population into three classes—those who own carriages, merchants and professionals, and craftsmen; he did not notice the city's poor.

25. Bridenbaugh, *Rebels and Gentlemen*, 21-22; Warner, *The Private City*, 20–21; J. Thomas Scharf and Thompson Westcott, *History of Philadelphia, 1609–1884*, 3 vols, (Philadelphia: 1884), II, 982–984; Whitfield J. Bell, Jr., "Some Aspects of the Social History of Pennsylvania, 1760–1790," *PMHB*, LXII (July, 1938), 281–308. Social clubs sprang from these social gatherings and ranged from eating clubs to fire companies. Clubs became important centers for promoting public projects and focusing attention on political candidates and issues.

26. See John C. Miller, *The Federalist Era, 1789-1801* (New York: 1960). See especially William Chambers, *Political Parties in a New Nation: The American Experience, 1776-1809* (New York: 1963); Joseph Charles, *The Origins of the American Party System* (Williamsburg: 1956); Noble Cunningham, *The Jeffersonian Republicans: The Formation of Party Organization, 1789-1801* (Chapel Hill: 1957); Manning Dauer, *The Adams Federalists* (Baltimore: 1953). For sectional studies see Lisle A. Rose, *Prologue to Democracy: The Federalists in the South, 1789-1800* (Lexington: 1968), and William A. Robinson, *Jeffersonian Democracy in New England* (New Haven: 1916). For state studies see Harry Tinkcom, *The Republicans and Federalists in Pennsylvania, 1790-1801; A Study in National Stimulus and Local Response* (Harrisburg: 1950). For other excellent state studies see James M. Banner, Jr., *To the Hartford Convention: The Federalists and the Origins of the Party in Massachusetts, 1789-1815* (New York: 1970); and Paul Goodman, *The Democratic-Republicans of Massachusetts: Politics in a Young Republic* (Cambridge: 1964), for examples of the development

of the first American party system.

27. See Table 6; although the total sample for Federalists was larger than for Republican candidates (139 to 110), the percentage difference remained approximately the same. The total assessed wealth came from the United States Direct Tax of 1798; Tax lists for Philadelphia, from the United States National Archives.

28. Data on the religious affiliation came from a variety of sources, chiefly from genealogical and church records in the Historical Society of Pennsylvania. Other sources included the *PMHB,* and William Wade Hinshaw, *Encyclopedia of American Quaker Genealogy,* vol. 2 (Ann Arbor: Edwards Brothers Index, 1938); church membership was available for 152 of the 262 candidates. See Rasmusson, "Capital on the Delaware," 55-58.

29. Minute Books of the Bank of North America, 1782-1801, HSP; Rasmusson, "Capital on the Delaware," 58, 63.

30. Roland M. Baumann, "The Democratic-Republicans of Philadelphia: The Origins, 1776-1797" (unpublished Ph.D. dissertation, Pennsylvania State University, 1970); Roland M. Baumann, "John Swanwick: Spokesman for 'Merchant-Republicanism' in Philadelphia, 1790-1798," *PMHB,* XCVII (April, 1973), 131-182.

31. Gary Nash, *Quakers and Politics, Pennsylvania, 1681-1726* (Princeton: 1968); Theodore Thayer, *Pennsylvania Politics and the Growth of Democracy* (Harrisburg: 1953); Frederick Tolles, *Meeting House and Counting House: The Quaker Merchants of Colonial Philadelphia, 1682-1763* (Chapel Hill: 1948); Rasmusson, "Capital on the Delaware;" Robert C. Alberts, *The Golden Voyage: The Life and Times of William Bingham, 1752-1804* (Boston: 1969); Judith M. Dimondstone, "Philadelphia Corporation, 1701-1776," (unpublished Ph.D. dissertation, University of Pennsylvania, 1969).

32. See Edward Pessen, "The Egalitarian Myth and the American Social Reality: Wealth, Mobility, and Equality in the 'Era of the Common Man,' " *American Historical Review,* LXXVI (Oct., 1971), 989-1034; Edward Pessen, "A Social and Economic Portrayal of Jacksonian Brooklyn," *New York Historical Quarterly,* LV (Oct., 1971), 318-353; Frank Otto Gatell, "Money and Party in Jacksonian America: A Quantitative Look at New York City's Men of Quality," *Political Science Quarterly,* LXXXII (June, 1967), 235-252; Stuart M. Blumin, "Mobility in a Nineteenth-Century American City: Philadelphia, 1820-1860" (unpublished Ph.D. dissertation, University of Pennsylvania, 1968).

2: The Origins of the Federalist and Republican Parties, 1776-1790

1. Seymour M. Lipset, *Political Man: The Social Basis of Politics* (Garden City: 1963), 287.

2. Warner, *The Private City,* 23; David Hawke, *In the Midst of a Revolution* (Philadelphia: 1961); Robert Brunhouse, *The Counter-Revolution in Pennsylvania, 1776-1790* (Philadelphia: 1942), 60-68; Geib, "A History of Philadelphia," 1-10.

3. Rasmusson, "Capital on the Delaware,"58-63; Mary Jamar, *Hollingsworth Family* (Philadelphia: 1944), 41-42; H.E. Wallace, "Sketch of John Innskeep," *PMHB*; XXVIII (April, 1904), 129-135; Henry Flanders, "Thomas Fitzsimons,"*PMHB*; II (July, 1878), 306-314; Robert F. Oaks, "Philadelphians in Exile: The Problem of Loyalty During the American Revolution," *PMHB*; XCVI (July, 1972), 298-325.

4. William Bingham to Benjamin Rush, May 3, 1784, Gratz Collection, HSP; Bingham to Richard Price, December 1, 1786, *Proceedings of the*

Massachusetts Historical Society; 2nd series XVII, 361; Jackson Turner Main, *Political Parties Before the Constitution* (Chapel Hill: 1973), 174-211.

5. Brunhouse, *The Counter-Revolution in Pennsylvania,* 190-192; Geib, "A History of Philadelphia," 268-290.

6. For the story of Pennsylvania's ratification of the Constitution see *Pennsylvania and the Federal Constitution, 1787-88,* ed. John B. McMaster and Frederick D. Stone (Philadelphia: 1888), 89-106; Brunhouse, *The Counter-Revolution in Pennsylvania,* 203-204.

7. Tench Coxe to James Madison, April 5, 1789, Madison Papers, LC; Richard Peters to John Adams, April 14, 1789, Adams Papers, MHS, vol. 372; William Bradford to Elias Boudinot, September 22, 1789, Wallace Papers, HSP; Robert Morris to Richard Peters, September 25, 1789; and Alexander Hamilton to Richard Peters, October 11, 1789, Richard Peters Papers, HSP. Men associated with the Federalist junto were appointed to a wide variety of Federal posts; e.g., Thomas Willing, president of the Bank of the United States; William Bradford, United States attorney for eastern Pennsylvania; William Lewis, federal judge; Tench Coxe, comptroller of the treasury; Richard Peters, federal judge; William Rawley, United States attorney; William MacPherson, U.S. surveyor, later inspector of the revenue for the Port of Philadelphia; Samuel Meredith, treasurer of the U.S.; Sharp Delany, collector of the port of Philadelphia; Clement Biddle, U.S. marshall for Philadelphia; Robert Patton, postmaster of Philadelphia.

8. Charles Biddle, *Autobiography of Charles Biddle, Vice-President of the Supreme Executive Council of Pennsylvania, 1745-1821,* ed. James Biddle (Philadelphia: 1883), 251-253; Raymond Walters, "The Origins of the Jeffersonian Party in Pennsylvania," *PMHB;* LXVI (Oct., 1942), 443.

9. Brunhouse, *The Counter-Revolution in Pennsylvania,* 176-190; Geib, "A History of Philadelphia," 273-280; Baumann, "The Democratic-Republicans of Philadelphia," 56-59.

10. Benjamin Rush to John Adams, February 24, 1790, in *The Letters of Benjamin Rush,* ed. Lyman H. Butterfield, 2 vols. (Princeton: 1951), I, 532-538; John McKean to George Washington, April 27, 1790, Hampton and Carson Collection, HSP.

11. *Columbian Magazine,* 1788, quoted in Scharf and Westcott, *History of Philadelphia,* II, 910.

12. *Statutes at Large of Pennsylvania, 1682-1801* (Harrisburg: 1908), XIII, 197-205; Tench Coxe to William Irvine, March 13, 1789, Irvine Papers, HSP; Samuel Miles to Tench Coxe, February 4, 1789; and Daniel Coxe to Tench Coxe, February 12, 1789, Coxe Papers, HSP; *Pennsylvania Gazette,* February 4, 1789.

13. *Independent Gazetteer,* March 26, 1789.

14. *Federal Gazette,* February 26, March 28, 30, April 3, 6, 7, 8, 1789; *Independent Gazetteer,* March 28, April 6, 9, 1789; *Pennsylvania Gazette,* April 15, 1789.

15. *Independent Gazetteer,* March 26, 27, 28, April 14, 1789; *Federal Gazette,* March 28, 30, April 8, 13, 1789.

16. *Independent Gazetteer,* April 16, 1789; *Federal Gazette,* April 15, 1789; Brunhouse, *The Counter-Revolution in Pennsylvania,* 220-221. The percentage of eligible voters who went to the polls was calculated by dividing the total votes cast in a specific election by the number of taxable in the 1793 Pennsylvania Septennial Census. The percentage is a close approximation allowing for the increase in Philadelphia's population and the women listed in the census (see appendix).

17. *Diary of Jacob Hiltzheimer,* March 19, 1789, ed. Jacob Cox Parsons (Philadelphia: 1893), 151; Levi Hollingsworth to Richard Spaigt, March 24, 1789, Levi Hollingsworth Letterbook, Hollingsworth Correspondence, HSP.
18. Petition to the Pennsylvania Assembly, 1789, Bryan Papers, HSP.
19. Francis Hopkinson to Thomas Jefferson, April 2, 1789, in *Papers of Thomas Jefferson,* ed. Julian Boyd, 19 vols. (Princeton: 1950–1974), XV, 16-17.
20. Committee to Timothy Pickering, April 18, 1789, Pickering Papers, Vol. 19, MHS; *Pennsylvania Packet,* March 24, 26, 1789. Members of the committee included James Wilson, George Latimer, Benjamin Rush, Tench Coxe, and William Bingham.
21. *Federal Gazette,* May 2, June 6, 1789.
22. *Independent Gazetteer,* May 18, 29, June 6, August 1, 1789.
23. William Bradford to Elias Boudinot, September 6, 1789, Wallace Papers, HSP.
24. *Minutes of the General Assembly of Pennsylvania,* 241-242, 249-251, 254-257.
25. *Federal Gazette,* March 11, October 12, 1789. For the assembly Federalists named Lawrence Seckle, wealthy Lutheran merchant; Jacob Hiltzheimer, wealthy Lutheran lawyer, William Bingham; and Henry Drinker.
26. Journal of William Rawle, October 13, 1789, William Rawle Papers, HSP.
27. *Independent Gazetteer,* October 15, 1789; *Pennsylvania Packet,* October 15, 1789; *Pennsylvania Gazette,* October 21, 1789.
28. *Federal Gazette,* December 11, 1789; John Mifflin to John Penn, November 10, 1789, John Mifflin Letterbook, Penn Papers, HSP; Thomas Fitzsimons to Benjamin Rush, August 20, 1789, Miscellaneous Manuscripts, APS.
29. Tinkcom, *The Republicans and Federalists in Pennsylvania,* 8-17.
30. William Maclay to Benjamin Rush, March 7, 1790; same to same May 12, 1790, Rush Papers, LC.
31. Samuel Bryan, Jr., to Albert Gallatin, May 13, 1790, Gallatin Papers, NYHS; James Hutchinson to Albert Gallatin, June 11, 1790; and Samuel Bryan to Albert Gallatin, May 13, 1790, Gallatin Papers, NYHS; Kenneth Rossman, "Thomas Mifflin, Revolutionary Patriot," *Pennsylvania History,* XV (Jan., 1948), 9-23.
32. William Maclay, in *The Journal of William Maclay,* ed. Edgar Maclay (New York: 1927), 254-255; Thomas Fitzsimons to Benjamin Rush, May 21, 1790, Gratz Collection, HSP.
33. *Journal of Maclay,* 271; Frederick Muhlenberg to Benjamin Rush, May 30, 1790, Society Collection, HSP; Thomas Fitzsimons to Rush, July 23, 1790, Gratz Collection, HSP.
34. Allen Johnson and Dumas Malone, eds., *Dictionary of American Biography,* 20 vols. (New York: 1928-1958), XVI, 293-295.
35. Broadside, September 6, 1790, Broadside Collection, HSP; *Pennsylvania Packet,* September 15, 1790; *Independent Gazetteer,* September 18, 1790. Philadelphians signing the appeal included: Thomas Fitzsimons, Robert Morris, George Clymer, Benjamin Rush, and Frederick Muhlenberg.
36. Thomas Fitzsimons to St. Clair, n.d., 1790, in *The Life and Public Services of Arthur St. Clair: With His Correspondence and Other Papers,* ed. William H. Smith, 2 vols., (Cincinnati: 1882), II, 191-192; Tench Coxe to Benjamin Rush, September 10, 1790, Rush Papers, LC.
37. *Federal Gazette,* September 15, 1790; *Pennsylvania Packet,* September 18, 1790; *Independent Gazetteer,* September 18, 1790; Thomas Fitz-

simons to Samuel Meredith, September 24, 1790, Dreer Collection, HSP; St. Clair to Fitzsimons, October 12, 1790, Gratz Collection, HSP.
38. *Federal Gazette,* September 17, 1790; *Independent Gazetteer,* September 18, 1790; *Autobiography of Charles Biddle,* 244-245; *Independent Gazetteer,* September 25, 1790.
39. *Pennsylvania Packet,* October 5, 1790; *Federal Gazette,* October 11, 1790; *General Advertiser,* October 11, 1790. For the assembly Federalists agreed to support Lawrence Seckle, an Anglican merchant; Francis Gurney, a Quaker merchant; Richard Wells, and William Bingham; for the Senate they selected Samuel Powel and Richard Peters.
40. *General Advertiser,* October 11, 12, 13, 14, 1790; *Pennsylvania Packet,* October 12, 1790; *Pennsylvania Gazette,* October 20, 1790.
41. *General Advertiser,* October 13, 1790; *Federal Gazette,* October 13, 1790; Ward returns were not available.
42. Samuel Bryan to Albert Gallatin, December 18, 1790, Gallatin Papers, NYHS; Robert Morris to Gouverneur Morris, October 31, 1790, Jared Sparks, *The Life of Gouverneur Morris: With Selections from his Correspondence & Miscellaneous Papers,* 3 vols. (New York: 1832), III, 19.
43. *General Advertiser,* October 13, 1790; *Federal Gazette,* October 13, 1790; *Independent Gazetteer,* October 16, 1790.
44. Samuel Bryan to Gallatin, December 18, 1790, Gallatin Papers, NYHS; *Autobiography of Charles Biddle,* 245-248.
45. Levi Hollingsworth to Benjamin Contee, July 6, 1789, Thomas Hollingsworth to Levi Hollingsworth, October 3, 1789, Hollingsworth Correspondence, HSP; John Mifflin to John Penn, May 28, 1790, John Mifflin Letterbook, Penn Papers, HSP; Thomas Fitzsimons to Rush, April 20, 1789, Gratz Collection, HSP; Jacob E. Cook, "The Compromise of 1790," *William and Mary Quarterly,* Third Series XXVII (Oct., 1970), 523-546; Boyd, *Papers of Thomas Jefferson,* ed. Boyd, XIX, 3–73.
46. Tench Coxe to James Madison, July 23, 1788, Madison Papers, LC; see also Tench Coxe to Samuel Miles, July 29, 1790, Coxe Papers, HSP; Robert Morris to Mary Morris, August 28, 1789, Robert Morris Papers, HL (Morris describes a dinner he had with Thomas McKean and other Philadelphians lobbying for removal of the capital). Benjamin Rush to John Adams, February 21 and March 19, 1789, Butterfield, *Letters of Benjamin Rush,* I, 501-501, 506-509.
47. Peter Muhlenberg to Benjamin Rush, March 18, 1789, Gratz Collection, HSP; Peter Muhlenberg to Rush, April 2, 1789, Society Collection, HSP; Peter Muhlenberg to Rush, August 10, 1789, Gratz Collection, HSP; Kenneth R. Bowling, "Politics in the First Congress, 1789-1791," (unpublished Ph.D. dissertation, University of Wisconsin, 1968), 184-189.
48. Robert Morris to Richard Peters, September 13, 1789; and Richard Peters to William Lewis, September, 1789, Peters Papers, HSP. Robert Morris to Mary Morris, September 6, 1789; and same to same, September 9, 1789, Robert Morris Papers, HL.
49. *Federal Gazette,* May 28, June 16, 1789, March 25, July 12, September 22, 1790.
50. Thomas Fitzsimons to Miers Fisher, June 15, 1790; same to same, July 16, 1790, Miers Fisher Papers, HSP; Minutes of the City Council, July 12, 16, 23, September 9, November 22, 1790, HSP; *Federal Gazette,* September 22, 1790. Robert Morris to Mary Morris, July 2, 1790, Robert Morris Papers, HL;
51. *Journal of Maclay,* 230-231, 234; William Bradford to Elias Boudinot, September 20, 1789, Wallace Papers, HSP; Richard Peters to Thomas Jefferson, June 20, 1790, Boyd, *Papers of Thomas Jefferson,* XVI, 345;

Samuel Miles to Tench Coxe, 1790; Daniel Coxe to Tench Coxe, February 12, 1789; William Coxe to Tench Coxe, Coxe Papers, HSP; John DeNormandie to Thomas Clifford, August 17, 1790, Clifford Correspondence, HSP; Isaac Harvey to William Chadwick, December 8, 1790, Isaac Harvey Letterbook, HSP; E. James Ferguson, *The Power of the Purse: A History of American Public Finance, 1776-1790* (Chapel Hill, N.C.: 1961), 319-320.

52. *Annals of Congress,* 1st Congress, 2nd Session, 1308-1325; Thomas Hartley to Tench Coxe, April 9, 1789; same to same, September 13, 1789; William Maclay to Coxe, April 30, 1790; William Irvine to Coxe, August 20, 1790, Coxe Papers, HSP.

53. To William Irvine, August, 1790, Irvine Papers, HSP. See Cooke, "Compromise of 1790," who contends that "Fitzsimons' . . . persistence and lobbying won" the move of the capital to Philadelphia, 539.

3: Ferment and Opposition, 1789-1792

1. Clement Biddle to Robert Gilchrist, May 8, 1789, Clement Biddle Letterbook, HSP; see Ferguson, *The Power of the Purse,* for the best account of the financial question.

2. *Federal Gazette,* September 3, 1789; Clement Biddle to George Joy, September 8, 1789, Clement Biddle Letterbook, HSP; those signing the petition included Matthew Clarkson, Jonathan Sergeant, Joseph Ball, Samuel Miles, John Nixon, Thomas McKean, and Blair McClenachan. Only McClenachan and Sergeant had been Constitutionalists.

3. William Bingham to Alexander Hamilton, November 25, 1789, in *Papers of Alexander Hamilton,* ed. Harold Syrett, 21 vols. (New York: 1961-1974), X, 539; Thomas Fitzsimons to Samuel Meredith, December 21, 1789, Dreer Collection, HSP; see *Annals of Congress,* 1st Congress, 2nd Session, 1345-1373, for some Philadelphians' proposal that the interest rate be set at six percent.

4. William Bradford to Elias Boudinot, January 17, 1790, Wallace Papers, HSP; see also Clement Biddle to Robert Gilchrist, January 6, 1790, Clement Biddle Letterbook, HSP, for a similar argument of national interest and self-interest as one and the same.

5. William Bradford to Elias Boudinot, January 21, 1790, and same to same, January 17, 1790, Wallace Papers, HSP; Clement Biddle to Robert Gilchrist, January 24, 1790, and same to same, January 31, 1790, Clement Biddle Letterbook, HSP; *Federal Gazette,* February 11, 1790; *Annals of Congress,* 1st Congress, 2nd Session, 1305, 1376.

6. William Bradford to Elias Boudinot, March 21, 1790, Wallace Papers, HSP; Clement Biddle to Robert Gilchrist, March 11, 1790; Clement Biddle to William Rogers, May 27, 1790, Clement Biddle Letterbook, HSP; Tench Coxe to Hamilton, March 5, 1790, in *Papers of Alexander Hamilton,* ed. Syrett, VI, 291.

7. Clement Biddle to William Rogers, July 7, 1790, Clement Biddle Letterbook, HSP; William Bradford to Elias Boudinot, June 17, 1790, Wallace Papers, HSP; *Pennsylvania Packet,* July 9, 1790; *Federal Gazette,* July 12, 1790; Tench Coxe to Hamilton, July 9, 1790; and same to same, July 10, 1790, in *Papers of Alexander Hamilton,* ed. Syrett, VI, 486-487, 490-491. The committee consisted of Federalists William Bingham, John Nixon, Matthew Clarkson, Joseph Ball, and William Bradford; Republicans included Charles Pettit, Thomas McKean, Jonathan Sergeant, and Blair McClenachan.

8. *Independent Gazetteer,* March 11, 1789; Lance Banning, "Republican Ideology and the Triumph of the Constitution, 1789 to 1793," *William*

and Mary Quarterly, Third Series XXXI (April, 1974), 167-188.

9. Madison to Benjamin Rush, March 7, 1790, Madison Papers, LC; Miller, *The Federalist Era,* 41-43; *Federal Gazette,* February 16, 1790.

10. *Federal Gazette,* February 16, 1790; Clement Biddle to John Jones, February 16, 1790, Clement Biddle Letterbook, HSP; see also Matthew McConnell to William Irvine, February 24, 1790, Irvine Papers, HSP; Thomas Fitzsimons to Benjamin Rush, July 21, 1790, Society Collection, HSP.

11. Rush to Fitzsimons, August 5, 1790, in *Letters of Benjamin Rush,* ed. Butterfield, I, 569; Benjamin Rush to James Madison, February 27, 1790; see also unknown to Madison, March 2, 1790; J. Dawson to Madison, March 14, 1790, Madison Papers, LC.

12. Benjamin Rush to James Madison, April 10, 1790, Madison Papers, LC; Rush to Elias Boudinot, April 18, 1790; Rush to Fitzsimons, August 5, 1790, in *Letters of Benjamin Rush,* ed. Butterfield, I, 563, 569; Daniel Heister to James Hutchinson, March 30, 1790, Hutchinson Papers, APS; Moses Brown to Samuel Coates, April 27, 1790, Coates-Reynell Papers, HSP.

13. *Pennsylvania Packet,* June 25, 1790; *General Advertiser,* January 15, 1791; Susan Dillnyn to William Dillnyn, January 28, 1790, Dillnyn Papers, LCP; James T. Callender, *A Short History of the Nature and Consequence of Excise Laws* (Philadelphia: 1795).

14. *Pennsylvania Packet,* June 25, 1790; *General Advertiser,* January 15, 1791; Thomas Hollingsworth to Levi Hollingsworth, January 19, 1791, Hollingsworth Correspondence, HSP; Scharf and Westcott, *History of Philadelphia,* I, 467; Petition from the merchants and traders to the Pennsylvania senate, April 11, 1791, against the excise tax, Manuscript Collection, LCP; *Independent Gazetteer,* July 23, 1791.

15. *Journal of the House of Representatives,* 2nd House, 110-111; *Dunlap's American Daily Advertiser,* February 2, 1791.

16. *Gazette of the United States,* February 2, 1791; *Journal of the Senate,* 1st Senate, 131. Thomas Fitzsimons supported the excise tax in Congress; in the years to come this proved a powerful weapon against him. See *Annals of Congress,* 1st Congress, 1st Session, 127, 135.

17. *Gazette of the United States,* April 2, 1791; Clement Biddle to Francis Rotch, March 25, 1791; and Biddle to William Campbell, June 19, 1791, Clement Biddle Letterbook, HSP; Jasper Yeates to Edward Burd, December 27, 1790, Shippen Family Papers, HSP; Tench Coxe to Thomas Fitzsimons, July, 1790; Coxe to Fisher Ames, June 7, 1790, Coxe Papers, HSP.

18. James Madison to Thomas Jefferson, July 13, 1791, Madison Papers, LC; George Washington to David Humphreays, July 20, 1791, in *Writings of George Washington,* ed. John Fitzpatrick, 39 vols. (Washington: 1931-1944), XXXI, 318.

19. Benjamin Rush to his wife, August 12, 1791, in *Letters of Benjamin Rush,* ed. Butterfield, I, 602-603; Thomas Smith to William Irvine, August 15, 1791, Irvine Papers, HSP; Tench Coxe to A. Lee, June 10, 1791, Coxe to Fisher Ames, June 7, 1791; Coxc to Joseph Bartlett, July 9, 1791; Coxe to John Pintard, July 15, 1791, Coxe Papers, HSP.

20. Benjamin Rush, *The Autobiography of Benjamin Rush: His "Travels Through Life" Together with his "Commonplace Book" for 1789-1813,* ed. George W. Conner (Princeton: 1948), 204; Jefferson to Edward Rutledge, August 29, 1791, in *The Writings of Thomas Jefferson* ed. Paul L. Ford, 10 vols. (New York: 1892-1899), V, 376.

21. *General Advertiser,* April 17, 1792; *National Gazette,* April 19, 1792; Corner, *Autobiography of Rush,* 217; Clement Biddle to William Campbell,

March 11, 1792, Clement Biddle Letterbook, HSP; Tench Coxe to James McClung, August 31, 1791, Coxe papers, HSP.

22. Fisher Ames to George Minor, May 3, 1792, in *Works of Fisher Ames With a Selection from His Speeches and Correspondence,* ed. Seth Ames, 2 vols. (Boston: 1854), I, 118-119; Tench Coxe to John Adams, June 10, 1792, vol. 375, Adams Papers, MHS.

23. Political tract in the Papers of William Irvine, HSP; *Journal of the House of Representatives,* 1st House, 151; *Journal of the Senate,* 1st Senate, 124.

24. James Hutchinson to Albert Gallatin, June 11, 1790, Gallatin Papers, NYHS; William Jackson to Washington, October 9, 1791, Washington Papers, vol. 101, LC; Clement Biddle to William Rogers, August 5, 1791, Clement Biddle Letterbook, HSP; Thomas Smith to William Irvine, August 15, 1791, Irvine Papers, HSP; Benjamin Rush to his wife, August 12, 1791, *Letters of Benjamin Rush,* ed. Butterfield, I, 602-603.

25. *Independent Gazetteer,* July 23, 1791; Nathaniel Irvine to George Logan, August 31, 1791, Logan Papers, HSP; *General Advertiser,* September 27, October 9, 10, 1791; William Jackson to Washington, October 9, 1791, Washington Papers, vol. 101, LC; Clement Biddle to William Campbell, November 17, 1791, Clement Biddle Letterbook, HSP; David Campbell to Jefferson, November 19, 1791, Jefferson Papers, LC.

26. *Journal of the House of Representatives,* 2nd House, 284, 300; *Journal of the Senate,* 2nd Senate, 237.

27. *National Gazette,* May 3, 1792; *General Advertiser,* May 4, 1792; Clement Biddle to George Lewis, April 15, 1792, Clement Biddle Letterbook, HSP; Joseph Gilpin to William Tilghman, May 3, 1792, Tilghman Papers, HSP; William Bingham to Wilcocks, April 19, 1792, Bingham Letterbook, HSP; John Adams to Henry Marchant, March 3, 1792, Adams Letterbook, Adams Papers, MHS.

28. Frederick Tolles, *George Logan* (New York: 1953), 122-123; *General Advertiser,* January 16, 20, 1792; *National Gazette* January 23, 1792; Thomas Hartley to Tench Coxe, June 24, 1792, Coxe Papers, HSP.

29. William Bingham to Nichols, June 20, 1792, and Bingham to unknown, July 22, 1792, William Bingham Letterbook, HSP; Tench Coxe to John Adams, June 10, 1792, Adams Papers, vol. 375, MHS; Henry Drinker to Lane Hopkins, July 26, 1792, Henry Drinker Letterbook, Henry Drinker Papers, HSP; Margaret Brown, "William Bingham, Eighteenth-Century Magnate," *PMHB* LXI (Oct., 1937), 392; Walters, "The Origins of the Jeffersonian Party In Pennsylvania," 444-446; Abigail Adams to Mary Cranch, March 29, 1792, in "New Letters of Abigail Adams," *Proceeding of the American Antiquarian Society,* V, 192-193.

30. Walters, "The Origins of the Jeffersonian Party in Pennsylvania," 444-446; Raymond Walters, *Alexander James Dallas: Lawyer-Politician-Financier, 1759-1817* (Philadelphia: 1943), ch. 4.

31. Tench Coxe to John Adams, July 28, 1792; Thomas Adams to John Adams, July 29, 1792; and same to same, August 16, 1792, Adams Papers, vol. 375, MHS; *General Advertiser,* July 27, 30, 31, August 1, 30, 1792; *Independent Gazetteer,* August 18, 1792; James Hutchinson to Albert Gallatin, August 19, 1792, Gallatin Papers, NYHS; *Federal Gazette,* August 1, 1792; John Beckley to James Madison, August 1, 1792, Madison Papers, LC. *Independent Gazetteer,* August 4, 18, 1792; circular letter of the Federalists issued August, 1792, Broadside Collection, HSP; Scharf and Westcott, *History of Philadelphia,* I, 468.

32. Edmund Randolph to Washington, August 5, 1792, Washington Papers, vol. 102, LC; Thomas Adams to John Adams, August 15, 1792, Adams

Papers, vol. 375, MHS; *Gazette of the United States,* August 4, 1792; Washington to Edmund Randolph, August 26, 1792, Gratz Collection, HSP.
33. John Beckley to James Madison, August 1, 1792, Madison Papers, LC; Noble Cunningham, "John Beckley: An Early American Party Manager," *William and Mary Quarterly,* Third Series XIII (Jan., 1956), 41-52; Philip March, "John Beckley, Mystery Man of the Early Jeffersonians," *PMHB,* LXXI (Jan., 1947), 54-69.
34. James Hutchinson to Albert Gallatin, August 19, 1792; William Findley to Gallatin, August 20, 1792, Gallatin Papers, NYHS; circular letter August 3, 1792, issued by the Correspondence Committee headed by Thomas McKean, Alexander Dallas, and James Hutchinson, Broadside Collection, HSP; Committee of Correspondence to Jeasper Yeates, August 3, 1792, Stauffer Collection, vol. XII, 806, HSP.
35. James Hutchinson to Albert Gallatin, September 14, 1792, Gallatin Papers, NYHS. The Hutchinson ticket included Charles Thomson and John Barclay of Philadelphia.
36. Alexander Dallas to Albert Gallatin, September 25, 1792, Gallatin Papers, NYHS; John Beckley to James Madison, September 10, 1792, Madison Papers, NYPL.
37. *National Gazette,* September 26, 1792; circular to the "Freemen of Pennsylvania" issued in 1792, Broadside Collection, HSP; *Independent Gazetteer,* August 4, 1792; *General Advertiser,* September 5, 6, 7, 1792.
38. *General Advertiser,* September 27, 1792; *Independent Gazetteer,* September 29, 1792.
39. Rufus King to Gouverneur Morris, September 1, 1792, King Papers, NYHS; *Gazette of the United States,* September 26, 1792; *General Advertiser,* September 25, 1792; *Independent Gazetteer,* September 29, 1792; Thomas Hartley to Tench Coxe, October 24, 1792, Coxe Papers, HSP; Tench Coxe to John Adams, September 25, 1792, Adams Papers, vol. 375, MHS. Federalists nominated two Philadelphians, Thomas Fitzsimons and William Bingham.
40. James Hutchinson to Albert Gallatin, September 25, 1792, Gallatin Papers, NYHS; broadside issued to the "Independent Electors of Pennsylvania," in 1792, Broadside Collection, HSP.
41. *Federal Gazette,* October 3, 1792; *Independent Gazetteer,* October 6, 1792; *General Advertiser,* October 8, 1792.
42. Broadside issued October 9, 1792, Broadside Collection, HSP; *General Advertiser,* October 3, 5, 8, 9, 1792; Baumann, "John Swanwick," 131-139, 148-149.
43. The seven candidates common to both slates were: Frederick Muhlenberg, Peter Muhlenberg, Thomas Hartley, John Kittera, William Findley, William Irvine, Daniel Heister. The six Federalists were: Thomas Fitzsimons, William Bingham, Samuel Sitgreaves, James Armstrong, Thomas Scott, and Henry Wynkoop. The Republicans were: John Barclay, Charles Thomson, John Smilie, Jonathan Sergeant, Andrew Gregg, and William Montgomery.
44. *General Advertiser,* October 11, 1792; *Independent Gazetteer,* October 13, 1792; Tinkcom, *Republicans and Federalists of Pennsylvania,* 65-66; Scharf and Westcott, *History of Philadelphia,* I, 469.
45. *General Advertiser,* October 11, 1792; *Independent Gazetteer,* October 13, 1792; John Beckley to Madison, October 17, 1792, Madison Papers, NYPL; James Hutchinson to Albert Gallatin, October 24, 1792, Gallatin Papers, NYHS.
46. Thomas Adams to John Adams, October 7, 1792; Tench Coxe to John Adams, October 28, 1792; Samuel Otis to John Adams, October 29, 1792, Adams Papers, vol. 375, MHS; William Bradford to Elias Boudinot,

October 13, 1792, Wallace Papers, HSP.

47. James Hutchinson to Albert Gallatin, October 24, 1792, Gallatin Papers, NYHS; John Beckley to James Madison, October 17, 1792, Madison Papers, NYPL.

48. *Dunlap's American Daily Advertiser,* August 27, 1792; *Independent Gazetter,* September 29, 1792; Alexander Hamilton to Rufus King, September 23, 1792, *King Correspondence,* I, 427–28; James Hutchinson to Albert Gallatin, October 24, 1792, Gallatin Papers, NYHS; John Beckley to James Madison, October 17, 1792, Madison Papers, NYPL; Walters, *Alexander J. Dallas,* 41.

49. Samuel Otis to John Adams, October 3, 1792; Tench Coxe to John Adams, November 8, 1792, Adams Papers, vol. 375, MHS; Alexander Hamilton to John Steele, October 15, 1792, in *Papers of Alexander Hamilton,* ed. Syrett, XII, 567-568; *Independent Gazetteer,* November 10, 1792; Scharf and Westcott, *History of Philadelphia,* I, 469.

50. *Independent Gazetteer,* November 10, 1792; Cunningham, *Jeffersonian Republicans,* 38, 44-45.

4: The Politics of Neutrality and Excise Taxes, 1793-1794

1. See especially Alexander DeConde, *Entangling Alliances: Politics and Diplomacy under George Washington* (Durham: 1958), chs. 3 & 4; Jerald Combs, *The Jay Treaty: Political Battleground of the Founding Fathers* (Berkeley: 1970), ch. 7; Richard Buel, Jr., *Securing the Revolution: Ideology in American Politics, 1790–1815* (Ithaca: 1972), chs. 3 & 4; Ralph L. Ketcham, "France and American Politics, 1763-1793," *Political Science Quarterly,* LXXVIII (June, 1963), 198-223; Albert H. Bowman, *The Struggle for Neutrality: Franco-American Diplomacy During the Federalist Era* (Knoxville: 1974), chs. 2 & 3.

2. *Federal Gazette,* October 26, 1790; *National Gazette,* July 18, 1792; *Dunlap's American Daily Advertiser,* January 3, 1793; Donald H. Stewart, *The Opposition Press of the Federalist Period* (Albany: 1969), ch. 4.

3. *Federal Gazette,* January 8, 1790; William Bingham to Lafayette, April 8, 1791; Society Collection, HSP; William Bingham to Unknown, October 22, 1791, William Bingham Letterbook, HSP; John Sitgreaves to Dommik Terry, April 23, 1791, John Sitgreaves Letterbook, Thomas Biddle Business Papers, HSP; Thomas Hartley to Tench Coxe, March 26, 1793, Coxe Papers, HSP; Samuel F. Bemis, *Jay's Treaty: A Study in Commerce and Diplomacy* (New Haven: 1962).

4. William Bingham to W. & J. Willink, April 1, 1793; and Bingham to John Wilcocks, April 11, 1793, Bingham Letterbook, HSP; Combs, *The Jay Treaty,* 107-108.

5. Memorial presented by the merchants of Philadelphia in support of neutrality, May, 1793, Washington Papers, LC; *Independent Gazetteer,* May 25, 1793; Thomas Hartley to Tench Coxe, July 9, 1793; and same to same, August 12, 1793, Coxe Papers, HSP (Federalists who signed the memorial included John Nixon, Thomas Willing, Miers Fisher, Joseph Ball, Frederick Kuhl, and Isaac Wharton; Republicans who signed were John Swanwick, Charles Pettit, Jacob Morgan, and Samuel Miles; Minutes of the City Council, June 3, 1793, HSP.

6. *General Advertiser,* April 25, 1793; Hamilton Notes, May 14, 1793, Hamilton Papers, LC.

7. Thomas Adams to Abigail Adams, May 5, 1793, Adams Papers, vol. 376, MHS; Jefferson to Thomas Mann Randolph, May 6, 1793, Jefferson Papers, LC; Jefferson to Monroe, May 5, 1793, in *Writings of Jefferson,*

ed. Ford, VI, 238; *Dunlap's American Daily Advertiser,* May 3, 1793.

8. *General Advertiser,* May 17, 1793; *Independent Gazetteer,* May 25, 1793; Jefferson to Madison, May 19, 1793, Madison Papers, LC; Scharf and Westcott, *History of Philadelphia,* I, 473; Harry Ammon, *The Genet Mission* (New York: 1973), 57-58.

9. Hamilton to Anon., May 18, 1793, Hamilton Papers, LC; see John Adams to Jefferson, June 30, 1813, in *The Works of John Adams* ed. Charles Francis Adams, 10 vols. (Boston: 1850-56), X, 47, for the fear many Federalists had of Genet and the support given the French cause in Philadelphia during the spring and summer of 1793.

10. William Bradford to Elias Boudinot, June 7, 1793; and same to same, July 14, 1793, Wallace Papers, HSP; Hamilton to Rufus King, August 13, 1793, in *Papers of Hamilton,* ed. Syrett, XV, 239-242; *Dunlap's American Daily Advertiser,* July 10, 1793; *Independent Gazetteer,* July 13, 1793; Scharf and Westcott, *History of Philadelphia,* I, 474; Ammon, *Tbe Genet Mission,* 86-89; Bowman, *Struggle for Neutrality,* 71-75.

11. *General Advertiser,* July 22, 1793; *Dunlap's American Daily Advertiser,* May 1, 1793, May 3, 1794; Francis Childs, *French Refugee Life in the United States, 1790-1800: An American Chapter of the French Revolution* (Baltimore: 1940); John Earl III, "Talleyrand in Philadelphia, 1794-1796," *PMHB,* XCI (July, 1967), 282-298.

12. *General Advertiser,* July 30, 31, August 3, 1793; Charles Page Smith, *James Wilson: Founding Father, 1742-1798* (Chapel Hill: 1956), 362-364; Francis Wharton, *State Trials of the United States* (Philadelphia: 1849), 51, 89; Charles M. Thomas, *American Neutrality in 1793: A Study in Cabinet Government* (New York: 1931), 171-174.

13. *Dunlap's American Daily Advertiser,* July 30, August 5, 1793; Jefferson to Madison: August 3, 1793, August 25, 1793; and September 1, 1793, in *Writings of Jefferson,* ed. Ford, VI, 361, 379-398, 401-402; DeConde, *Entangling Alliances,* 227-230.

14. Jefferson to Madison, May 12, 1793, Madison Papers, LC.

15. Jefferson to Madison, June 28, 1793, in *Writings of Jefferson,* ed. Ford, VI, 323, same to same, August 11, 1793; and same to same, September 1, 1793, Madison Papers, LC; Francis Johnstone to Anthony Wayne, July 24, 1793, Wayne Papers, HSP; *Federal Gazette,* July 31, August 8, 1793; Thomas Fisher to unknown, August, 1793, Logan-Fisher-Fox Collection, HSP.

16. Eugene Link, *Democratic Republican Societies, 1790–1800* (New York: 1942), 15, 71-72; Cunningham, *The Jeffersonian Republicans,* 65; *Independent Gazetteer,* July 13, 1793; Minutes of the Democratic Society of Pennsylvania, HSP. Prominent local Republicans in the membership included: David Rittenhouse, Charles Biddle, William Coates, James Hutchinson, Alexander Dallas, Michael Leib, Jonathan Sergeant, Israel Israel, Peter Duponceau, and David Jackson.

17. *General Advertiser,* April 15, 1793; Tinkcom, *Republicans and Federalists in Pennsylvania,* 82–83.

18. *Gazette of the United States,* July 17, 1793; *National Gazette,* July 20, 1793.

19. Powel, *Bring Out Your Dead;* Pernick, "Politics, Parties, and Pestilence," 559-587; Carey, *Short Account of Yellow Fever;* Tench Coxe to Pennsylvania's Congressmen, November 16, 1793, Coxe Papers, HSP.

20. Powel, *Bring Out Your Dead,* 255; Tinkcom, *Republicans and Federalists in Pennsylvania,* 137-138.

21. *Federal Gazette,* December 10, 1793.

22. John C. Miller, *Alexander Hamilton and the Growth of the New*

Nation (New York: 1959), 399-400; Callender, *A Short History of the Excise,* 11, 20, 56-69, 111-116; Tench Coxe, *A View of the United States of America . . .* (Philadelphia: 1794), chs. 11-16; Tench Coxe to John Pintard, August 2, 1794, Coxe Papers, HSP; Samuel Hodgdon to Hamilton, May 9, 1794, *The Papers of Alexander Hamilton,* ed. Syrett, XVI, 397–398.

23. *General Advertiser,* May 8, 18, 26, 1794; Callender, *A Short History of the Excise,* 75-86. The wealth of Leiper and Morgan clearly made them among the most affluent men in Philadelphia. In 1798 Leiper had assessed real property in the Philadelphia area worth $54,350; while Morgan's was $39,402 (United States Direct Tax of 1798, Tax List for Philadelphia).

24. Minutes of the Democratic Society of Pennsylvania, 75-76, HSP; *General Advertiser,* May 12, 1794; William Miller, "The Democratic Societies and the Whiskey Insurrection," *PMHB* LXII (July, 1938), 324–349; *Annals of Congress,* 3rd Congress, 1st Session, 620-661, 740-741.

25. Madison to Jefferson, March 9, 1794, Jefferson Papers, LC; Charles, *The Origins of the American Party System,* 99, 101-102.

26. John Clifford to Thomas Clifford, December 10, 1793, Clifford Correspondence, Pemberton Papers, HSP; Clement Biddle to Armstrong & Barnwell, December 19, 1793; and Biddle to Essingham Lawrence, February 16, 1794, Clement Biddle Letterbook, Thomas Biddle Business Papers, HSP; Thomas Adams to John Adams, March 23, 1793, Adams Papers, vol. 376, MHS.

27. *Dunlap's American Daily Advertiser,* August 27, 30, September 7, 1793; *General Advertiser,* January 17, 18, February 8, May 28, 1794; Bemis, *Jay Treaty,* 158-159; John B. McMaster, *The Life and Times of Stephen Girard: Mariner and Merchant* 2 vols. (Philadelphia: 1918), I, 272.

28. Robert Henderson to Patrick Hart, March 10, 1794, Robert Henderson Letterbook, HSP; *Independent Gazetteer,* March 12, 1794; *General Advertiser,* March 10, 11, 13, 1794; Madison to Jefferson, March 2, 9, 10, 12, 14, 1794, Madison Papers, LC.

29. *Independent Gazetteer,* March 22, 1794; *General Advertiser,* March 18, 21, 1794; Albert Gares, "Stephen Girard's West Indian Trade," *PMHB,* LXXII (October, 1948), 311-343; Scharf and Westcott, *History of Philadelphia,* I, 476-477. During the 1790s Philadelphia merchants were expanding their trade with countries other than Great Britain. In the period 1792 to 1794, 47 ships were cleared for French ports, as opposed to 126 for the British Isles; this represents a sharp turn around since the Revolution (Baumann, "Democratic-Republicans of Philadelphia," 411).

30. Clement Biddle to Armstrong & Barnwell, March 20, 1794; Biddle to William Campbell, March 28, 1794; and Biddle to Armstrong & Barnwell, March 31, 1794, Clement Biddle Letterbook, Thomas Biddle Business Papers, HSP; *General Advertiser,* May 23, 26, June 6, 1794; Tench Coxe to J. London, May 25, 1794, Coxe Papers, HSP; Benjamin Barton to Thomas Pennant, March 26, 1794, Barton Papers, HSP; William Irvine to his son, March 24, 1794, Irvine Papers, HSP.

31. Clement Biddle to William Campbell, April 11, 1794; and same to same, April 16, 1794, Clement Biddle Letterbook, Thomas Biddle Business Papers, HSP; John Adams to Abigail Adams, April 1, 1794, Adams Papers, vol. 377, MHS.

32. *Independent Gazetteer,* May 7, 1794; John B. McMaster, *A History of the People of the United States,* 8 vols. (New York, 1883-1913), II, 109; Earl, "Talleyrand in Philadelphia," 283-84; *Dunlap's American Daily Advertiser,* July 7, 1794; *General Advertiser,* July 8, 9, 10, 30, 1794.

33. James Monroe to unknown, April 11, 1794, Gratz Collection, HSP;

Clement Biddle to Randolph Latimer, May 14, 1794, Clement Biddle Letterbook, Thomas Biddle Business Papers, HSP; Scharf and Westcott, *History of Philadelphia,* I, 478; Henry Drinker to Samuel Preston, June 4, 1794, Henry Drinker Letterbook, Drinker Papers, HSP; Combs, *The Jay Treaty,* 125-128; DeConde, *Entangling Alliances,* ch. 4.

34. Henry Drinker to Enoch Edwards, July 17, 1794; and Drinker to Samuel Preston, July 22, 1794, Henry Drinker Letterbook, Drinker Papers, HSP; Clement Biddle to Armstrong & Barnwell, August 25, 1794, Clement Biddle Letterbook, Thomas Biddle Business Papers, HSP.

35. Tinkcom, *Republicans and Federalists in Pennsylvania,* 95-97; *Independent Gazetteer,* August 9, 1794; *Gazette of the United States,* September 1, 1794.

36. *Pennsylvania Archives,* 9th series, II, 851–852; *Dunlap's American Daily Advertiser,* September 19, 1794; Hamilton to Rufus King, September 17, 1794, in *The Life and Correspondence of Rufus King,* ed. Charles King, 6 vols. (New York: 1895), I, 573-574; Richard H. Kohn, "The Washington Administration's Decision to Crush the Whiskey Rebellion," *The Journal of American History,* LIX (December, 1972), 578-584; Rufus King to Hamilton, September 17, 1794, in *Papers of Alexander Hamilton,* ed. Harold C. Syrett, XVIII, 241; Leland D. Baldwin, *Whiskey Rebels: The Story of a Frontier Uprising* (Pittsburgh: 1939); Jacob E. Cooke, "The Whiskey Insurrection: A Re-evaluation," *Pennsylvania History,* XXX. (July, 1963), 316-346.

37. *Journal of the House of Representatives,* 4th House, 225-227; *Diary of Jacob Hiltzheimer,* 201; Thomas Hartley to Tench Coxe, October 22, 1793, Coxe Papers, HSP.

38. *Philadelphia Gazette,* January 13, 1794; *Gazette of the United States,* October 11, 1794.

39. *Philadelphia Gazette,* October 14, 1794. See also *Papers of Alexander Hamilton,* XVI, n. 235, for Fitzsimons' position on his shipping.

40. *General Advertiser,* September 19, 27, October 10, 11, 14, 1794; *Philadelphia Gazette,* October 13, 1794.

41. *Gazette of the United States,* September 27, October 9, 11, 14, 1794.

42. Washington to Henry Lee, August 26, 1794, in *The Writings of George Washington,* ed. John C. Fitzpatrick, 39 vols. (Washington D.C.: 1931-1944), XXXIII, 475-476.

43. Kearny Wharton to Levi Hollingsworth, October 12, 1794, Hollingsworth Correspondence, HSP.

44. *Philadelphia Gazette,* October 13, 14, 1794; *Gazette of the United States,* October 14, 1794.

45. Clark to William Jones, October 14, 1794, Uselma Clark Smith Collection, HSP; *Dunlap's American Daily Advertiser,* November 12, 1794.

46. Edmund Randolph to Washington, October 15, 1794; same to same, October 16, 1794, and William Bradford to Washington, October 17, 1794, Washington Papers, vol. 106, LC; Alfred Hicks to Samuel Coates, October 24, 1794, Coates-Reynell Papers, HSP; Tench Coxe to Francis Conbain, November 8, 1794, Coxe Papers, HSP; *Dunlap's American Daily Advertiser,* November 12, 1794; *General Advertiser,* November 1, 1794; Daniel Katz and Samuel J. Eldersveld, "The Impact of Local Party Activity Upon the Electorate," *The Public Opinion Quarterly,* XXV (Spring, 1961), 1-24.

47. Pearson for the product-moment correlation is one of the most useful of the correlation coefficients and is the best suited for the type of data used in this study where all variables are interval in nature. It varies between -1 (perfect negative correlation) and +1 (perfect positive correlation). Coefficients which are near 0 the variables might possibly be strongly

related but are not associated in a linear form, e.g., Federalist voting and misc. trades +.01. See Charles M. Dollar and Richard T. Jensen, *Historian's Guide to Statistics: Quantitative Analysis and Historical Research* (New York: 1971), 61-87. For the problems which inhere in correlations of this type, see W.S. Robinson, "Ecological Correlations and the Behavior of Individuals," *American Sociological Review,* 15 (Feb., 1950), 351–357.

48. Mary Meredith to David Meredith. December 6, 1794; Robert Andrews to David Meredith, December 6, 1794; and William Meredith to David Meredith. December 7, 1794, Meredith Papers, HSP; William Bradford to Elias Boudinot, October 17, 1794, Wallace Papers, HSP; *Gazette of the United States.* November 8, 1794.

49. Madison to James Monroe, December 4, 1794; and Madison to Jefferson, November 16, 1794, Madison Papers, LC.

50. *General Advertiser,* October 16, 1794.

51. *Ibid.,* November 8, December 23, 1794.

5: "This Damn Treaty"

1. William Meredith to David Meredith, March 13, 1795, Meredith Papers, HSP; Fisher Ames to Thomas Dwight, February 3, 1795, in *The Works of Fisher Ames,* ed. Seth Ames, 2 vols. (Boston: 1845) I, 166; William Atlee to Anthony Wayne, December 5, 1794, Wayne Papers, HSP; William Bradford to Samuel Bayard, March 30, 1795, Gratz Collection, HSP.

2. William Bradford to unknown, June 4, 1795, Gratz Collection, HSP; Clement Biddle to William Morbary, June 24, 1795, Clement Biddle Letterbook, Thomas Biddle Business Papers, HSP; Robert Henderson to Patrick Hart, June 24, 1795, Robert Henderson Letterbook, HSP.

3. *Aurora,* June 26, July 1, 1795; Alexander Dallas to Jonathan Dayton, April 13, 1795, Gratz Collection, HSP; Alexander Dallas to William Irvine, June 13, 1795, Irvine Papers, HSP; Alexander J. Dallas, *Features of Mr. Jay's Treaty* (Philadelphia: 1795); DeConde, *Entangling Alliances,* 116-140; Bowman, *Struggle for Neutrality,* 219-227.

4. *Aurora,* July 3, 7, 9, 10, 13, 16, 1795; *Independent Gazetteer,* July 4, 8, 23, 1795; *Gazette of the United States,* July 7, 17, 1795; William Bradford to Hamilton, July 2, 1795, in *Papers of Alexander Hamilton,* ed. Syrett, XVIII, 393–397. The Republicans that organized the Jay Treaty protest included: Thomas McKean, Alexander Dallas, John Swanwick, Stephen Girard, Blair McClenachan, Moses Levy, Charles Pettit, Thomas Lee Shippen.

5. *Independent Gazetteer,* July 23, 1795; John Beckley to DeWitt Clinton, July 24, 1795, DeWitt Clinton Papers, CUL; Swanwick to Madison, July 26, 1795, Madison Papers, LC; T.L. Shippen to Swanwick, July 1795, Shippen Family Papers, LC; Tench Coxe to Jefferson, July 20, 1795, Coxe Papers, HSP; Scharf and Westcott, *History of Philadelphia,* I, 481.

6. *Aurora,* July 25, 27, 1795; *Gazette of the United States,* July 26, 1795; Tench Coxe to William Murray, July 1, 1795, Coxe Papers, HSP; *Independent Gazetteer,* July 29, 1795; *Gazette of the United States,* July 27, 1795; Scharf and Westcott, *History of Philadelphia,* I, 481.

7. Petition from the general meeting of the citizens of Philadelphia, July 25, 1795, Washington Papers, vol. 107, LC; Stephen Girard to Paul Post, July 10, 1795; Girard to John Berenberg, Gossler, & Co., August 8, 1795; and same to same, August 8, 1795, Girard Letterbook No. 5, Girard Papers, Girard College; Matthew Carey to B. Gomez, July 29, 1795, Lea and Febiger Letterbook, HSP; George M. Dallas, ed., *The Life and Writings of Alexander J. Dallas* (Philadelphia: 1871), 160; Presley Nevill to William Irvine, August 22, 1795, Irvine Papers, HSP.

8. *Dunlap's American Daily Advertiser,* June 27, 1795; *Gazette of the United States,* July 8, 1795; William Bingham to Henry Knox, June 27, 1795, Henry Knox Papers, MHS; Oliver Wolcott, Jr., to Hamilton, September 26, 1795, in *Papers of Hamilton,* ed. Syrett, XIX, 294-295.
9. *Philadelphia Gazette,* August 22, 1795; Fitzsimons to Hamilton, July 14, 1795, in *Papers of Hamilton,* ed. Syrett, XVIII, 464-466; Wolcott to Hamilton, July 30, 1795, in *Memoirs of the Administration of Washington and John Adams,* 2 vols. (New York: 1846), ed, Gibbs, I, 219. The local Federalist merchant committee included: Thomas Willing, Matthew Clarkson, Thomas Fitzsimons, Robert Morris, Levi Hollingsworth, George Latimer, Israel Whelen, Robert Waln, and Francis Gurney.
10. *Aurora,* August 15, 1795; Jefferson to Madison, September 21, 1795, Madison Papers, LC.
11. Elizabeth Meredith to David Meredith, July 12, 1795, Meredith Papers, HSP; Samuel Hodgdon to Henry Knox, July 7, 1795, Henry Knox Papers, MHS; Edward Shippen to William Arnold, July 14, 1795, Edward Shippen Letterbook, Burd-Shippen-Hubley Papers, HSP; *Gazette of the United States,* July 24, 1795.
12. Oliver Wolcott to Washington, July 26, 1795; and Wolcott to his wife, July 26, 1795, in *Memoirs of Wolcott,* ed. Gibbs, I, 218; Timothy Pickering to Washington, July 27, 1795; and Pickering to Timothy Williams, July 17, 1795, in Charles Upham, *The Life of Timothy Pickering,* 4 vols. (Boston: 1867-1873), III, 181, 182-183; Edmund Randolph to Washington, July 27, 1795, Washington Papers, vol. 107, LC; Wolcott to Hamilton, July 30, 1795, in *Papers of Hamilton,* ed. Syrett, XVIII, 526-532.
13. Washington to Alexander Hamilton, July 29, 1795, Hamilton Papers, LC; Washington to Edmund Randolph, July 29, 1795, Gratz Collection, HSP; *Gazette of the United States,* September 12, 1795; Timothy Pickering to Stephen Higginson, August 8, 1795, in Upham, *Life of Timothy Pickering,* III, 187-188.
14. Clement Biddle to Adam Gilchrist, August 23, 1795, Clement Biddle Letterbook, Thomas Biddle Business Papers, HSP; William Bingham to Henry Knox, September 5, 1795, Knox Papers, MHS.
15. John Beckley to DeWitt Clinton, September 13, 1795, DeWitt Clinton Papers, CUL; Clement Biddle to Adam Gilchrist, August 23, 1795, Clement Biddle Letterbook, Thomas Biddle Business Papers, HSP; Thomas Hartley to Anthony Wayne, February 6, 1795, Wayne Papers, HSP; Alexander McGregor to Samuel Coates, September 23, 1795, Coates-Reynell Papers, HSP. See Beckley to Madison, September 10, 1795, Madison Papers, NYPL, where Beckley accuses Dallas of being a trimmer and a man who could not be trusted. But Dallas believed that since Washington had signed the treaty, it should not become a political issue. Consequently, Dallas remained inactive in the elections of 1795 and 1796.
16. *Aurora,* October 3, 6, 8, 13, 19, 1795. See John Swanwick, *A Rub from Snub: or a Cursory Analytical Epistle* (Philadelphia: 1795).
17. *Aurora,* October 6, 8, 1795; Moses Brown to Samuel Coates, September 25, 1795, Coates-Reynell Papers, HSP; *Independent Gazetteer,* October 10, 1795.
18. The Pennsylvania Legislature elected Bingham on February 25, 1795 to rcplace Robert Morris, who retired. In a special election to fill Bingham's state senate seat, Federalist Israel Whelen, a wealthy Quaker merchant, won easily over three Republican candidates. Madison to Jefferson, January 11, 1795, Madison Papers, LC; *Journal of the House of Representatives,* 5th House, 205; William Bradford to Samuel Bayard, March 30, 1795, Gratz Collection, HSP; William Meredith to David Meredith, March 13,

1795, Meredith Papers, HSP; *Aurora,* March 16, 17, 19, 1795; *Dunlap's American Daily Advertiser,* March 14, 16, 19, 1795.

19. *Aurora,* October 3, 8, 1795; *Independent Gazetteer,* October 10, 1795; *The Philadelphia Jockey Club or Mercantile Influence Weighted* (Philadelphia: 1795).

20. *Independent Gazetteer,* October 10, 1795; *Gazette of the United States,* October 6, 1795; Lemuel Hopkins, *The Democratial, A Poem in Retaliation, For the "Philadelphia Jockey Club" By a Gentleman of Connecticut* (Philadelphia: 1796).

21. Henry Drinker to John Canan, October 15, 1795, Henry Drinker Letterbook, Drinker Papers, HSP; Jeremiah Brown to Levi Hollingsworth, October 12, 1795, Hollingsworth Correspondence, HSP; Samuel Coates to Moses Brown, October 12, 1795, Samuel Coates Letterbook, HSP; William Cobbett, *A bone to Gnaw for the Democrats: or Observations on a Pamphlet entitled "The Political Progress of Britain"* (Philadelphia: 1795).

22. *Aurora,* October 13, 14, 1795; Elizabeth Drinker Diary, October 12, 1795, HSP; *Independent Gazetteer,* October 17, 1795; Angus Campbell, "Surge and Decline: A Study of Election Change," *Public Opinion Quarterly,* XIV (Fall, 1960), 397-418.

23. *Gazette of the United States,* October 14, 1795; Elizabeth Drinker Diary, October 13, 1795, HSP; Robert Henderson to Alex Glen, October 30, 1795, Robert Henderson Letterbook, HSP; Levi Hollingsworth to Philip Samson, November 7, 1795, Hollingsworth Letterbook, Hollingsworth Correspondence, HSP; John Mifflin to Ann Penn, November 11, 1795, John Mifflin Letterbook, Penn Papers, HSP; Elizabeth Meredith to David Meredith, November 8, 1795, Meredith Papers, HSP.

24. *Aurora,* October 15, 16, 1795. See also James Madison to James Monroe, December 20, 1795, Madison Papers, LC.

25. Robert Andrews to David Meredith, December 14, 1795; same to same, December 19, 1795, Meredith Papers, HSP; Benjamin Rush to Jefferson, March 1, 1795, Jefferson Papers, LC; Sim Sansculotte (John Swanwick), *A Roaster or a Check to the Progress of Political Blasphemy: Intended as a Brief Reply to Peter Porcupine and Billy Cobler* (Philadelphia: 1796); *Aurora:* March 28, April 7, 20, 21, 23, 30, 1796; Rush to Griffith Evans, March 4, 1796, Society Miscellaneous Collection, HSP.

26. S. Rochefontaine to Timothy Pickering, December 6, 1795, Pickering Papers, vol. 20, MHS; *Gazette of the United States,* February 26, March 29, April 16, 18, 19, 20, 1796; *Independent Gazetteer,* April 20, 1796; *Aurora,* April 20, 21, 22, 1796; Thomas Hollingsworth to Levi Hollingsworth, April 18, 1796, and Levi Hollingsworth to Abraham Pierce, April 27, 1796, Hollingsworth Correspondence, HSP; Hamilton to Rufus King, April 15, 1796; King to Hamilton, April 17, 1796; same to same April 20, 1794, in *Papers of Alexander Hamilton,* ed. Syrett, XX, 112-125.

27. *Annals of Congress,* 4th Congress, 1st Session, 1140-1190; Levi Hollingsworth to Robert McCulloch, May 18, 1796; Levi Hollingsworth to Robert Barr, May 18, 1796; Levi Hollingsworth to unknown, April 21, 1796; Herman Stump to Levi Hollingsworth, May 19, 1796; and Levi Hollingsworth to Philip Samson, May 30, 1796, Hollingsworth Letterbook, Hollingsworth Correspondence, HSP; Elizabeth Meredith to David Meredith, May 17, 1796, Meredith Papers, HSP; *Gazette of the United States,* April 26, 1796; *Aurora,* April 16, 19, 21, 1796; Andrew Elliott to William Irvine, April 23, 1796, Irvine Papers, HSP; Samuel Coates to Moses Brown, May 5, 1796, Coates Letterbook, HSP.

28. Madison to Jefferson, May 1, 1796, Jefferson Papers, LC; Madison to James Monroe, May 14, 1796, Madison Papers, LC; Hawthorn and Kerr to

George Ellis, May 18, 1796, Hawthorn & Kerr Letterbook, Meredith Papers, HSP; *Aurora*, April 21, 23, 1796.
29. *Journal of the House of Representatives*, 6th House, 429, 433-434; John Adams to Abigail Adams, February 10, 1796, Adams Papers, vol. 381, MHS; Elizabeth Meredith to David Meredith, March 10, 1796, Meredith Papers, HSP; *Gazette of the United States*, February 26, March 29, 1796.
30. Washington to Jefferson, July 6, 1796, Jefferson Papers, LC; Elizabeth Meredith to David Meredith, March 10, 1796, Meredith Papers, HSP; *Aurora*, June 8, 1796; Tench Coxe to N. Gilman, July 23, 1796, Coxe Papers, HSP.
31. *Independent Gazetteer*, August 31, 1796; William Meredith to David Meredith, September 24, 1796, Meredith Papers, HSP; Wolcott to Washington, July 6, 1796, in *Memoirs of Oliver Wolcott*, ed. Gibbs, I, 366; Washington to Wolcott, July 6, 1796, in *Writings of Washington*, ed. Fitzpatrick, XXXV, 126, *Gazette of the United States*, October 5, 6, 1796. Tilghman owned assessed real property in Philadelphia valued at $5,500.
32. *Aurora*, September 8, 17, October 11, 1796; John Beckley to William Irvine, September 30, 1796, Irvine Papers, HSP.
33. *Journal of the House of Representatives*, 6th House, 1st Session, 178-179, 355; *Pennsylvania Statutes at Large*, XV, 462-464.
34. Minutes of the City Council, April 24, 28, May 4, 22, June 8, August 6, 1795, PCA; *Aurora*, May 7, 1795; *Philadelphia Gazette*, May 30, 1795; Susan Dillnyn to William Dillnyn, July 2, 1791, Dillnyn Papers, LCP.
35. *Aurora*, September 29, 1796. For the select council Republicans named Stephen Girard, John Dunlap, William Van Phil, Matthew Carey, Conrad Hanse, David Jackson, Issac Pennington, Abraham Shoemaker, Joseph Erwin, James Sarawood, Thomas Leiper, and William Adcock.
36. *Aurora*, October 4, 1796; *Gazette of the United States*, October 5, 6, 1796.
37. *Aurora*, September 17, 23, 29, October 6, 1796; John Beckley to William Irvine, September 30, 1796, Irvine Papers, HSP.
38. *Aurora*, October 6, 10, 11, 1796.
39. *Aurora*, October 13, 1796; Scharf and Westcott, *History of Philadelphia*, I, 485; Carter, "Naturalization in Philadelphia," 331-346; *Annals of Congress*, 4th Congress, 1st Session, 1227, 1297, 1359-1360, 1406-1415.
40. *Aurora*, October 13, 1796.
41. *Aurora*, October 13, 14, 1796; Minutes of the City Council, October 14, 1796, PCA.
42. *Aurora*, October 13, 1796; Elizabeth Meredith to David Meredith, April 14, 1796, Meredith Papers, HSP.
43. *Aurora*, October 19, 1796; John Beckley to William Irvine, October 17, 1796, Irvine Papers, HSP.
44. Circular letter concerning the Federalist ticket in the Hollingsworth Correspondence, HSP; Andrew Gregg to William Irvine, May 24, 1796, Irvine Papers, HSP.
45. Washington to Hamilton, June 26, 1796, Hamilton Papers, LC; John Beckley to William Irvine, September 15, 1796, Irvine Papers, HSP; James McHenry to Washington, September 25, 1796, Washington Papers, vol. 109, LC; William Harthorn to Samuel Coates, September 28, 1796, Coates-Reynell Papers, HSP; Thomas Hollingsworth to Levi Hollingsworth, October 20, 1796, Hollingsworth Correspondence, HSP.
46. John Beckley to William Irvine, September 15, 1796; and same to same, September 22, 1796, William Irvine Papers, HSP.
47. John Beckley to William Irvine, September 22, 1796, Irvine Papers,

HSP; broadside issued October 3, 1796, from "Republican." Circular letter from Michael Leib with the Republican ticket, September 25, 1796, Broadside Collection, HSP; *Claypoole's American Daily Advertiser,* November 1, 1796.
48. *Aurora,* October 26, 1796; *Claypoole's American Daily Advertiser,* October 31, 1796; *Philadelphia Gazette,* October 31, November 1, 1796; Levi Hollingsworth to Philip Swanson, October 29, 1796, Hollingsworth Letterbook, Hollingsworth Correspondence, HSP; *Gazette of the United States,* November 3, 4, 1796.
49. *Aurora,* November 2, 1796; John Beckley to William Irvine, November 2, 1796, Irvine Papers, HSP; Stephen Kurtz, *The Presidency of John Adams: The Collapse of Federalism, 1795-1800* (Philadelphia: 1957), 106-113; Samuel Emlen to William Dillnyn, November 9, 1796, Dillnyn Papers, LCP; Samuel Coates to Alexander McGregor, November 10, 1796, Samuel Coates Letterbook, HSP.
50. *Aurora,* November 7, 1796.
51. *Aurora,* November 7, 1796. Forty-one percent of Philadelphia's eligible voters cast ballots in this election, down slightly from the congressional race one month before.
52. William Smith to Ralph Izard, November 8, 1796, "South Carolina Federalists' Correspondence," *American Historical Review,* XIV (July, 1909), 784-785; William Bingham to Rufus King, November 29, 1796, *King Correspondence,* II, 112–113; John Adams to John Q. Adams, December 5, 1796, Adams Papers, vol. 382, MHS.
53. *Gazette of the United States,* November 5, 1796.

6: A Question of Survival

1. Bowman, *The Struggle for Neutrality,* 275-278; Kurtz, *The Presidency of John Adams,* 285-286; Marvin R. Zahniser, *Charles Cotesworth Pinckney: Founding Father* (Chapel Hill: 1967), 136-164.
2. William Smith to Rufus King, April 3, 1797, King Papers, NYHS; Miller, *The Federalist Era,* 207-208; Jeremiah Yellott to Levi Hollingsworth, May 20, 1797, Hollingsworth Correspondence, HSP; Richard Hofstadter, *The Idea of a Party System: The Rise of Legitimate Opposition in the United States, 1780-1840* (Berkeley: 1969), 102-111.
3. *Aurora,* May 27, 1797; Thomas McKean to John Dickinson, June 6, 1797, R.R. Logan Collection, HSP; Tench Coxe to unknown, April 5, 1797, Coxe Papers, HSP; Stewart, *The Opposition Press of the Federalist Period,* 297-305.
4. Benjamin Rush to John Montgomery, June 16, 1797, Rush Papers, LCP; Tench Coxe to William Erwin, May 16, 1797, Coxe Papers, HSP; *Aurora,* June 29, 1797.
5. Eben Wheelwright to Samuel Coates, February 8, 1797, Coates-Reynell Papers, HSP; Elizabeth Meredith to David Meredith, April 23, 1797, Meredith Papers, HSP; William Bingham to Henry Knox, May 22, 1797, Knox Papers, vol. 40, MHS; same to same, December 11, 1797, Knox Papers, vol. 41, MHS; Bingham to Rufus King, July 10, 1797, *King Correspondence,* II, 199; Hawthorn and Kerr to Samuel Rainey, December 12, 1796, Hawthorn and Kerr Letterbook, Meredith Papers, HSP.
6. William Meredith to David Meredith, August 4, 1797, Meredith Papers, HSP; Hawthorn and Kerr to Samuel Rainey, December 12, 1797, Hawthorne and Kerr Letterbook, Meredith Papers, HSP; for details of the losses to Philadelphia's commerce and its political effects see Robert Henderson to William Galt, April 12, 1797, Robert Henderson Letterbook, HSP;

Samuel Coates to Samuel Coffin, May 5, 1797, Samuel Coates Letterbook, HSP; Albert Stuart to Levi Hollingsworth, April 2, 1797, Hollingsworth Correspondence, HSP; Stephen Girard to John Bernberg, November 17, 1796, Girard Letterbook No. 6, Girard Papers, Girard College.

7. Samuel Coates, Jr., to Samuel Coates, February 4, 1797, Coates-Reynell Papers, HSP; John Adams to Elbridge Gerry, May 3, 1797; and same to same, May 30, 1797, Adams Letterbook, Adams Papers, MHS.

8. William Smith to Ralph Izard, May 23, 1797, "South Carolina Federalist Letters," 788; William Spencer to Levi Hollingsworth, February 24, 1797, Hollingsworth Correspondence, HSP.

9. Zachey Poulson, Jr., to Samuel Coates, September 25, 1797; William Rawle, *et al.*, to Samuel Coates, *et al.*, October 7, 1797, Coates-Reynell Papers, HSP; Henry Drinker to Elizabeth Drinker, July 2, 1797, Drinker-Sandwith Collection, HSP.

10. *Gazette of the United States*, October 2, 1797.

11. Benjamin Bache to James Monroe, September 7, 1797, Monroe Papers, LC; *Aurora*, October 6, 7, 10, 1797; *Claypoole's American Daily Advertiser*, August 30, September 5, October 4, 10, 1797; Alexander, "Poverty, Fear, and Community," 22-23; Carter, "Naturalization in Philadelphia," 331-346.

12. *Aurora*, October 9, 10, 1797; *Gazette of the United States*, October 9, 1797.

13. *Aurora*, October 12, 1797; Minutes of the Select Council, October 13, 1797, PCA.

14. *Aurora*, October 12, 1797.

15. *Ibid.*, October 16, 1797.

16. *Porcupine's Gazette*, October 16, 1797; John Coates to Samuel Coates, October 14, 1797, Coates-Reynell Papers, HSP.

17. *Journal of the Senate*, 8th Senate, 1st Session, 22; *Philadelphia Gazette*, January 23, 1798; *Aurora*, January 31, February 3, 1798; *Porcupine's Gazette*, February 2, 1798.

18. *Journal of the Senate*, 8th Senate, 1st Session, p. 111.

19. Broadside issued February 12, 13, 1798, Broadside Collection, HSP; *Porcupine's Gazette*, February 19, 1798.

20. *Porcupine's Gazette*, February 20, 1798; broadside issued February 21, 1798, Broadside Collection, HSP; William Cobbett, *The Detection of Bache; or French Diplomatic Skill Developed* . . . (Philadelphia: 1798); *Gazette of the United States*, February 16, 17, 21, 1798; *Pennsylvania Gazette*, February 21, 1798.

21. *Aurora*, February 12, 16, 17, 18, 19, 1798; *Porcupine's Gazette*, February 20, 1798; *Gazette of the United States*, February 16, 1798; *Federal Gazette*, February 13, 17, 1798; *Claypoole's American Daily Advertiser*, February 19, 20, 21, 1798.

22. Diary of Elizabeth Drinker, February 22, 1798, HSP; *Gazette of the United States*, February 19, 20, 1798.

23. *Aurora*, February 24, 1798; *Porcupine's Gazette*, February 24, 1798; Diary of Elizabeth Drinker, February 24, 1798, HSP; Israel received 69 percent of the vote in Eastern Northern Liberties, 76 percent in Western Northern Liberties, and 74 percent in Southwark.

24. *Aurora*, February 24, 1798; *Porcupine's Gazette*, February 24, 1798.

25. *Porcupine's Gazette*, February 24, 1798; *Gazette of the United States*, February 24, 1798; Thomas Hollingsworth to Levi Hollingsworth, March 1, 1798, and Jeremiah Yellott to Levi Hollingsworth, March 17, 1798, Hollingsworth Correspondence, HSP; William Hemsely to William

Tilghman, March 5, 1798, Tilghman Papers, HSP; W. Harthorn to Samuel Coates, March 14, 1798, Coates-Reynell Papers, HSP.

26. *Aurora*, February 22, 26, 1798.

27. Stephen Girard to William Douglas, January 17, 1798; same to same, January 22, 1798; and Girard to John Berenberg, January 16, 1798, Girard Papers, Girard College; Albert Gallatin to his wife, January 16, 1798, Gallatin Papers, NYSH; *Papers of Thomas Jefferson*, ed. Boyd XVIII, 261, XIX, 122-126; Tench Coxe to J. Taylor, January 10, 1798, Coxe Papers, HSP.

28. Andrew Gregg to William Irvine, March 22, 1798, Irvine Papers, HSP; Alexander DeConde, *The Quasi-War: The Politics and Diplomacy of the Undeclared War with France, 1797-1801* (New York: 1966), 66-108.

29. James Douglas to Levi Hollingsworth, March 14, 1798, Hollingsworth Correspondence, HSP; *Gazette of the United States*, April 13, 14, 1798; Jefferson to Madison, April 12, 1798; Madison Papers, LC; Minutes of the Select Council of Philadelphia, April 19, 1797, PCA; Scharf and Westcott, *History of Philadelphia*, I, 492.

30. *Aurora*, March 20, April 16, May 12, June 4, 1798; James Douglas to Levi Hollingsworth, April 17, 1798, Hollingsworth Correspondence, HSP; Stephen Girard to Sebastion Lesa, April 17, 1798, Girard Letterbook No. 7, Girard Papers, Girard College.

31. Petition from the Quakers of Philadelphia to Congress, March 23, 1798, Logan Papers, HSP; *Porcupine's Gazette*, March 26, 27, 28, 1798.

32. *Claypoole's American Daily Advertiser*, May 1, 1798; Scharf and Westcott, *History of Philadelphia*, I, 493; Diary of Elizabeth Drinker, May 7, 1798, HSP; Abigail Adams to John Q. Adams, May 1, 1798, Adams Papers, vol. 388, MHS.

33. Abigail Adams to John Q. Adams, May 1, 1798, Adams Papers, vol. 388, MHS; Robert Waln to Bainbridge Ambey, April 26, 1798, Waln Letterbook; see also Robert Waln to Thomas Bulkley, April 25, 1798, Waln Letterbook; and Robert Waln to Rathbone Hughes, April 26, 1798, Waln Letterbook, Waln Family Papers, LCP; William Bingham to Rufus King, April 2, 1798, *King Correspondence*, II, 298-300.

34. *Aurora*, May 9, 10, 12, 1798; William MacPherson to Alexander Dallas, May 5, 1798, W.H. Hornor Collection, HSP; Jefferson to Thomas Mann Randolph, May 9, 1798, Jefferson Papers, LC.

35. *Porcupine's Gazette*, May 7, 1798, *Gazette of the United States*, May 10, 1798; William Bingham to Rufus King, June 5, 1798, *King Correspondence*, II, 331-332; Thomas Hollingsworth to Levi Hollingsworth, May 22, 1798, Hollingsworth Correspondence, HSP.

36. Thomas Hollingsworth to Levi Hollingsworth, June 9, 1798; and same to same, June 15, 1798, Hollingsworth Correspondence, HSP; *Gazette of the United States*, June 14, 1798; *Claypoole's American Daily Advertiser*, June 15, 1798; Robert Waln to John Buckley, June 16, 1798, Waln Letterbook, Waln Family Papers, LCP.

37. James M. Smith, *Freedom's Fetters: The Alien and Sedition Laws and American Civil Liberties* (Ithaca: 1956), 38-39, 145-146, 150-151; Carter, "Naturalization in Philadelphia," 339-341.

38. Abigail Adams to Thomas Adams, July 21, 1798, Adams Papers, vol. 390, MHS; James Douglas to Levi Hollingsworth, July 10, 1798, Hollingsworth Correspondence, HSP; Thomas McKean to John Dickinson, June 24, 1798, McKean Papers, HSP.

39. Waln and Gurney owned assessed real property in the amounts of $83,391 and $8,306 respectively (United States Direct Tax of 1798, Tax Lists for Philadelphia). *Aurora*, August 27, 1798; *Philadelphia Gazette*,

August 27, 1798; *Gazette of the United States,* September 24, 1798; *Claypoole's American Daily Advertiser,* September 28, 1798; broadside, "Sir, A Numerous Meeting of the Freemen of the City . . ." Gratz Collection, HSP.
40. Richard Peters to Timothy Pickering, August 24, 1798; and same to same, August 30, 1798, Pickering Papers, vol. 23, MHS; Pickering to Peters, August 27, 1798, Peters Papers, HSP; James M. Smith, "Benjamin Bache and the Alien and Sedition Law," *PMHB* (Jan., 1953), 21-22.
41. *Gazette of the United States,* September 24, 1798; Tinkcom, *Republicans and Federalists in Pennsylvania,* 197.
42. Benjamin Rush to William Marshall, September 15, 1798, Rush Papers, LC; Jefferson to Wise, February 12, 1798, Sparkmen Papers, HSP.
43. *Claypoole's American Daily Advertiser,* September 20, October 1, 8, 1798; Walters, *Dallas,* 76; Tinkcom, *Republicans and Federalists in Pennsylvania,* 187.
44. *Claypoole's American Daily Advertiser,* September 1, 6, October 8, 1798; William Bingham to Rufus King, September 30, 1798, *King Correspondence,* II, 425.
45. Samuel Hodgdon to Timothy Pickering, October 16, 1798, vol. 42; and Pickering to Alexander Dallas, November 17, 1798, Pickering Papers, vol. 19, MHS; *Gazette of the United States,* October 16, 1798; Thomas Hollingsworth to Levi Hollingsworth, October 16, 1798, Hollingsworth Correspondence, HSP; *Claypoole's American Daily Advertiser,* October 10, 1798.
46. *Claypoole's American Daily Advertiser,* October 10, 11, 1798; *Porcupine's Gazette,* October 10, 1798.

7: The Crest of Federalism

1. Tolles, *George Logan,* 184-186; Frederick B. Tolles, "Unofficial Ambassador: George Logan's Mission to France, 1798," *William and Mary Quarterly,* Third Series VII (Jan., 1950), 4-25; Bowmann, *Struggle for Neutrality,* 353-357.
2. *Aurora,* December 19, 21, 24, 26, 1798; W. S. Shaw to Abigail Adams, December 30, 1798, Adams Papers, vol. 392, MHS.
3. Jefferson to James Monroe, December 27, 1797, Jefferson Papers, LC; Levi Hollingsworth to James Heron, March 28, 1798, Levi Hollingsworth Letterbook; Thomas Hollingsworth to Levi Hollingsworth, November 18, 1798, Hollingsworth Correspondence, HSP; Samuel Hodgdon to Timothy Pickering, October 26, 1798, Pickering Papers, vol. 42, MHS; John Beckley to William Irvine, January 2, 1799, Irvine Papers, HSP; Gail S. Rowe, "Power, Politics, and Public Service: The Life of Thomas McKean, 1734-1817" (Unpublished Ph.D. dissertation, Stanford University, 1969).
4. Walters, *Dallas,* 88-89; James Peeling, "Governor McKean and the Pennsylvania Jacobins, 1799-1808," *PMHB,* LIV (Oct., 1930), 321-322; *Aurora,* April 16, 1799; John Beckley to William Irvine, March 22, 1799, Irvine Papers, HSP; Michael Leib to Tench Coxe, January 25, 1799, Coxe Papers, HSP; Rowe, "The Life of Thomas McKean," 325-332.
5. *General Advertiser,* March 23, 1793; Rowe, "The Life of Thomas McKean," 325-335; G.S. Rowe, "Thomas McKean and the Coming of the Revolution," *PMHB,* XCVI (Jan., 1972), 3-47; Peeling, "McKean and the Pennsylvania Jacobins," 320-324.
6. A. Brodie to William Bingham, November 22, 1798, Pickering Papers, vol. 23, MHS; William McHenry to John Adams, December 2, 1798, Adams

Papers, vol. 392, MHS; *Gazette of the United States,* December 4, 1798; *Journal of the Senate,* 9th Senate, 42-44; *Journal of the House of Representatives,* 9th House, 58-59; Samuel Coates to Matthew Hart, December 20, 1798; Samuel Coates Letterbook, HSP; *Philadelphia Gazette,* March 18, 1799; Robert Waln to Rathbone, February 16, 1799, Robert Waln Letterbook, Waln Family Papers, LCP.

7. Herman Stamp to Levi Hollingsworth, March 12, 1799, Hollingsworth Correspondence, HSP.

8. Tench Coxe to unknown, May 8, 1799, Tench Coxe Letterbook, Coxe Papers, HSP; *Aurora,* February 11, 1799.

9. Walters, *Dallas,* 78; Scharf and Westcott, *History of Philadelphia,* I, 496-497; William Duane, *A Report of the Extraordinary Transactions Which Took Place at Philadelphia in February, 1799, in Consequences of a Memorial from Certain Natives of Ireland to Congress Praying Repeal of the Alien Bill* (Philadelphia: 1799). Reynolds, Duane, Robert Morre, and Samuel Cuming had taken the petition to various Catholic and Presbyterian churches attended by Irish immigrants. William Cobbett, *Porcupine's Works,* 12 vols. (London: 1801), X, 97; Smith, *Freedom's Fetters,* 279.

10. William Bingham to Rufus King, December 8, 1798, *King Correspondence,* II, 482-483; *Gazette of the United States,* March 30, April 3, 1799.

11. Carter, "Naturalization in Philadelphia," 338-339, 342. Professor Carter has calculated that between 1790 and 1800 Philadelphia's population, including its suburbs increased by 13,240 immigrants, of whom 7,415 were Irish. *Aurora,* October 13, 1798; *Claypoole's American Daily Advertiser,* October 10, 1798; *Aurora,* October 16, 1796; Kenneth Keller, "Diversity and Democracy; Ethnic Politics in Southeastern Pennsylvania, 1788-1799" (unpublished Ph.D. dissertation, Yale University, 1971), 183-184.

12. *Aurora,* April 11, 1799; *Philadelphia Gazette,* August 8, 1799. Federalist election committees were headed by Levi Hollingsworth and wealthy merchants Robert Wharton and Henry Pratt. Wharton, a Quaker, was mayor of Philadelphia and owned real property assessed at $27,431; while Pratt, an Anglican, served on the select council and owned real property assessed at $33,390.

13. *Gazette of the United States,* April 13, 27, 1799.

14. *Aurora,* April 16, 1799; Tench Coxe to Albert Gallatin, April 12, 1799, Gallatin Papers, NYHS.

15. Tench Coxe to Albert Gallatin, April 12, 1799, Gallatin Papers, NYHS; John Beckley to William Irvine, April 22, 1799, Irvine Papers, HSP; *Journal of the Senate,* 9th Senate, 259-260; *Journal of the House of Representatives,* 9th House, 391; Leonard J. Sneddon, "From Philadelphia to Lancaster: The First Move of Pennsylvania's Capital," *Pennsylvania History* XXXVIII (October, 1971), 349-360.

16. Tench Coxe to Albert Gallatin, April 26, 1799, Gallatin Papers, NYHS; Jebidiah Morse to his wife, May 18, 1799, Morse Collection, Yale University Library; John Beckley to William Irvine, May 17, 1799, Irvine Papers, HSP; Scharf and Westcott, *History of Philadelphia,* I, 497; Girard to John Berenberg, April 27, 1799, Girard Letterbook, Girard Papers, Girard College.

17. Tench Coxe to Alexander Pattes, June 18, 1799, Coxe Papers, HSP; broadside addressed to the "Citizen of the County of Philadelphia," signed by *Franklin,* issued in 1799, Broadside Collection, HSP; Broadside issued in support of McKean in 1799, Broadside Collection, LC.

18. Kurtz, *The Presidency of John Adams,* 335-337; Miller, *The Federalist Era,* 245-246. Hofstadter, *The Idea of a Party System,* 104-111; Dauer, *The Adams Federalists,* ch. 14; Bowmann, *Struggle for Neutrality,* 366-374.

19. L.R. Morris to William Meredith, May 29, 1799, Meredith Papers, HSP; unknown to Levi Hollingsworth, June 10, 1799, Hollingsworth Correspondence, HSP; Alexander Addison to Washington, July 6, 1799, Washington Papers, vol. 114, LC; *Porcupine's Gazette,* August 15, 17, 1799; Oliver Wolcott to Frederick Wolcott, April 2, 1799, in *Memoirs of Wolcott,* ed. Gibbs, II, 230-231; Carter, "Naturalization in Philadelphia."
20. John Coates to Samuel Coates, June 25, 1799, Coates-Reynell Papers, HSP; *Gazette of the United States,* July 21, 1799; Richard Peters to Pickering, September 12, 1799, Pickering Papers, vol. 25, MHS.
21. Thomas Adams to Abigail Adams, August 26, 1799, Adams Papers, vol. 396, MHS; William Bingham to Rufus King, September 2, 1799, *King Correspondence,* III, 93–94; Washington to Jonathan Trumbull, July 21, 1799; and same to same, August 30, 1799, in *Writings of Washington,* ed. Fitzpatrick, XXXVII, 313, 349.
22. *Gazette of the United States,* August 14, 15, 24, September 6, 1799; Israel Israel to Tench Coxe, September 17, 1799; Michael Leib to Tench Coxe, September 26, 1799; and same to same, September, 1799, Coxe Papers, HSP; *Claypoole's Daily American Advertiser,* August 8, 1799; Thomas Dick to Levi Hollingsworth, July 13, 1799, Hollingsworth Correspondence, HSP; *Pennsylvania Gazette,* August 21, 1799; *Porcupine's Gazette,* September 6, 1799; *Aurora,* August 17, September 4, 1799; Scharf and Westcott, *History of Philadelphia,* I, 497.
23. *Porcupine's Gazette,* September 27, 1799; letter from the Republican Campaign Committee, September 22, 1799; see also Tench Coxe to Jefferson, June 21, 1799, Jefferson Papers, LC; Alexander Dallas to Tench Coxe, October 6, 1799, Coxe Papers, HSP.
24. *Aurora,* September 19, 20, 30, 1799; Israel Israel to Tench Coxe, September 12, 1799, Coxe Papers, HSP; Tench Coxe to Albert Gallatin, August 2, 1799, Gallatin Papers, NYHS; John Hall to Levi Hollingsworth, September 22, 1799; and Jeremiah Brown to Hollingsworth, September 23, 1799, Hollingsworth Correspondence, HSP.
25. David Meredith to William Meredith, October 8, 1799, Meredith Papers, HSP; Benjamin Rush to Timothy Pickering, September 30, 1799, Pickering Papers, vol. 25, MHS; Scharf and Westcott, *History of Philadelphia,* I, 498.
26. *Claypoole's American Daily Advertiser,* October 9, 1799; *Aurora,* October 9, 1799; *Journal of the House of Representatives,* 10th House, 35.
27. *Journal of the House of Representatives,* 10th House, 35.
28. *Gazette of the United States,* October 9, 1799; *Claypoole's American Daily Advertiser,* October 12, 1799; Minutes of the Select Council, October 11, 1799, PCA.
29. *Aurora,* October 9, November 7, 1799; *Journal of the House of Representatives,* 10th House, 35.
30. *Gazette of the United States,* October 9, 1799; *Claypoole's American Daily Advertiser,* October 12, 1799.
31. W.S. Shaw to John Adams, October 12, 1799, Adams Papers, vol. 396, MHS; John Fenno to Timothy Pickering, October 16, 1799, Pickering Papers, vol. 25, MHS; John Hollingsworth to Levi Hollingsworth, October 14, 1799, Hollingsworth Correspondence, HSP; *Gazette of the United States,* November 27, 1799.
32. William Bingham to Timothy Pickering, October 21, 1799, Pickering Papers, vol. 25, MHS; *Porcupine's Gazette,* October 11, 1799; Joseph Wallace to Levi Hollingsworth, October 19, 1799; see also David Ritter to

Hollingsworth, October 15, 1799; and Jeremiah Brown to Hollingsworth, October 19, 1799, Hollingsworth Correspondence, HSP.
33. Fisher Ames to Thomas Dwight, October 20, 1799, in *Works of Ames,* ed. Ames, I, 259; *Gazette of the United States,* November 27, 1799.
34. Elizabeth Drinker Diary, October 28, 1799, HSP; *Aurora,* October 26, 1799; Scharf and Westcott, *History of Philadelphia,* I, 498; Stewart, *The Opposition Press,* 581-582.

8: A Minority No Longer

1. Edward Riley, "Philadelphia, the Nation's Capital, 1790-1800," *Pennsylvania History,* XX (Oct., 1953), 357-380; Thomas Fitzsimons to Oliver Wolcott, August 20, 1800, in *Memoirs of Wolcott,* ed. Gibbs, II, 405-406.
2. Tench Coxe to Michael Leib, January 23, 1800; Leib to Coxe, January 29, 1800, Coxe Papers, HSP; Tinkcom, *Republicans and Federalists in Pennsylvania,* 245-247.
3. Michael Leib to Tench Coxe, January 13, 1800; and Henry Drinker, Jr., to Coxe, March 17, 1800, Coxe Papers, HSP.
4. Samuel Preston to Levi Hollingsworth, November 16, 1799, Hollingsworth Correspondence Supplementary, HSP; Jeremiah Brown to Hollingsworth, December 12, 1799; and same to same, January 1, 1800, Hollingsworth Correspondence, HSP; *Philadelphia Gazette,* December 24, 1799; *Gazette of the United States,* January 1, 1800.
5. Albert Gallatin to James Nicholson, December 7, 1799, Gallatin Papers, NYHS; Jefferson to McKean, January 9, 1800, McKean Papers, HSP; Michael Leib to Tench Coxe, February 12, 1800; and Coxe to Leib, January 23, 1800, Coxe Papers, HSP.
6. Jeremiah Brown to Levi Hollingsworth, December 23, 1799; and same to same, January 14, 1800, Hollingsworth Correspondence, HSP; Samuel Coates to William Barttet, February 3, 1800, Samuel Coates Letterbook, HSP; *Gazette of the United States,* January 22, 1800; *Philadelphia Gazette,* June 13, 1800.
7. McKean to John Dickinson, June 23, 1800, R.R. Logan Collection, HSP; James Monroe to McKean, July 12, 1800, McKean Papers, HSP.
8. Alexander Dallas to James Monroe, January 19, 1800, Monroe Papers, NYPL; McKean to Sara McKean, January 19, 1800, McKean Papers, HSP; John Beckley to James Monroe, August 26, 1800, Monroe Papers, NYPL.
9. Thomas Adams to John Q. Adams, April 1, 1800; and same to same, May 11, 1800, Adams Papers, vol. 397, MHS; see also William Bingham to Rufus King, March 5, 1800, *King Correspondence,* III, 205; Theodore Sedwick to King, May 11, 1800, King Papers, NYHS.
10. Thomas Fitzsimons to Oliver Wolcott, July 10, 1800; and Fitzsimons to Wolcott, July 24, 1800; in *Memoirs of Wolcott,* ed. Gibbs, II, 378-379, 388, 390.
11. William Bingham to Wolcott, July 23, 1800, *Ibid.,* II, 387-388; Robert Waln to William McHenry, May 7, 1800, Robert Waln Letterbook, LCP; Bingham to Rufus King, March 5, 1800, *King Correspondence,* III, 205; Henry Drinker to Samuel Preston, June 16, 1800, Henry Drinker Letterbook, Drinker Papers, HSP.
12. Michael Leib to Tench Coxe, January 13, 1800; and Coxe to Alexander Dallas, July 13, 1800, Coxe Papers, HSP; unknown to William Meredith, January 15, 1800, Meredith Papers, HSP; *Claypoole's American Daily Advertiser,* April 17, 1800, *Aurora,* July 25, 28, 1800.
13. *Aurora,* July 25, 28, August 16, 1800. Jones owned real property in Philadelphia assessed at $45,000. Pearson, a carpenter, owned property

assessed at $1,000 and had been a candidate for the select council in 1799.
14. *Philadelphia Gazette*, July 28, 1800.
15. *Aurora*, July 25, August 16, 1800; John Beckley to James Monroe, August 26, 1800, Monroe Papers, NYPL; Cunningham, *Jeffersonian Republicans*, 159-160.
16. *Claypoole's American Daily Advertiser*, July 28, 30, 1800; Thomas Fitzsimons to James McHenry, August 2, 1800, Society Miscellaneous Collection, HSP; Fitzsimons to Wolcott, July 24, 1800, in *Memoirs of Wolcott*, ed. Gibbs, II, 388-390. The Federalist campaign committee consisted of Fitzsimons, Levi Hollingsworth, William Rawle, and John Innskeep. Gurney owned assessed real property valued at $8,306.
17. *Aurora*, August 5, 1800.
18. Thomas Fitzsimons to James McHenry, August 2, 1800, Society Miscellaneous Collection, HSP; William Bingham to Rufus King, August 6, 1800, *King Correspondence*, III, 284-286; Bingham to Wolcott, August 6, 1800, in *Memoirs of Wolcott*, ed. Gibbs, II, 397-398.
19. William Bingham to Rufus King, August 6, 1800, *King Correspondence*. III, 285; Henry Drinker to Rosewell Wells, February 7, 1800, Henry Drinker Letterbook, Drinker Papers, HSP; Thomas Fitzsimons to Oliver Wolcott, August 20, 1800; and Wolcott to Fisher Ames, August 10, 1800, in *Memoirs of Wolcott*, ed. Gibbs, II, 400, 405-406.
20. *Claypoole's American Daily Advertiser*, September 20, 1800; Thomas Adams to John Adams, August 30, 1800; Adams Papers, vol. 398, MHS.
21. Thomas Adams to John Adams, September 20, 1800, Adams Papers, vol. 398, MHS; *Aurora*, August 8, 1800; *Claypoole's American Daily Advertiser*, September 20, 1800; *An Ordinance Providing for the Raising of a Sum of Money for Supplying the City of Philadelphia with Wholesome Water (Philadelphia: 1799); A Report to the Select and Common Council on the Progress and State of the Water Works on the 24th of November, 1799* (Philadelphia: 1799). The city proposed to spend $150,000 to bring the water from the Schuylkill River to center square. The cost included two steam engines to pump the water.
22. *Aurora*, July 28, October 12, 1800; Tench Coxe to Alexander Dallas, July 13, 1800, Coxe Papers, HSP.
23. *Gazette of the United States*, August 16, 1800; *Philadelphia Gazette*, September 24, October 11, 13, 1800.
24. Thomas Adams to John Q. Adams, October 12, 1800, Adams Papers, vol. 399, MHS; see also Samuel Hodgdon to Timothy Pickering, October 13, 1800, Pickering Papers, vol. 42, MHS.
25. Minutes of the Select Council, February 13, 1800, and Minutes of the Common Council, February 13, 1800, PCA, for the petitions requesting the increase in the city's wards; *Pennsylvania Statutes at Large*, XVI, 423-424; *Poulson's American Daily Advertiser*, October 16, 1800. Coefficient of correlations could not be calculated because census and tax data were not available for the new ward structure in 1800.
26. *Poulson's American Daily Advertiser*, October 16, 1800.
27. *Ibid.*
28. *Ibid.*
29. Andrew Elliot to Jefferson, October 17, 1800, Jefferson Papers, LC.
30. *Gazette of the United States*, October 30, 1800; Thomas Leiper to Jefferson, October 16, 1800, Jefferson Papers, LC; Jeremiah Brown to Levi Hollingsworth, October 26, 1800, Hollingsworth Correspondence, HSP.
31. *Aurora*, November 1, 1800; Michael Leib to Tench Coxe, April 25, 1800; and Henry Drinker, Jr. to Coxe, June 13, 1800, Coxe Papers, HSP;

Tinkcom, *Republicans and Federalists in Pennsylvania,* 247; Sanford W. Higginbotham, *The Keystone in the Democratic Arch: Pennsylvania Politics, 1800-1816* (Harrisburg: 1952), 28-29; William B. Wheeler, "Pennsylvania and the Presidential Election of 1800: Republican Acceptance of the 8-7 Compromise," *Pennsylvania History,* XXXVI (Oct. 1969), 424-429.

32. *Aurora,* October 25, November 1, 1800; John Beckley to Alexander Dallas, November 7, 1800, Dallas Papers, HSP.

33. Timothy Pickering to Samuel Gardner, June 21, 1800, Pickering Papers, vol. 13, MHS; Charles Ogden to David Meredith, May 3, 1800; and same to same, May 25, 1800, Meredith Papers, HSP; *Autobiography of Charles Biddle,* 288-289; *Gazette of the United States,* October 14, 1800. The four senators representing the Philadelphia district split along party lines; Federalists Francis Gurney and John Jones opposed a joint vote, while Republicans James Pearson and Benjamin Say favored a joint vote.

34. *Philadelphia Gazette,* October 9, 15, 1800; Jacob Cooke, "Tench Coxe; Tory Merchant," *PMHB,* XCVI (Jan. 1972), 48-88.

35. *Aurora,* November 10, 1800; Jeremiah Brown to Levi Hollingsworth, November 7, 1800, Hollingsworth Correspondence, HSP; McKean to Jefferson, December 15, 1800, McKean Papers, HSP. The Federalist committee consisted of Thomas Fitzsimons; William Rawle; Anglican lawyer Joseph Hopkinson, and James Milnor.

36. *Aurora,* November 17, 22, 1800; Alexander Dallas to McKean, November 28, 1800, McKean Papers, HSP; *Philadelphia Gazette,* November 22, 1800; Thomas Adams to Abigail Adams, October 19, 1800, and Thomas Adams to John Adams, November 1, 1800, Adams Papers, vol. 399, MHS; David Ogden to William Meredith, October 23, 1800; and same to same, October 30, 1800, Meredith Papers, HSP.

37. William Penrose to Alexander Dallas, n.d., 1800, Dallas Papers, HSP; Andrew Gregg to William Irvine, December 6, 1800, Irvine Papers, HSP; Dallas to McKean, December 8, 1800, McKean Papers, HSP; Jeremiah Brown to Levi Hollingsworth, November 21, 1800; Roger Kirke to Hollingsworth, November 25, 1800, and Francis Gurney to Hollingsworth, November 30, 1800, Hollingsworth Correspondence, HSP; *Journal of the Senate,* 23; *Gazette of the United States,* November 18, 1800.

38. Jeremiah Brown to Levi Hollingsworth, December 12, 1800, Hollingsworth Correspondence, HSP; Samuel Coates to unknown, November 24, 1800, Samuel Coates Letterbook, HSP; William Meredith to David Meredith, December 2, 1800; and L.R. Morris to William Meredith, December 10, 1800, Meredith Papers, HSP; Richard Peters to Rufus King, January 10, 1801, *King Correspondence,* III, 371; for the struggle in South Carolina see Rose, *Prologue to Democracy,* ch. 8.

39. William Irvine to unknown, December 22, 1800, Irvine Papers, HSP; McKean to Jefferson, December 15, 1800, McKean Papers, HSP; Jefferson to William Barton, February 14, 1801, Barton Papers, HSP; *Gazette of the United States,* August 11, October 22, 1801. John Smith was named Marshall for eastern Pennsylvania.

40. *Gazette of the United States,* August 11, September 30, October 5, 16, 29, 30, 1801; *Aurora,* August 13, 18, 1801.

41. *Aurora,* August 13, 18, 22, September 5, 8, 21, October 1, 3, 6, 9, 11, 12, 1801; *Poulson's American Daily Advertiser,* October 5, 10, 1801.

42. *Gazette of the United States,* October 14, 1801; *Aurora,* October 15, 1801; *Poulson's American Daily Advertiser,* October 15, 1801.

NOTES

9: Conclusion

1. See William Chambers, *Political Parties in a New Nation: The American Experience* (New York: 1963); Cunningham, *The Jeffersonian Republicans;* Charles, *The Origins of the American Party System;* Goodman, *The Democratic-Republicans of Massachusetts;* and Tinkcom, *The Republicans and Federalists in Pennsylvania,* for examples of this thesis.

BIBLIOGRAPHY

Primary Sources

Manuscripts

Information about politics in Philadelphia in private correspondence is scattered through numerous collections. Almost without exception the letters are from the leading political figures of the day, with little or none from the average citizen. The Federalists wrote more letters to and from Philadelphia during the 1790s. At the HSP, the Hollingsworths' correspondence is a valuable source for the entire period. In addition, the Coates-Reynell Papers, the Meredith Papers, and the Henry Drinker Papers are useful for Federalists' views. For the early part of the decade the William Bingham Papers, the Miers Fisher Papers, the Thomas Fitzsimons Papers, the Robert Henderson Letterbook, the William Rawle Papers, and the Wallace Papers are useful. For the latter part of the decade, the papers of Robert Waln, and Richard Peters and the William Tilghman Correspondence are of some help. Also, the HL has the Robert Morris Papers, which are valuable for the politics behind moving the capital to Philadelphia. The LCP has the Waln Family and the Dillnyn Family Papers. There are numerous letters from Philadelphia Federalists in many of the national political leaders' correspondence. A very valuable source at the MHS is the Adams Family Papers and the Timothy Pickering Papers. At the LC the Alexander Hamilton Papers and the George Washington Papers are of some value.

Sources for the Republicans are scattered through many collections. The most useful for this study at the HSP were the Coxe Papers, the William Irvine Papers, the Thomas McKean Papers, and the Clement Biddle Business Papers. At the LC the most helpful collection, containing valuable political news for the entire decade, was the Thomas Jefferson Papers; other sources that were useful included the James Madison Papers and the Benjamin Rush Papers. Collections of only limited value were the James Monroe Papers and the Charles Thomson Papers. The APS contains the James Hutchinson Papers and the microfilm copy of the Stephen Girard Papers, which are valuable sources for the period. The Albert Gallatin Papers, the James Madison Papers, and the James Monroe Papers housed at the NYHS and NYPL are important sources for Republican politics.

The PCA contains the manuscript of the minutes of the city council, the common council and the select council. In addition, the tax records for almost all of the period are available.

There are miscellaneous collections which contain letters from Federalist and Republicans. At the HSP they are: The Greer Collection, the Gratz Collection and the Society Collection; and at the APS, the miscellaneous manuscripts. In addition there are scattered letters in many other collections, which are cited in the footnotes.

Newspapers

Aurora-General Advertiser
Claypoole's American Daily Advertiser
Federal Gazette
Gazette of the United States
Independent Gazetteer
National Gazette
Pennsylvania Gazette
Pennsylvania Packet
Philadelphia Gazette
Poulson's American Daily Advertiser
Broadside Collection, HSP
Broadside Collection, LC

Government Documents

Annals of Congress
First Census of the United States, 1790. Washington, D.C.: 1907-1908.
Second Census of the United States, 1800. Washington, D.C.: 1907-1908.
Journal of the Pennsylvania House of Representatives
Journal of the Pennsylvania Senate
Minutes of the General Assembly

Memoirs, Printed Correspondence, and Travel Accounts

Adams, Charles F. *The Works of John Adams.* 10 vols. Boston: 1850-1856.

Ames, Seth ed. *Works of Fisher Ames with a Selection from his Speeches and Correspondence.* 2 vols. Boston: 1854.

Bayard, Ferdinand M. *Travels of a Frenchman in Maryland and Virginia with a Description of Philadelphia and Baltimore.* Edited and translated by Benjamin C. McCary. Ann Arbor: 1950.

Biddle, Charles, *Autobiography of Charles Biddle, Vice President of the Supreme Executive Council of Pennsylvania, 1745-1821.*

Boudinot, J.J., ed. *The Life and Public Services, Addresses and Letters of Elias Boudinot.* 2 vols. Boston: 1896.

Boyd, Julian, ed. *The Papers of Thomas Jefferson.* 19 vols. Princeton: 1950 to present.

Butterfield, Lyman, ed. *Letters of Benjamin Rush.* 2 vols. Princeton: 1951.

Cobbett, William. *Porcupine's Works.* 12 vols. London: 1801.

Dallas, George M., ed. *The Life and Writings of Alexander J. Dallas.* Philadelphia: 1871.

Fitzpatrick, John, ed. *Writings of George Washington.* 39 vols. Washington: 1931-1944.

Foner, Philip. *The Complete Writings of Thomas Paine.* 2 vols. New York: 1945.

Ford, Paul L., ed. *The Writings of Thomas Jefferson.* 10 vols. New York: 1892-1899.

Gibbs, George, ed. *Memoirs of the Administration of Washington and John Adams, edited from the Papers of Oliver Wolcott.* 2 vols. New York: 1846.

Hazard, Samuel, ed. *Register of Pennsylvania, Devoted to the Preservation of Facts and Documents, and Every Other Kind of Useful Information Respecting the State of Pennsylvania.* 16 vols. Philadelphia: 1828-1836.

King, Charles, ed. *The Life and Correspondence of Rufus King.* 6 vols. New York: 1894-1900.

Lodge, Henry C., ed. *The Works of Alexander Hamilton.* 12 vols. New York: 1904.

Maclay, Edgar, ed. *The Journal of William Maclay.* New York: 1927.

Padelfor, Philip, ed. *Colonial Panorama–Dr. Robert Honeyman's Journal for March and April, 1775.* San Marino: 1939.

Pearson, Jacob, ed. *Extracts from the Diary of Jacob Hiltzheimer of Philadelphia, 1765-1798.* Philadelphia: 1893.

Phillips, Ulrich, ed. "South Carolina Federalists' Correspondence." *American Historical Review* XIV (July, 1909): 731-744.

Rush, Benjamin. *The Autobiography of Benjamin Rush: His "Travels Through Life" Together with his "Common Place Book" for 1789-1813.* Edited by George W. Conner. Princeton: 1948.

Smith, William, ed. *The Life and Public Services of Arthur St. Clair: with his Correspondence and Other Papers.* 2 vols. Cincinnati: 1882.

Sparks, Jared, ed. *The Life of Gouverneur Morris: with selections from his Correspondence and Miscellaneous Papers.* 3 vols. Boston: 1832.

Syrett, Harold, ed. *Papers of Alexander Hamilton.* 21 vols. New York: 1961 to present.

Upham, Charles. *The Life of Timothy Pickering.* 4 vols. Boston: 1867-1873.

Wansey, Henry. *Journal of an Excursion to the United States of North America.* Salisbury, England: 1796.

Secondary Works

Books

Alberts, Robert. *The Golden Voyage: The Life and Times of William Bingham, 1752-1804.* Boston: 1969.

Ammon, Harry. *The Genet Mission.* New York: 1973.

Baldwin, Leland D. *Whiskey Rebels: The Story of a Frontier Uprising.* Pittsburgh: 1939.

Banner, James M. *To the Hartford Convention: The Federalists and the Origins of the Party in Massachusetts, 1789–1815.* New York: 1970.

BIBLIOGRAPHY

Barber, Bernard. *Social Stratification: A Comparative Analysis of Structure and Process.* New York: 1957.

Beard, Charles. *The Economic Origins of Jeffersonian Democracy.* New York: 1915.

Bemis, Samuel F. *Jay's Treaty: A Study in Commerce and Diplomacy.* New Haven: 1962.

Bowman, Albert H. *The Struggle for Neutrality: Franco-American Diplomacy During the Federalist Era.* Knoxville: 1974.

Bridenbaugh, Carl and Jessica. *Rebels and Gentlemen: Philadelphia in the Age of Franklin.* New York: 1942.

Bridenbaugh, Carl. *Cities in Revolt.* New York: 1955.

Brown, Robert E. *Middle-Class Democracy and the Revolution in Massachusetts, 1691–1780.* Ithaca: 1955.

Brunhouse, Robert. *The Counter-Revolution in Pennsylvania, 1776–1790.* Philadelphia: 1942.

Buel, Richard. *Securing the Revolution: Ideology in American Politics, 1790–1815.* Ithaca: 1972.

Callender, James T. *A Short History of the Nature and Consequence of Excise Laws.* Philadelphia: 1795.

Carey, Matthew. *A Short Account of the Malignant Fever Lately Prevalent in Philadelphia.* Philadelphia: 1794.

Chambers, William. *Political Parties in a New Nation: The American Experience, 1776–1809.* New York: 1963.

Charles, Joseph. *The Origins of the American Party System.* Williamsburg: 1956.

Childs, Francis. *French Refugee Life in the United States, 1790–1800: An American Chapter of the French Revolution.* Baltimore: 1940.

Combs, Jerald. *The Jay Treaty: Political Battleground of the Founding Fathers.* Berkeley: 1970.

Coxe, Tench. *A View of the United States of America . . .* Philadelphia: 1794.

Cunningham, Noble. *The Jeffersonian Republicans: The Formation of Party Organization, 1789–1801.* Chapel Hill: 1957.

Dallas, Alexander J. *Features of Mr. Jay's Treaty.* Philadelphia: 1795.

Dauer, Manning. *The Adams Federalists.* Baltimore: 1953.

Davis, Allen F., and Haller, Mark, eds. *The Peoples of Philadelphia: A History of Ethnic Groups and Lower Class Life.* Philadelphia: 1973.

DeConde, Alexander. *Entangling Alliances: Politics and Diplomacy under George Washington.* Durham: 1958.

__________, *The Quasi-War: The Politics and Diplomacy of the Undeclared Naval War with France, 1777–1801.* New York: 1966.

Dollar, Charles M. and Jensen, Richard T. *Historian's Guide to Statistics: Quantitative Analysis and Historical Research.* New York: 1971.

Ferguson, James. *The Power of the Purse: A History of American Public Finance, 1776–1790.* Chapel Hill: 1961.

Gilchrist, David, ed. *The Growth of the Seaport Cities, 1790–1825.* Charlottesville: 1967.

Goodman, Paul. *The Democratic Republicans of Massachusetts: Politics in a Young Republic.* Cambridge: 1964.

Handlin, Oscar, and Burchard, John, eds. *The Historian and the City.* Cambridge: 1964.

Hawke, David. *In the Midst of a Revolution.* Philadelphia: 1961.

Hensen, Marcus Lee. *The Atlantic Migration, 1607–1860.* Cambridge: 1940.

Higginbotham, Sanford. *The Keystone in the Democratic Arch: Pennsylvania Politics, 1800–1816.* Harrisburg: 1952.

Hofstadter, Richard. *The Idea of a Party System: The Rise of Legitimate Opposition in the United States, 1780–1840.* Berkeley: 1969.

Jackson, Kenneth, and Schultz, Stanley, eds. *Cities in American History.* New York: 1972.

Jamar, Mary. *The Hollingsworth Family.* Philadelphia: 1944.

King, Moses. *Philadelphia and Notable Philadelphians.* New York: 1902.

Konkle, Burton. *Benjamin Chew, 1722–1810.* Philadelphia: 1932.

Kurtz, Stephen. *The Presidency of John Adams: The Collapse of Federalism, 1795–1800.* Philadelphia: 1957.

Link, Eugene. *Democratic-Republican Societies, 1790–1800.* New York: 1942.

Lipset, Seymour M. *Political Man: The Social Basis of Politics.* Garden City: 1963.

Main, Jackson Turner. *The Social Structure of Revolutionary America.* Princeton: 1965.

____________, *Political Parties Before the Constitution.* Chapel Hill, 1973.

McMaster, John B., and Stone, Frederick D., eds. *Pennsylvania and the Federal Constitution, 1787–1788.* Philadelphia: 1888.

McMaster, John B. *The Life and Times of Stephen Girard: Mariner and Merchant.* 2 vols. Philadelphia: 1918.

____________, *A History of the People of the United States.* 8 vols. New York: 1883–1913.

Miller, John C. *Alexander Hamilton and the Growth of the New Nation.* New York: 1959.

Mohl, Raymond A. *Poverty in New York, 1783–1825.* New York: 1971.

Morison, Samuel. *The Life and Letters of Harrison Gray Otis, Federalist, 1765–1848.* 2 vols. Boston: 1913.

Nash, Gary. *Quakers and Politics: Pennsylvania, 1681–1726.* Princeton: 1968.

____________, *Class and Society in Early America.* New York: 1970.

Oberholtzer, Ellis. *Philadelphia: A History of the City and Its People, a record of 225 years.* 4 vols. Philadelphia.

Powell, J. H. *Bring Out Your Dead: The Great Plague of Yellow Fever in Philadelphia in 1793.* Philadelphia: 1949.

Ritter, Abraham. *Philadelphia and Her Merchants, as Constituted Fifty @ Seventy Years Ago.* Philadelphia: 1860.

Robinson, William A. *Jeffersonian Democracy in New England.* New Haven: 1916.

Rose, Lisle A. *Prologue to Democracy: The Federalist in the South, 1789–1800.* Lexington: 1968.

Scharf, Thomas, and Westcott, Thompson. *History of Philadelphia, 1609–1884.* 3 vols. Philadelphia: 1884.

Simpson, Henry. *The Lives of Eminent Philadelphians.* Philadelphia: 1859.

Smith, Charles Page. *James Wilson: Founding Father, 1742-1798.* Chapel Hill: 1956.

Smith, James Morton. *Freedom's Fetters: The Alien and Sedition Laws and American Civil Liberties.* Ithaca: 1956.

Stewart, Donald H. *The Opposition Press of the Federalist Era.* Albany: 1969.

Thayer, Theodore. *Pennsylvania Politics and the Growth of Democracy.* Harrisburg: 1953.

Thomas, Charles M. *American Neutrality in 1793: A Study in Cabinet Government.* New York: 1931.

Thomas, Earl. *Political Tendencies in Pennsylvania, 1783-1794.* Philadelphia: 1939.

Tinkcom, Harry. *The Republicans and Federalists in Pennsylvania, 1790-1801.* Harrisburg: 1950.

Tolles, Frederick. *Meeting House and Counting House: The Quaker Merchants of Colonial Philadelphia, 1682-1763.* Chapel Hill: 1948.

______________, *George Logan of Philadelphia.* New York: 1953.

Walters, Raymond. *Alexander James Dallas: Lawyer-Politician-Financier, 1759-1817.* Philadelphia: 1943.

Warner, Sam Bass, Jr. *The Private City: Philadelphia in Three Periods of its Growth.* Philadelphia: 1968.

Wharton, Francis. *State Trials of the United States.* Philadelphia: 1849.

Woodbury, Margaret. *Public Opinion in Philadelphia, 1789-1801.* Smith College: 1937.

Zahniser, Marvin R. *Charles Cotesworth Pinckney: Founding Father.* Chapel Hill: 1967.

Articles

Adams, Donald R., Jr. "Wage Rates in the Early National Period: Philadelphia, 1785-1830." *The Journal of Economic History* XXVIII (Sept., 1968): 404-417.

Banning, Lance. "Republican Ideology and the Triumph of the Constitution, 1789 to 1793." *William and Mary Quarterly* Third Series XXXI (April, 1974): 167-188.

Baumann, Roland. "John Swanwick: Spokesman for 'Merchant Republicanism' in Philadelphia, 1790-1798." *PMHB* XCVII (April, 1973): 131-182.

Bell, Whitfield J. "Some Aspects of the Social History of Pennsylvania, 1760-1790." *PMHB* LXII (July, 1938): 281-308.

Brown, Margaret. "William Bingham, Eighteenth-Century Magnate." *PMHB* LXI (Oct., 1937): 388-398.

Carter, Edward. "A 'Wild Irishman' Under Every Federalist's Bed: Naturalization in Philadelphia, 1789-1806." *PMHB* XCIV (July, 1970): 331-347.

Cooke, Jacob E. "The Compromise of 1790." *William and Mary Quarterly* Third Series XXVII (Oct., 1970): 523-546.

______________, "The Whiskey Insurrection: A Re-evaluation." *Pennsylvania History* XXX (July, 1963): 316-346.

_____________, "Tench Coxe: Tory Merchant." *PMHB* XCVI (Jan., 1972): 48–88.

Cunningham, Noble. "John Beckley: An Early American Party Manager." *William and Mary Quarterly* Third Series XIII (Jan., 1958): 41–52.

Dorpalen, Andreas. "The German Element in Early Pennsylvania Politics, 1789-1800." *Pennsylvania History* IX (April, 1942): 176–190.

Dumbauld, Edward. "Thomas Jefferson and Pennsylvania." *Pennsylvania History* V (April, 1938): 157–167.

Earl, John. "Talleyrand in Philadelphia, 1794–1796." *PMHB* XCI (July, 1967).

Egle, William. "The Federal Constitution of 1787: Biographical Sketches of the Members of the Pennsylvania Convention." *PMHB* X & XI (1886, 1887).

Fay, Bernard. "Early Party Machinery in the United States: Pennsylvania in the Election of 1796." *PMHB* LX (July, 1936): 375–390.

Flanders, Henry. "Thomas Fitzsimons." *PMHB* II (July, 1878): 306-314.

Gares, Albert. "Stephen Girard's West Indian Trade." *PMHB* LXXII (Oct., 1948): 311–343.

Gatell, Frank Otto. "Money and Party in Jacksonian America: A Quantitative Look at New York City's Men of Quality." *Political Science Quarterly* LXXXII (June, 1967): 235-252.

Henretta, James A. "Economic Development and Social Structure in Colonial Boston." *William and Mary Quarterly* Third Series XXII (Jan., 1965): 75-102.

Ketcham, Ralph L. "France and American Politics, 1763–1793." *Political Science Quarterly* LXXVIII (June, 1963): 198-223.

Kohn, Richard H. "The Washington Administration's Decision to Crush the Whiskey Rebellion." *The Journal of American History* LIX (Dec., 1972): 567–584.

Kulikoff, Allan. "The Progress of Inequality in Revolutionary Boston." *William and Mary Quarterly* Third Series XXVIII (July, 1971): 375-413.

Lemon, James. "Urbanization and Development of Eighteenth-Century Southeastern Pennsylvania and Adjacent Delaware." *William and Mary Quarterly* Third Series XXIV (Oct., 1967): 501–542.

Lemond, James T., and Nash, Gary B. "The Distribution of Wealth in Eighteenth-Century America: A Century of Change in Chester County, Pennsylvania, 1693–1802." *Journal of Social History* II (Fall, 1968): 1-24.

March, Philip. "Philip Freneau and His Circle." *PMHB* LXIII (Jan., 1939): 36–59.

_____________, "John Beckley, Mystery Man of the Early Jeffersonians." *PMHB* LXXXI (Jan., 1947): 54–69.

Miller, William. "The Democratic Societies and the Whiskey Insurrection." *PMHB* LXII (July, 1938): 324–349.

_____________, "First Fruits of Republican Organization: Political Aspects of the Congressional Election of 1794." *PMHB* LXIII (April, 1939): 118–143.

Montgomery, David. "The Working Class of the Pre-Industrial American City, 1780–1830." *Labor History* IX (Winter, 1968): 3–22.

Oaks, Robert F. "Philadelphians in Exile: The Problem of Loyalty During the American Revolution." *PMHB* XCVI (July, 1972): 298-325.

Peeling, James. "Governor McKean and the Pennsylvania Jacobins, 1799-1808." *PMHB* IV (Oct., 1930): 320-354.

Pendleton, O. A. "Poor Relief in Philadelphia, 1790-1840." *PMHB* LXX (April, 1946): 161-172.

Pernick, Martin C. "Politics, Parties, and Pestilence: Epidemic Yellow Fever in Philadelphia and the Rise of the First Party System." *William and Mary Quarterly* Third Series *XXIX (Oct., 1972): 559-587.*

Pessen, Edward. "The Egalitarian Myth and the Social Reality: Wealth, Mobility, and Equality in the 'Era of the Common Man.' " *American Historical Review* LXXVI (Oct., 1971): 989-1034.

______________, "A Social and Economic Portrayal of Jacksonian Brooklyn." *New York Historical Quarterly* LV (Oct., 1971): 381-353.

Pole, Jack. "Election Statistics in Pennsylvania, 1790-1840." *PMHB* LXXXII (April, 1958): 217-219.

Rasmusson, Ethel. "Democratic Environment: Aristocratic Aspirations." *PMHB* XC (April, 1966): 155-182.

Reitzel, William. "William Cobbett and Philadelphia Journalism, 1794-1800." *PMHB* LIX (April, 1935): 223-244.

Riley, Edward. "Philadelphia, The Nation's Capital, 1790-1800." *Pennsylvania History* XX (Oct., 1953): 357-380.

Risch, Erna. "Immigrant Aid Societies Before 1829." *PMHB* LX (Jan., 1936): 16-27.

Rossman, Kenneth. "Thomas Mifflin Revolutionary Patriot." *Pennsylvania History* XV (Jan., 1948): 9-23.

Rowe, Gail S. "Thomas McKean and the Coming of the American Revolution." *PMHB* XCVI (Jan., 1972): 3-47.

Smelser, Marshall. "The Federalist Period as an Age of Passion." *American Quarterly* X (Winter, 1958): 391-419.

Smith, James. "Benjamin Bache, The Philadelphia *Aurora*, and Sedition Libel." *PMHB* LXXVII (Jan., 1953): 391-419.

______________, "William Duane, the *Aurora*, and the Alien and Sedition Laws." *PMHB* LXXVII (April, 1953): 123-155.

Sneddon, Leonard J. "From Philadelphia to Lancaster: The First Move of Pennsylvania's Capital." *Pennsylvania History* XXXVIII (Oct., 1971): 349-360.

Tolles, Frederick. "Unofficial Ambassador: George Logan's Mission to France, 1798." *William and Mary Quarterly* Third Series VII (Jan., 1950): 3-26.

______________, "The Culture of Early Pennsylvania." *PMHB* LXXXI (Jan., 1957): 119-137.

Wallace, H. E. "Sketch of John Innskeep." *PMHB* XXVIII (April, 1904): 129-135.

Walters, Raymond. "The Origins of the Jeffersonian Party in Pennsylvania." *PMHB* LXVI (Oct., 1942): 440-458.

Wheeler, William B. "Pennsylvania and the Presidential Election of 1800: Republican Acceptance of the 8-7 Compromise." *Pennsylvania History* XXXVI (Oct., 1969): 424-429.

Unpublished Ph.D. Dissertations:

Baumann, Roland M. "The Democratic-Republicans of Philadelphia: The Origins, 1776-1797." Pennsylvania State University, 1970.

Blumin, Stuart M. "Mobility in a Nineteenth-Century City: Philadelphia 1820–1860." University of Pennsylvania, 1968.

Bowling, Kenneth. "Politics in the First Congress, 1789–1791." University of Wisconsin, 1968.

Dimondstone, Judith M. "Philadelphia Corporation, 1701–1776." University of Pennsylvania, 1969.

Duvall, Regin F. "Philadelphia's Maritime Commerce with the British Empire, 1738–1789." University of Pennsylvania, 1960.

Geib, George. "A History of Philadelphia, 1776–1790." University of Wisconsin, 1969.

Keller, Kenneth. "Diversity and Democracy: Ethnic Politics in Southeastern Pennsylvania, 1788–1799." Yale University, 1971.

Rasmusson, Ethel. "Capital on the Delaware: A Study of Philadelphia's Upper-Class, 1789-1800." Brown University, 1962.

Rowe, Gail S. "Power Politics and Public Service: The Life of Thomas McKean, 1734-1817." Stanford University, 1969.

Wheeler, William. "Urban Politics in Nature's Republic: The Development of Political Parties in the Seaport Cities in the Federalist Era." University of Virginia, 1967.

INDEX